Drumming in a Band: Stuff You Can Use

Written by Rob Mitzner
Musical Notation: Rob Mitzner
Video Editing: Rob Mitzner
Drums Recorded @ C-Room Studio, Brooklyn, NY
Audio Mixing: Charles Burst, Tracks 7 & 8 by Mitch Rackin
Camera & Lighting Consultant: Albert Bickley
Layout Design: Rob Mitzner
Production Designer: Ricky Hammerschmidt
Book Editor: Joe Bergamini
Front Cover Photo: Dmitry Ishenko
Back Cover Photo: Thomas Mester

Rob Mitzner appears courtesy of
Paiste Cymbals, Remo Drumheads & Hendrix Drums

To Download Audio & Video for this Book
Go To: halleonard.com/mylibrary
Enter Code: 7157-2497-7788-6036

HUDSON MUSIC

Table of Contents

Introduction 4
Groove Workshops 8

Groove Workshop 1: Rock
Loose HH Rock/Crash City 10
Rock Tight 11
The Sludge 12
Top O' The Beat 13
Toms Busy 13
Toms Sparse 14
4-On-The-Floor (Downbeats) 15
4-On-The-Floor (Upbeats) 16
Loose Heavy 17

Groove Workshop 2: Drum'n'bass, Reggae
Simple Drum'n'bass 18
Half-Time Drum'n'bass 19
Breakbeat 20
Reggae 21
Reggaeton 22

Groove Workshop 3: R&B, Funk & Soul
Barry 23
Bill Cobham 4-On-The-Floor 24
T.O.P. Linear 25
JB 26
Motown 27
'50s/Amy Winehouse 27
Steve Jordan 28
Old-School Hip-Hop 28
J Dilla/Glasper 29
Disco 29
Half-Time R&B Ballad 30
Regular Shuffle 31
Half-Time Shuffle 32
Slow & Sparse 33
6/8 Gospel/R&B Ballad 33
Gospel Trips 34

Groove Workshop 4: World Music
Irish Jig 35
Irish Reel 36
Soca 37
Jazzy Bossa Nova 38
Samba 39
Rhumba 40
Baião 41

Groove Workshop 5: Roots
Country/Bluegrass Train 42
New Orleans Second Line 43
New Orleans Funk 44
Boogaloo 44
Slow 12/8 Blues 45

Groove Workshop 6: Jazz
Brushes Medium Swing 46
Brushes 2-Feel 47
Brushes Waltz 48
Brushes Ballad 49
Jazz Shuffle (Art Blakey) 49
Afro-Cuban Jazz 50
Elvin 51

Groove Workshop 7: Odd-Time Signatures, Soloing, Backing a Soloist
5/4 (2-3 Subdivision) 52
5/4 (3-2 Subdivision) 53
7/4 (4-3 Subdivision) 54
7/4 (3-4 Subdivision) 55

Charts, Lead Sheets & Road Maps
Song Workshop #1: "Classic Breakdown" (Woodhead) 59
Song Workshop #2: "The Conjuration" (Woodhead) 62
Song Workshop #3: "July 1" (Woodhead) 68
Song Workshop #4: "Gowanus Mash" (Woodhead) 71
Song Workshop #5: "Our Funeral" (Simon Garrett) 76
Song Workshop #6: "Escape" (Simon Garrett) 86
Song Workshop #7: "Sleep" (Dave Ross) 92
Song Workshop #8: "Worn Away" (Dave Ross) 97
Song Workshop #9: "Famous" (Luke Buck) 104
Song Workshop #10: "Without You" (Luke Buck) 110
Song Workshop #11: "Always Leave Me Wanting More" (Andrea Capozzoli) 113
Song Workshop #12: "I'll Form The Head" (MC Frontalot) 118
Song Workshop #13: "Clickbait" (MC Frontalot) 126
Song Workshop #14: "Getting Closer" from the musical RADIOACTIVE
    (Will Reynolds/Eric Price) 132
Song Workshop #15: "The Violet Hour" from the musical THE VIOLET HOUR
    (Will Reynolds/Eric Price) 138
Song Workshop #16: "Insurrection" (Michael Gallant) 142
Song Workshop #17: "Modern Jazz Combo" (Lars Potteiger) 148
Song Workshop #18: "Blues for Bob" (Rob Mitzner) 157

Glossary of Musical Slang
.... 162

Full Track Listing
.... 166

Acknowledgements
.... 168

Introduction

Did you ever notice how when you're at a show and people are dancing, the drummer can make a small change in what he or she plays and everyone starts dancing harder? The audience, and even the other musicians might not know exactly what the drummer did technically, but they can feel a difference in the vibe. My first teacher Steve "Freelance" Larrance used to say that "the drummer drives the bus," which was a metaphor for our subtle ability to control the intensity, volume, texture and overall feel of the music. This book will pull back the curtain on some of these details and teach you not only the "how" of playing different grooves and styles, but the "why" of making good musical choices and jelling with the rest of the band. Solo practice is an undeniably important part of getting better, however the culmination of that practice leads us to the greatest joy of being a drummer: playing with others and making music as part of a group. The unspoken musical communication and interaction we experience with bass players, guitarists, pianists and singers can elevate us far beyond what we can achieve on our own. We are always stronger together, and every bus needs a driver.

Photo by Thomas Mester

In the backseat of my Subaru I have a duffel that I call my "oh sh*t" bag. It has wrenches, coolant, drumsticks, bungee cords, laundry detergent, quarter-inch cables, a long extension cord and other odds and ends that could conceivably save my butt in a variety of situations. I don't know how many jams I've gotten out of over the years thanks to the items in that bag. I hope this book serves as your "oh sh*t" bag when you're onstage or in rehearsal and the bandleader asks for something a little out of your comfort zone.

There are over 70 play-along exercises in this book covering many styles. I created all the music specifically for this project with the help of more than twenty of my closest musical collaborators on the New York music scene. Some are full-length songs with entire bands, while others are just drums and bass, which is the core foundation of the rhythm section. For each groove or tune, there is a corresponding video track of me playing and explaining what I'm doing, along with "drummer-less" audio tracks so you can play along with the rest of the band. When I set out to write this book, it was important to me that all the music be original. There are a great many volumes about how to play your favorite cover songs, and this book will teach you the skills to do that too. But as a drummer in New York, I mostly play with artists who are creating their own unique sounds. The process of recording the music for this book was so different with each artist! Some were really into the details of the drums and sent me charts, mp3s and programmed parts as suggestions. Others simply sent a musical idea and said "go." Both are valid approaches, and I think that the more people you play with in any style of music, the easier it is to adapt to anything that gets thrown your way.

Photo by Thomas Mester

Besides the charts and play-along tracks, each section includes a "Tip Jar" with suggestions from me, but also thoughts and quotes from the rest of the band. The artists in this book are not just my collaborators, they are also my friends and musical influences. I can't think of a better way to teach drums than to put you directly in my shoes and give you the experience of rocking out with this diverse and wildly creative crew. Most of all, I hope that their observations can help you understand how other musicians conceptualize the drums in their music. You don't necessarily need to know every chord change or melody note, but the more information you have about the non-drummer stuff, the easier you can turn that knowledge into *Stuff You Can Use* on the drums. You might notice that each of these artists talks about our instrument differently. Some are drummers themselves and can break down every detail of a pattern, while others talk about texture, space and vibe to explain their ideas. However, they all know how they want their music to feel, and they know when it's right and when it's not. Bands are a collaborative experience, and if you really want to learn about how the drums fit in, start by asking the other musicians. So I did!

While you definitely will need to "get in the shed" and work on some of this material before you play along, I hope the audio and video we created will allow you to take the next step and simulate the experience of playing it live with a band. Here's the drill: work on the patterns alone, grab some tips from the jar, watch the video, then use the charts and road maps as your guide to playing along.

You'd be amazed at the wide range of groove requests I get from different artists regardless of what style they play. You also might wonder, "why do I need to know what a rhumba is to play in an indie rock band?" or "what does a drum'n'bass groove have to do with my jazz gig?" The answer is that all these genres are connected, and having a little useful information about each is just another tool in the box you can use in rehearsal or onstage. Skills such as locking in with a bassist, playing rock-solid time without rushing or dragging, transitioning smoothly between sections, playing with dynamics and feel, soloing over a vamp and really listening to the other players transcend any individual style of music. This stuff is good for absolutely everything. The goal of this book is not only to teach you how to play this material, but to help you *learn how to learn* new tunes when they get thrown your way. It's all about developing a process that works for you and accumulating the technical ability and knowledge to handle any musical situation.

I think that developing the art of listening is the most important thing you can do to become a better drummer. This means hearing and interacting with other band members musically while you play, as well as checking out tunes on your own. Variety is the spice of life, and it's best to listen to lots of different music and keep an open mind. Here's a provocative thought: sometimes you can take major steps forward in your musical journey just by hearing music you don't like. This may seem counterintuitive, but the key is to discover *why* you don't like it and use that information to grow. Maybe you think the snare is tuned too tightly or you don't like the tone of the singer's voice. Maybe the bass is too muddy, the guitar doesn't have enough grit or the whole song is just…boring. Listening critically, but with an open mind will help you form opinions on these topics and talk about them with your peers. I've learned so much from sitting in vans, hotel rooms and basements talking about music with other members of the band. While critical listening is essential, I think it's even more important to identify the things you *do* like. Maybe the groove is perfectly in the pocket, the lyrics really speak to you, or that drum fill between the verse and the chorus makes you want to jump out of your seat and boogie. As you listen more, your ears will evolve and your tastes may change over time. I know that some of the music I was into as a teenager sounds totally ridiculous to me now, while other material I never liked took on a whole new meaning when I gave it another chance. You may not love every track in this book (although I hope you do)! However, I sincerely hope you'll give it a shot and find useful bits to take away from each and every section. Grabbing that perfect item out of the "oh sh*t" bag will make the music feel amazing and the other musicians happy. ***Stuff You Can Use!***

GROOVE WORKSHOPS

The first part of this book includes a series of "Groove Workshop" sections across many different styles. These beats are by no means a complete list from each genre, but include many concepts you may encounter in everyday band situations. There are so many different types of grooves in the world, including limitless variations and tweaks you can make on each one. Something as simple as the placement of a single bass drum note can totally change how a pattern fits within the rest of a song. How much volume difference is there between the accented and non-accented notes? How does the vibe change when you open the hi-hat slightly versus a lot? Is it really on top of the beat or more laid back? Is it swung or more straight? These details are so important. Working on these and using the play-along tracks to try them out with a bass player will give you some skills and vocabulary you can apply to the full-band tracks that come afterwards.

I've always felt that the best way to learn new patterns is to deconstruct them. If you can't play every limb in isolation, you won't be able to play the whole pattern together. Imagine that you're building a house. Begin with the foundation (your feet), then add the frame (your snare) and finish with the details (everything else). Playing every single combination of hands and feet on its own first will help you build that house strong. Sometimes it's tempting to skip these steps and try to play the whole pattern right away. However, this can be super-frustrating and waste a lot of time. When I was younger, I would always try to cut this corner. If you can get in the habit of running each new pattern through this set of procedures, you'll find that learning grooves gets easier every time.

For many grooves, I've written out a basic version plus a variation or two. However, the patterns on the page are not meant to be played in a vacuum. Work with these grooves and get comfortable with them. Move them around the kit and come up with your own variations. Be creative, play them with feeling and above all else, have fun with the stuff. I know I did. No two drummers sound exactly alike, so don't worry if you see me do it on the video and you don't sound the way I do. Put your own spin on these and find your voice.

Dmitry Ishenko & Rob Mitzner

Photo by Seth Block

On that topic, another musical voice you'll hear a lot throughout this book is bassist Dmitry Ishenko, who played on all these groove play-alongs and many of the full band songs. One common theme throughout every section of this book is the importance of locking in with the bass, and I've played with Dmitry for almost 20 years. We've traveled around the world and backed countless artists across so many styles. We've recorded over 30 albums together as a rhythm section and simply put, he's one of the most versatile and creative bassists around. He can play any style on acoustic or electric and knows more about music than almost anyone I've ever met. Playing with him for all these years has made me a better drummer and a stronger overall musician. I'm excited to share his talents and ideas with you, and I hope you'll enjoy grooving along with him as much as I do.

Now that we've gone over the the process and met our bassist, let's get started! Begin each groove slowly and speed up gradually until you reach the written tempo. Practice the hands and feet separately at first, try using a metronome and repeat as many times as necessary. Once you've got it down, use the play-alongs to rock out with Dmitry. Note that each play-along track has two measures of count-in.

STUFF YOU CAN USE

GROOVE WORKSHOP 1: ROCK

Groove #1a: Loose HH Rock
♪ = 150

Groove #1b: Crash City
♪ = 160

TIP JAR:

- Loosen the hi-hats a little, but not so much that it sounds sloppy. Picking up your toes slightly inside your shoe should do the trick.
- Really smack those accents on the snare to give the pattern some shape and definition. Try to make the buzzed snare notes on the "a" of beats 2 and 4 as crisp as possible.
- Often with rock grooves, your bass drum and the bass player should lock in and play the same rhythms. But sometimes, the two will diverge and do their own thing while lining up in strategic spots. This is one of those beats where the bassist plays 16th notes to propel the groove, while the drums are less busy and focused around those snare accents.
- From Dmitry: "There are some anticipated notes in the bass line that align with the accents of the drums. It would be good to hear the drummer play some of those with me (particularly the 'e' of beats 1 and 3 on the snare)."
- 1b is the same groove, but with the crash cymbal replacing the hi-hat. This variation will make it even heavier and fatter. You could conceivably use pattern 1a for the verse of a tune and switch to 1b for the chorus to kick up the intensity.

Groove Workshop 1: Rock

Groove #2: Rock Tight

(Variation A)

(Variation B)

TIP JAR:

- This one has a totally different texture than the last groove since the hi-hat is closed.
- The bass drum and the bass player are playing the exact same thing. Lock it in with Dmitry and try to keep the feel nice and relaxed.
- The 2b variation has the same kick/snare pattern, but moves the right hand over to the ride, adds a crash on beat 3 and a buzzed snare anticipation at the end. It's still a "tight" feel since the bass and drums are locked together, but the texture is a little more open. You'll hear me talk about texture a lot in this book. This is a small thing that makes a very big difference in your sound.
- You could use pattern 2a for the verse of a tune and 2b for the pre-chorus or chorus to create a texture change without altering the underlying rhythm.

STUFF YOU CAN USE

Groove #3: The Sludge

(Variation A)

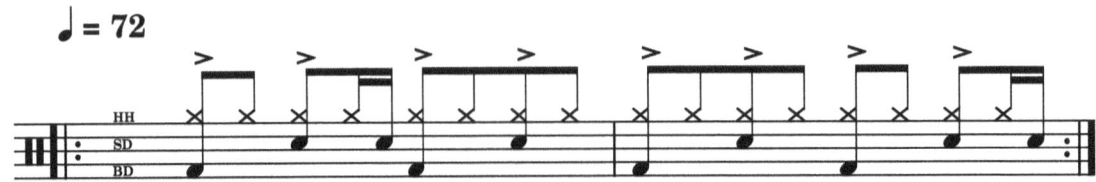

(Variation B)

TIP JAR:

- These grooves are meant to be played *waaaay* behind the beat to create the right feel. The patterns themselves are simple, but it's really about the beat placement.
- You almost need to split your body so the kick and snare are exactly with the metronome while the hi-hat creates the "sludgey" feel by playing a little behind. This is not easy! But it's so much fun.
- There is a ton of room for fills at this slow tempo, but…leaving space is good sometimes. It's just like having a conversation where not every moment has to be filled with talking. It's important not to fight the metronome and actually slow the tempo down so you sink into "the sludge."
- From Dmitry: "If it feels like the groove is starting to drag, I try to play it safe and simplify things so we don't lose the connection. Years ago I saw a clinic with the great bassist Carole Kaye who played with The Beach Boys, Simon & Garfunkel and on thousands of other famous albums. She talked about how there were sometimes moments of tension between the bass and drums, and her strategy was always to try to subtly nudge things in the right direction. I think the key is to relax and trust your internal metronome."
- 3b looks even more simple than 3a, but should be just as far behind the beat. Since this variation moves over to the crash cymbal, it creates an even heavier feel. "The sludge" has turned to total slop! But don't actually slow down.
- As we did on the play-along track, you can use 3a for a verse groove, switch to 3b for the chorus and then back.

Groove Workshop 1: Rock

Groove #4: Top O' The Beat

♩ = 158

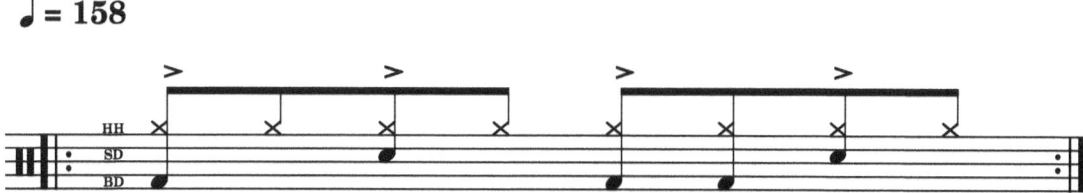

TIP JAR:

- This is the total opposite of the previous one in that both the bass and drums are playing extremely on top of the beat. This groove should almost feel like it's going to pull away from the metronome, but never should. This simple pattern is perfect for high-energy rock tunes, and you can loosen the hi-hat or switch to the ride for different textures and tones. When you play along with Dmitry, keep your foot on the gas but don't race away! The feel is everything.

Groove #5: Toms Busy

♩ = 175

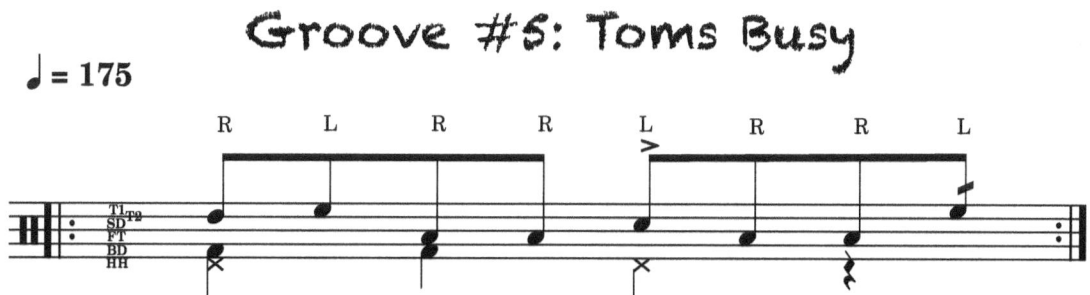

TIP JAR:

- Having a few tom-based grooves in the "oh sh*t" bag is really useful. Artists ask for these all the time as a way to create a darker tone in certain sections of the music (more on this later).
- The hands propel this groove while the feet are more sparse and steady. The right hand plays on tom 2 and the floor tom, while the left handles tom 1 and the snare. Try to get the sticking down first and then add the feet.
- From Dmitry: "The bass and drums are almost doing the same thing on different instruments. Playing on the toms thickens the groove, and we're still locking in on the accents. The bass guitar and toms have similar timbres, so depending on how the drummer tunes their drums, I'll sometimes play a bit higher so we don't clash. But the rhythm stays the same."

STUFF YOU CAN USE

Groove #6: Toms Sparse

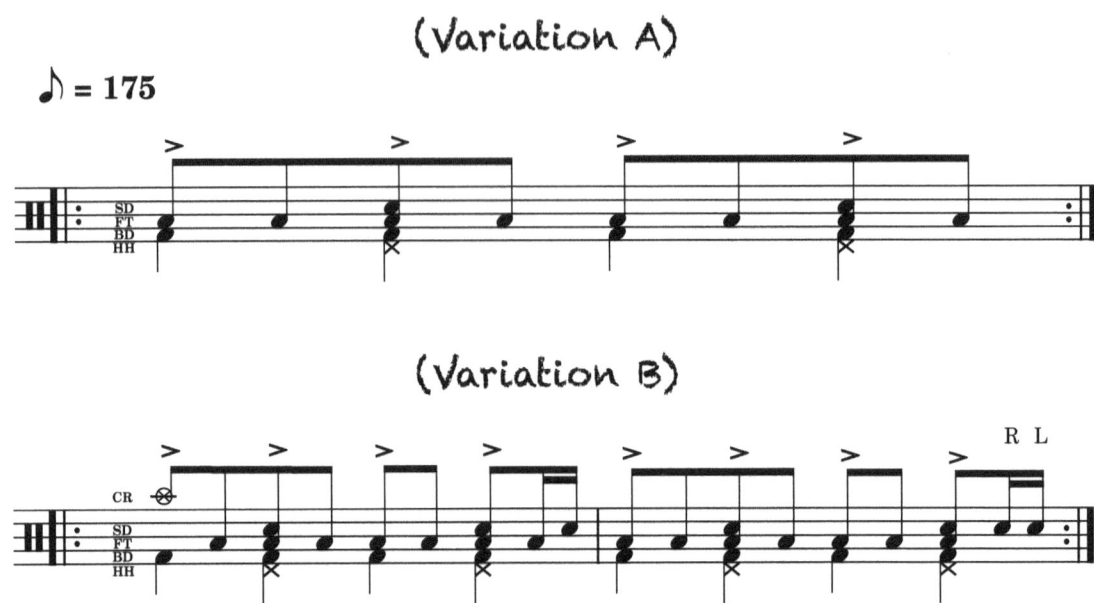

TIP JAR:

- These patterns are slower and less busy, but very driving. The bass drum quarter notes are the heartbeat and there is lots of room to add grace notes, small fills and variations. Experiment and have fun while keeping the bass drum and snare backbeat steady.

- Both grooves should be played with the right hand on the floor tom and the left on the snare. Use the notated "R L" sticking for the final snare lick of the variation to help smooth it out. Gotta keep a good flow!

- From Dmitry: "I feel like the bass and drums are kind of doing their own thing on this groove. Unlike the last groove where we're playing mostly together, this groove is more contrapuntal." *(Note: see the Glossary of Musical Slang at the end of the book if you're not sure what he's talking about, and watch the video for further explanation.)* This concept of the bass and drums sometimes playing the same rhythms and sometimes diverging is one of the most important subtleties in this important rhythm section relationship.

Photo by Thomas Mester

Groove Workshop 1: Rock

Groove #7: 4-On-The-Floor Downbeats

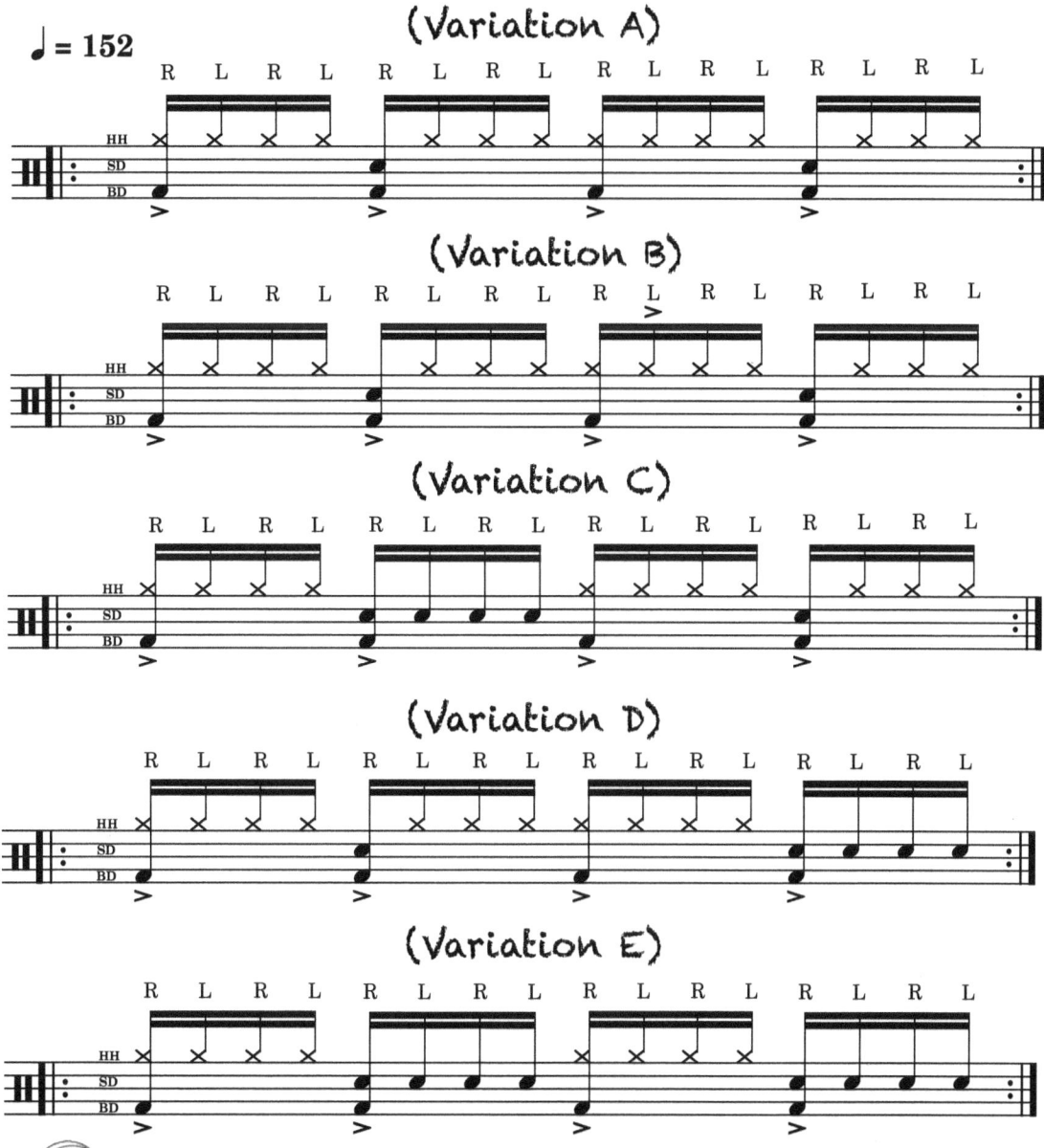

TIP JAR:

- This type of 16th-note dance/rock groove has become really popular in modern music. It may seem a bit like a disco beat, but it should be more driving with an emphasis on the downbeats rather than the upbeats.
- The variations are all on the snare and hi-hat, while the feet play "4-on-the-floor" (bass drum quarter notes on every beat). I like to keep a simple alternating sticking pattern going throughout and use my hands to create small fills.
- Play this one with a lot of energy and stay on top of the beat. This pattern should be super-crisp and tight, almost as if you are emulating the precision of a drum machine. *(Hint: lift your toes inside your shoe to get that perfect hi-hat sizzle.)*
- From Dmitry: "This beat is so steady and static in a positive sense. It really grooves and I feel like I have a lot of freedom to play and add ideas on top of what the drums are doing."

STUFF YOU CAN USE

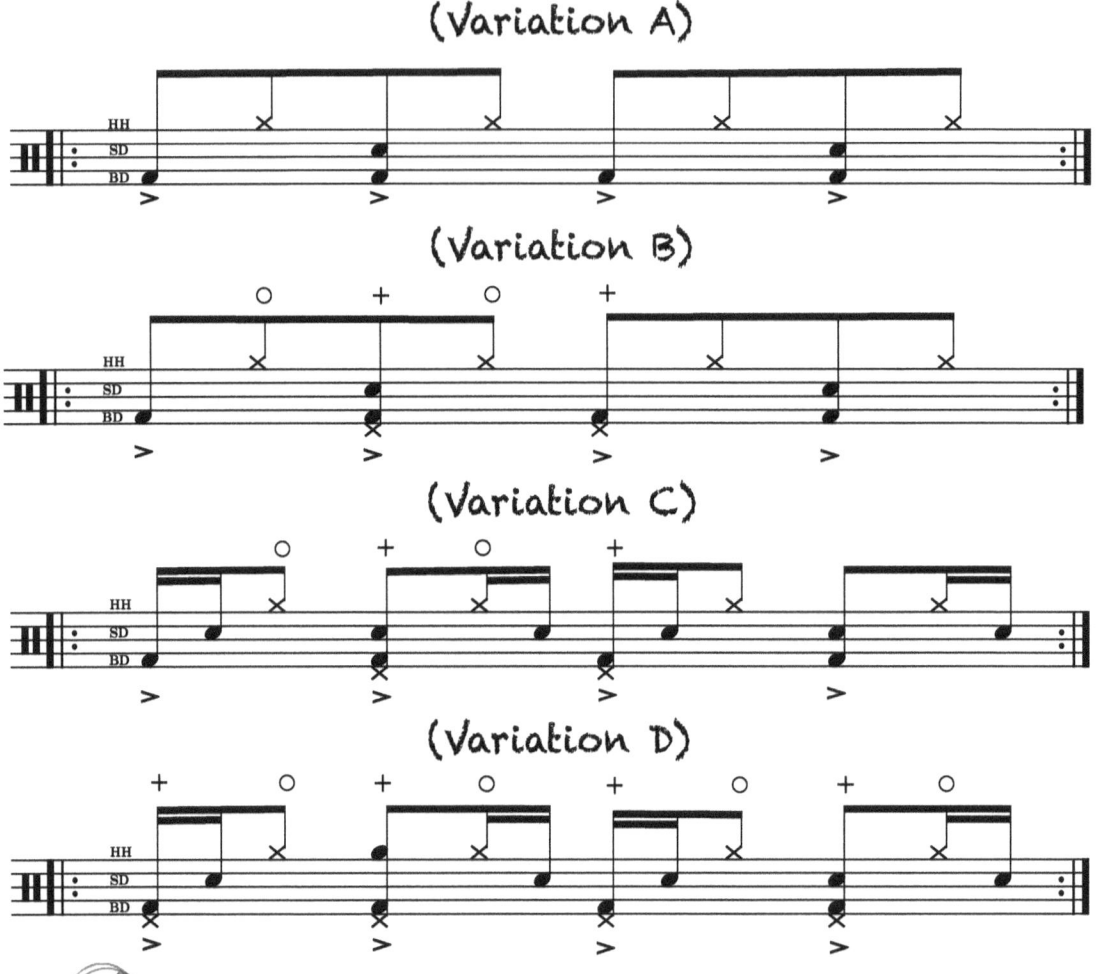

Groove #8: 4-On-The-Floor Upbeats
(Variation A)
(Variation B)
(Variation C)
(Variation D)

TIP JAR:

- This set also has a 4-on-the-floor backbeat, but with an emphasis on the upbeats to give it a funky, bouncy feel.
- Even though you're playing 8th notes on the hi-hat instead of 16ths, stay on top of the beat to keep it moving forward.
- Lift your toes inside your shoe for that tasty hi-hat sizzle (this is a recurring theme).
- Really nail down the first groove before you move on to the variations. All the ghost notes in the variations are just designed to add flavor.
- Listen closely to Dmitry in the play-along track since the drums and bass are playing a little "call-and-response." In the first part of the measure, I open the hi-hat and the bass plays in a lower octave, while the second part is the opposite: he goes up high while the drums "contract" and play tighter (particularly when I play variations B and C). This may seem like a tiny detail, but tonal interplay is an important concept.
- From Dmitry: "This is kind of a post-punk groove that reminds me of Talking Heads' *Remain in Light* album. I'm trying to play sparsely and let things breathe so the drummer can do their job and lay down the basic parts of the beat. It's very comfortable and I love this groove."

Groove Workshop 1: Rock

Groove #9: Loose Heavy

(Variation A)

♩ = 80

(Variation B)

(Variation C)

TIP JAR:

- The positioning of all these grooves relative to the metronome is the secret sauce that can make them sound super-hip. These patterns are played at a slower tempo and should be pretty far behind the beat.
- It's all about locking in the bass drum with Dmitry's bass notes throughout the 2-bar phrase. Everything else that's happening with the hands is more about adding color and texture.
- If you're playing onstage, it's easy to start this groove too fast or rush away when the adrenaline kicks in. Try to hold your body back and play with a relaxed feel.
- From Dmitry: "I want my bass to be right with those big fat bass drum notes since that's what I'm connecting to. And the tempo is pretty slow, so I can add layers in-between as long as I'm still locking in with the bass drum, which is a magical, time-proven technique over many decades of music. As far as the feel, you want to lay it back without getting too much into slop territory."

STUFF YOU CAN USE

GROOVE WORKSHOP 2: DRUM'N'BASS, REGGAE

Groove #10: Simple Drum'n'bass

TIP JAR:

- Drum'n'bass grooves feature a lot of tiny little notes that work together to propel the beat forward. The drums are usually tuned tightly and muffled using gels or tape to reduce overtones and create a super-dry tone.
- To get this sound, use primarily the bass drum, snare, closed hi-hat and cymbals that don't have a lot of decay.
- The key to making these beats work is to play them with a machine-like level of technical precision and control that almost mimics an electronic drum sound. Lift your toes inside your shoe for the hi-hat sizzle (again)!
- Even though it feels like there is a lot going on in the drum part, the underlying accents on beats 2 and the "and" of 3 are present the entire time and tie the whole thing together. Stick with that rhythm at first, then sprinkle in small fills and variations.
- Practice slowly and build the tempo as you get more comfortable.
- From Dmitry: "I'm much more free to play across the bar line and my parts are more sparse than on an R&B or funk groove. I'm playing lots of drone-y long notes while the drums frame everything and do most of the work."

Photo by Thomas Mester

Groove Workshop 2: Drum'n'bass, Reggae

Groove #11: Half-Time Drum'n'bass

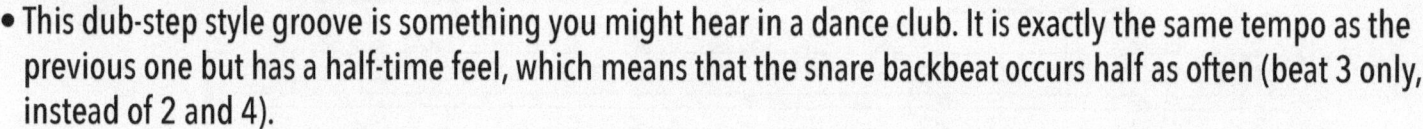

TIP JAR:

- This dub-step style groove is something you might hear in a dance club. It is exactly the same tempo as the previous one but has a half-time feel, which means that the snare backbeat occurs half as often (beat 3 only, instead of 2 and 4).

- The little notes on the hi-hat combined with the thumping 4-on-the-floor of the bass drum make this a driving and propulsive pattern. However, it's important not to play too loud, which could make it sound sloppy. Once you get comfortable, there are a lot of fun variations to explore as long as you keep that 4-on-the-floor and play on top of the beat. Keep your fills short and punchy while building and expanding on your ideas.

- This is another one where the goal is to emulate the sound of a drum machine. However, the groove should still be allowed to expand and breathe since, as Dmitry says, "we are inspired by machines, but we are not them…yet."

Dmitry and Rob after a show at The Blue Note. Photo by Rebecca Leach

STUFF YOU CAN USE

Groove #12: Breakbeat

(Variation A)

♩ = 140

(Variation B)

(Variation C)

TIP JAR:

- This breakbeat still has 4-on-the-floor (like we're at the club), and the snare notes other than beat 3 should be played as quiet "ghost notes" that add flavor and momentum.
- The bass and drums really lock in on the accented rhythm to form the backbone of this groove.
- If you add fills, make them staccato and crisp. Focus on the snare and other parts of the kit that don't have a lot of wash or sustain.
- (Hint: check out Jojo Mayer with his band *Nerve*. He is one of the icons of this style of drumming.)

Rob at American Music in Seattle, WA

Groove Workshop 2: Drum'n'bass, Reggae

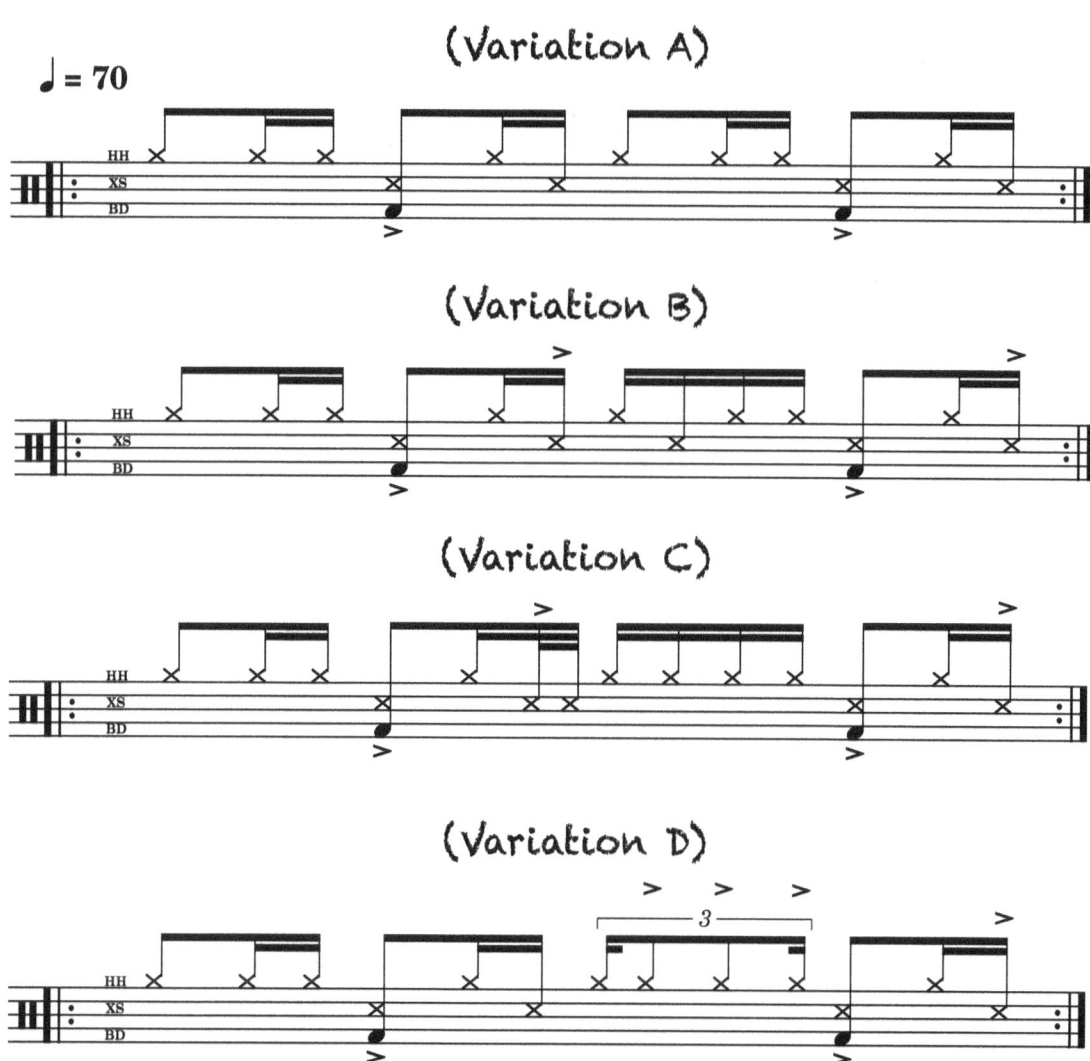

Groove #13: Reggae
(Straight or Swung)

(Variation A)

♩ = 70

(Variation B)

(Variation C)

(Variation D)

TIP JAR:

- The feel of these grooves is almost the polar opposite of the drum'n'bass, as the key to reggae is to play relaxed and behind the beat.
- The bass drum is played in unison with the cross-stick on beats 2 and 4 and generally avoids beat 1. This is very unique and sets this style apart from funk or rock. You can be creative with hi-hat and cross-stick variations as long as that bass drum part stays the same.
- All these variations work with a straight or swung 8th-note feel. Both are good to have in your repertoire, and the key is choosing the right one when someone asks for a reggae groove. Use your ears and give it your best shot!
- From Dmitry: "Stay simple, repetitive and pulled way back behind the beat."

STUFF YOU CAN USE

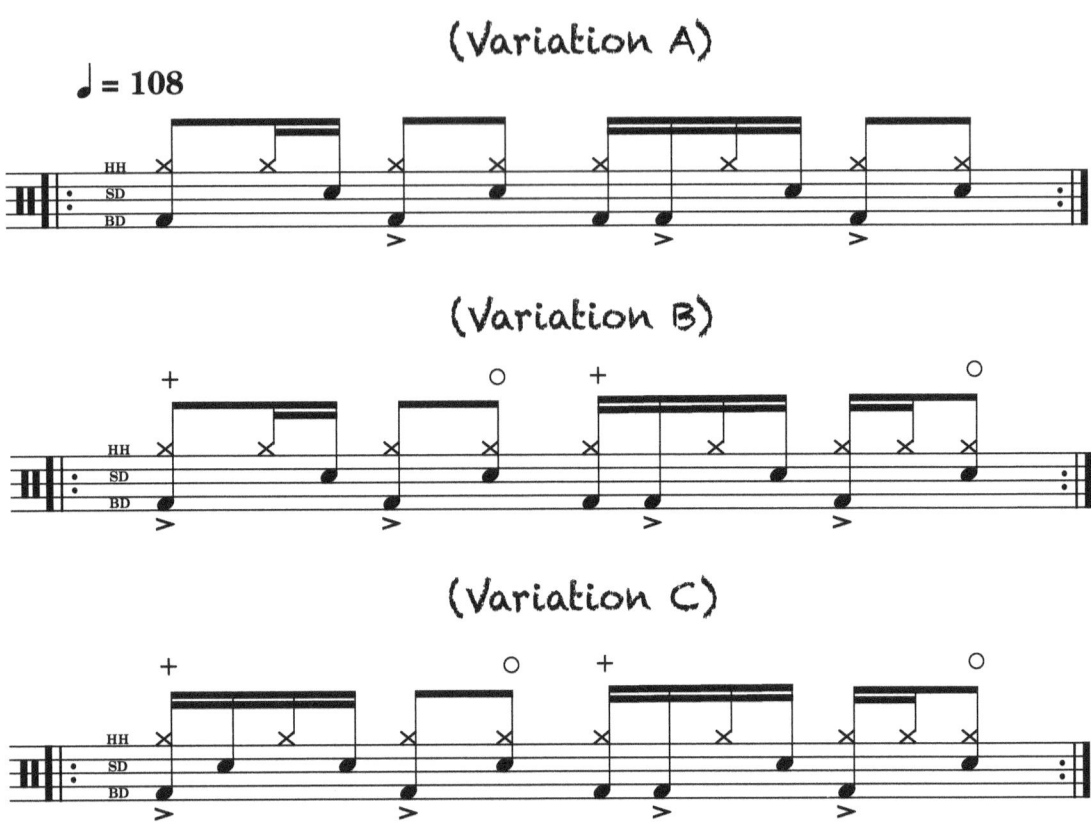

TIP JAR:

- Whenever someone has asked me for a dance-y, island, reggaeton-style beat, these have always fit the bill (they also differ slightly from a soca or calypso groove, which we'll dive into later).
- The bass drum and snare pattern are the engine that drives this one. Stick with that rhythm and keep it steady, hypnotic and grooving. If you do a fill, try to keep it within the framework of the pattern and don't deviate too much. Adding one extra note here or there will help the pattern breathe a little bit without detracting from the main rhythm.
- From Dmitry: "On this one, the bass and drums play the same rhythms. On the downbeat, I lock in with the kick drum and on the rest of the figure I lock in with the snare."

Photo by Thomas Mester

GROOVE WORKSHOP 3: R&B, FUNK & SOUL

Groove #15: Barry

(Variation A)

(Variation B)

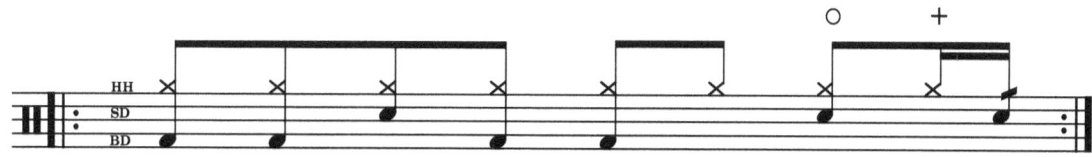

(Variation C)

TIP JAR:

- This groove was inspired by the famous Barry White album *Staying Power*, but you can find it in different forms and variations throughout modern and classic soul music. Play the 8th notes slightly swung and keep the feel bouncy and loose.
- The most important thing is to lock in the bass drum part with the bass player and keep a solid backbeat. All the other notes you're playing should support that interaction, such as the snare anticipation and open hi-hat in variation B, and the bounced bass drum in variation C. These are fun ornamentations that make it more funky.
- Try to stay slightly behind the beat but keep the feel crisp and confident.
- From Dmitry: "We're trying to play this really relaxed and not too on top, but very assertive. I'm mainly playing the same two-note rhythm and letting the drums do most of the work. In this groove, I'm really focusing on the kick drum."

STUFF YOU CAN USE

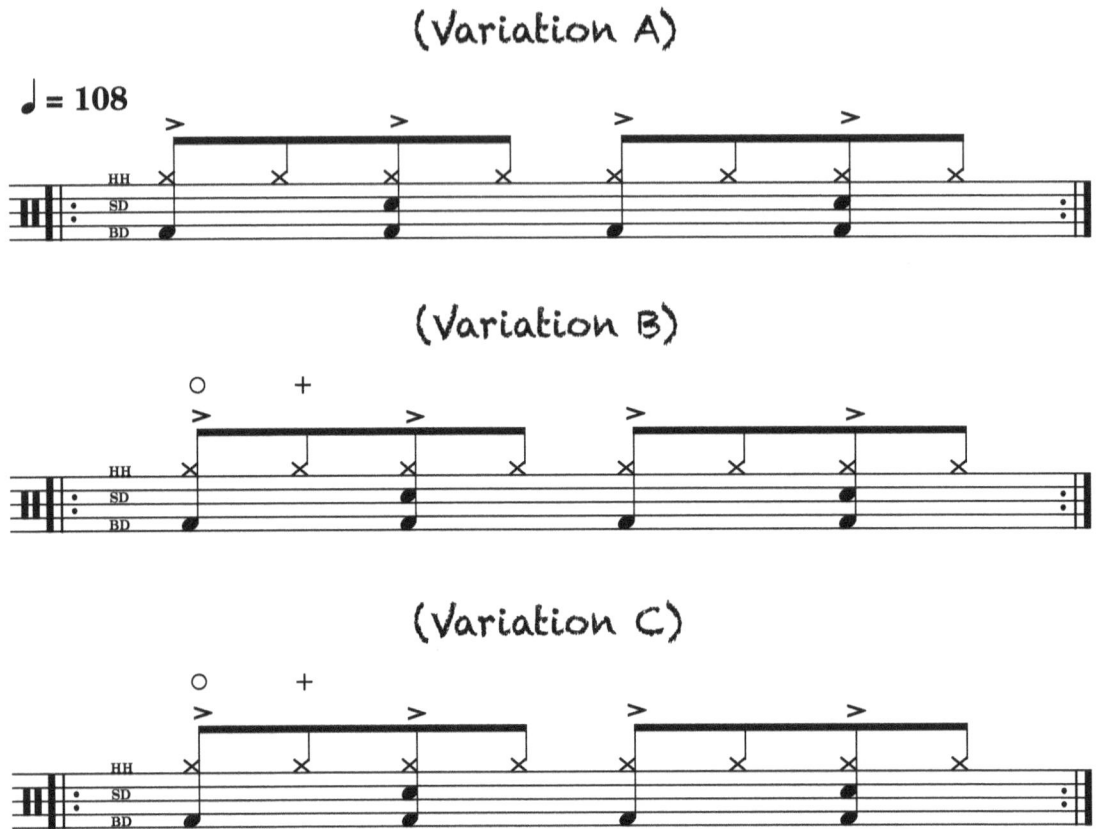

TIP JAR:

- This is a fun and important one since this groove pops up in so many situations. The key is to keep that 4-on-the-floor steady and solid. I named it after drumming legend Billy Cobham after hearing him play it on the tune "Hip Pockets" from his *'Live' on Tour in Europe* album with George Duke.
- Stay on top of the beat and give this one some energy. Use the "slap-tap" technique with your right hand to accent the downbeats on the closed hi-hat. This will make the pattern feel much more funky (see *Glossary of Musical Slang* for more info if you're not sure what that is).
- Variations B and C add some short moments where you open the hi-hat. Try to make them crisp and tight by lifting those toes inside your shoe.
- It's cool to add some little notes for flavor and color in-between the beats as long as your bass drum keeps playing the quarter-note pattern to drive the groove forward.
- From Dmitry: "I am playing along with the 4-on-the-floor, but I'm also going away from it a little. I do a lot of anticipated e's and a's to make it funky, but that kick drum is what I'm listening to. It's like my personal metronome."

Groove Workshop 3: R&B, Funk & Soul

Groove #17: T.O.P. Linear

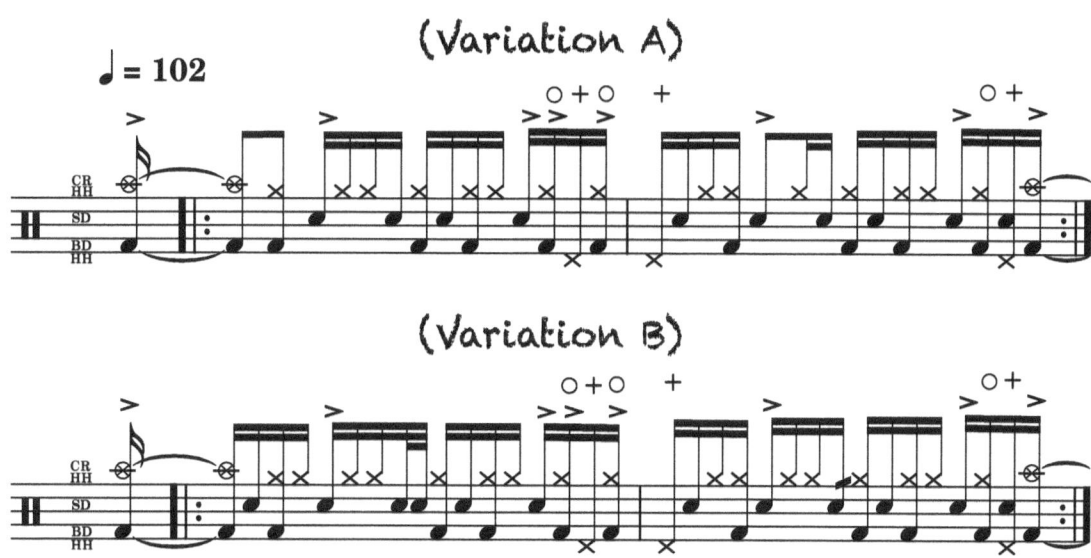

(Variation A) ♩ = 102

(Variation B)

TIP JAR:

- We call this a linear groove because the limbs are mostly playing one at a time to create a propulsive 16th-note feel. This groove is challenging since you never actually play on the downbeat of the measure.

- This concept was popularized by David Garibaldi of Tower of Power, along with The Headhunters' Mike Clark, and the accents are critical to getting it right. Try to create the biggest possible volume difference between your accented and non-accented notes. Instead of playing the accented notes louder, try reducing the level of the others so they feel almost like ghost notes. This will help the pattern have some shape and groove harder.

- The bass and drums are mostly doing their own thing but join each other at certain important parts of the groove, especially the last note of the second measure (the "a" of beat 4).

- From Dmitry: "It's the 16th note that matters. This groove is all even subdivisions and we aren't playing downbeats very often. It's very important to have your internal clock going the whole time because we aren't playing on the strong beats of the measure. It's vital to know exactly where you are and be very grounded."

Bacon-wrapped asparagus @ Karczma in Brooklyn, NY

STUFF YOU CAN USE

Groove #18: JB

(Variation A)

(Variation B)

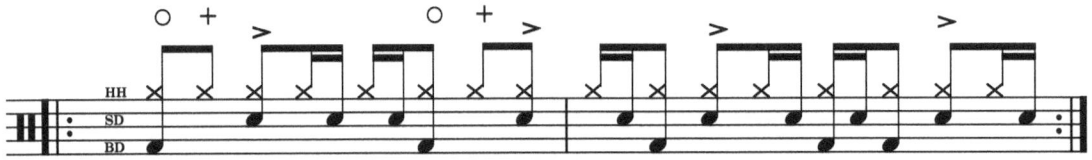

TIP JAR:

- The key to this groove is that the snare in the first measure is played on the "and" of 4 instead of on the beat. This displacement only happens in the first measure of the 2-bar phrase and the second measure almost serves as an opportunity to re-gather yourself before it comes back around.

- Keep the hi-hat really tight until you open it. Lift those toes for the sizzle!

- From Dmitry: "It's like you take a collection of notes and spread it out like a piece of butter. When you hear some of the James Brown sidemen talk about this groove, they always say that he was all about emphasizing the '1.' What he really meant was the downbeat every two bars. It's always reestablishing where you are and marking the territory. You play that '1,' then you go off and play the rest of it, then you play it again. We're also playing pretty on top of the beat."

Rob with legendary soul drummer Bernard Purdie at an event in NYC

Groove Workshop 3: R&B, Funk & Soul

Groove #19: Motown

TIP JAR:

- You can find this groove on countless Motown hits from the '50s and '60s ("Superfly" by Curtis Mayfield is one great example). The quarter-note pulse is very important and the bass drum and snare are playing it in unison.
- Keep this one super-simple and use the "slap-tap" technique on the hi-hat to accent the downbeats and give it some shape. In this groove, the bass and other instruments are more rhythmically active while the drums just lay it down. Opening the hi-hat on the "and" of beat 4 gives it a bit of breath, but it's mostly good to stick with the basic pattern and avoid playing a lot of fills.
- This one should be played right on the fat center of the beat as opposed to on top or behind.
- From Dmitry: "The bass part is more of its own melody and is pretty syncopated. It's fully relying on the drums to provide the momentum from those quarter notes."

Groove #20: '50s/Amy Winehouse

TIP JAR:

- This is a '50s-era groove that has enjoyed a renaissance in modern pop music. You can hear it on everything from Chuck Berry's classic "Johnny B. Goode" to "Rehab" by Amy Winehouse. The snare part is the key, so stick with it even if you add a few small fills.
- From Dmitry: "As a bass player, I'm definitely zeroing in on the downbeat and the 'and' of beat 2. That's the essence of the groove. The rest, I can fill in and the drums can too."

STUFF YOU CAN USE

Groove #21: Steve Jordan

TIP JAR:

- This one has a similar snare rhythm as the previous groove, but the feel is totally different. It's a far slower tempo and the 8th notes are slightly swung. It's almost as if the ride cymbal is played on the middle of the beat while the snare is a little behind to create a contrast. This might not seem hard at first glance, but these subtleties can make the difference between a tight pocket and a muddy mess!
- Sometimes it's hard to know how much to swing a groove or play it straight in different musical situations. There are so many different degrees of swing, and the more you play, the better you'll get at making the right decisions. Listen hard to the other musicians and trust your ears.
- I called this one the "Steve Jordan" because it's laid back and funky, but still assertive. (He plays a similar groove on "Waiting On the World to Change" by John Mayer.)
- From Dmitry: "Playing the swing grooves versus the straight ones is like being in completely different countries…or continents."

Groove #22: Old-School Hip-Hop

TIP JAR:

- This is a great one to have in the bag. The hi-hat 16th notes are slightly swung while the bass drum and snare are right on the beat.
- The articulation of those hi-hat notes on the "a" of beat 2 and the "e" of beat 4 gives this groove its funky flavor, while the bass drum should line up directly with the bass player.
- From Dmitry: "I'm really just locking in with the bass drum and providing a percussive punch. I'm also listening to the hi-hat for the time, but as far as connecting my notes with the drums, I'm concentrating on landing together with the kick drum and creating one tone. Since this is an old-school hip-hop beat, it's almost like we're emulating the sound of those vintage drum machines like the TR-808 or 909."

Groove Workshop 3: R&B, Funk & Soul

Groove #23: J Dilla/Glasper

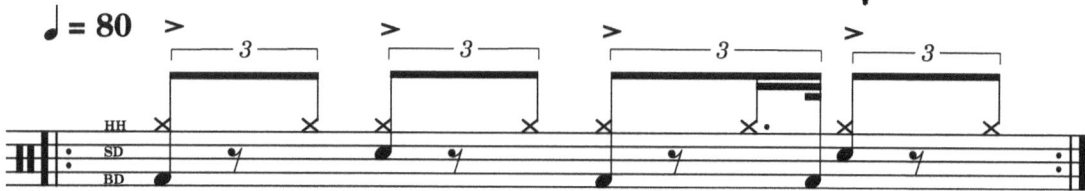

TIP JAR:

- This one is a real challenge! The groove feels a little stilted and uneasy as you play slightly ahead of, and behind the beat at different points. The note placement is the key to making it work. Avoid swinging the triplets on the hi-hat so much that it turns into a shuffle. The snare should be a tiny bit on top of the beat, while the hi-hat is more behind.
- You almost have to pull yourself apart and become comfortable with the idea that the time may not feel perfectly straight even as the tempo stays the same. The goal is to create a disorienting, washy effect with the bass player by not actually playing all the notes exactly together.
- This type of groove was popularized in the early 2000s by pioneer hip-hop producer J Dilla and used in jazz and hip-hop by artists like D'Angelo and Robert Glasper. It's very common in electronically produced music, but it's important for live drummers to be able to emulate it.
- From Dmitry: "It's funny, but I'm not looking to lock in with the drums on this particular groove. It's really behind the beat, and if you're playing to a click and you feel like it's a 32nd note ahead of you, that's maybe a good thing! You're displacing everything to such an extent that you're almost pulling the metronome behind you, but then you catch up and realign with it. You have to embrace the disparity of the feel and the fact that everybody is pulling on the beat. It's almost as if it's both straight and swung and everything is slightly exaggerated."

Groove #24: Disco

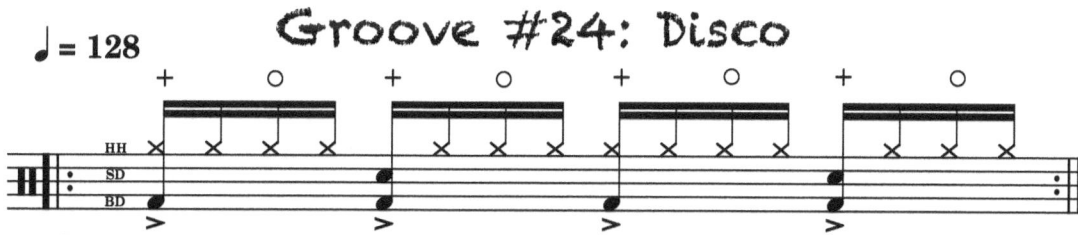

TIP JAR:

- This classic disco beat differs from the 16th-note, 4-on-the-floor rock grooves we covered earlier in that we're loosening the hi-hats on every upbeat. The hi-hat part really drives this pattern forward, and it's important to keep it super-tight and then loosen it just the right amount (toes inside the shoe)!
- There are a lot of notes here and the tempo is fast, so keep this pattern crisp and clean and avoid getting out of control. Try to play it slightly on top of the beat without rushing.
- The bass part is very active while the drums are holding it down with that 4-on-the-floor.
- From Dmitry: "I'm playing constant 8th notes with some 16ths mixed in. The connection point and main focus for me is that bass drum."

STUFF YOU CAN USE

Groove #25: Half-Time R&B Ballad

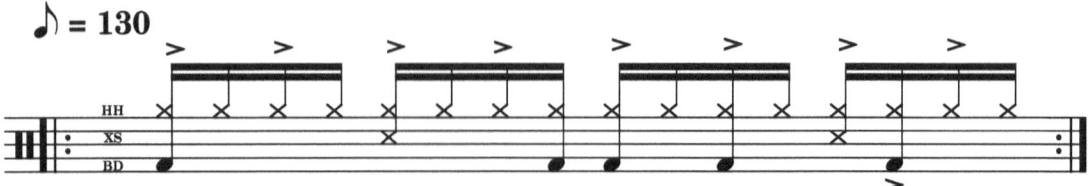

TIP JAR:

- This groove is very subtle and relaxed as the bass drum and the bass lock in, especially on the "e" of beat 4. That one little note gives this groove a lot of its flavor and buoyancy. Artists ask for this pattern all the time in R&B settings, but it applies to pop music too.

- Use the "slap-tap" technique with your right hand on the hi-hat to accent the downbeats and add articulation and color. This will make it groove way harder!

- To get the fattest cross-stick sound, flip your left stick upside down and position it on the hoop about 2 inches from the end. Grip firmly with your thumb and forefinger, keeping your other digits loose while resting them gently on the snare head. Use the tip of the stick (which should also be resting on the head) as a fulcrum and hit the rim firmly. Experiment with the positioning and grip until you find the most comfortable feel and best sound. This may seem like a small detail, but it's very important.

- From Dmitry: "I'm really trying to lay behind the beat on this one and keep it relaxed."

Recording @ Berklee College of Music in Boston, MA

Groove Workshop 3: R&B, Funk & Soul

Groove #26: Regular Shuffle

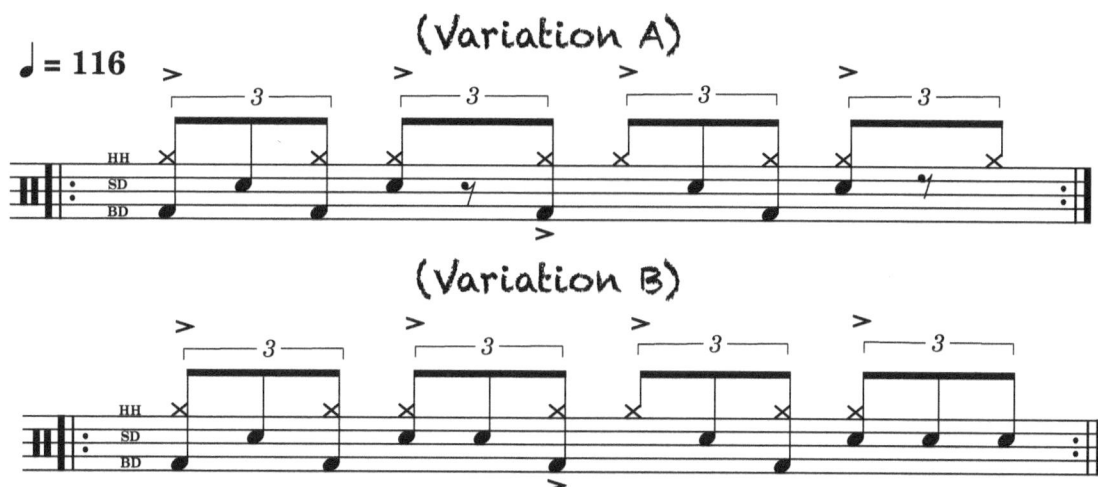

TIP JAR:

- This shuffle has a strong underlying triplet feel happening beneath the snare backbeat. The key is to have a big difference between your accented and non-accented notes so they all don't sound the same. It's just like having a conversation and emphasizing certain words and phrases to give them more meaning.
- Try to play the groove more in the center of the beat rather than behind. It should be relaxed, but assertive and not too sloppy.
- This groove is applicable to a lot of different musical situations such as blues, rock, R&B and even pop. Once you're comfortable, try moving your right hand over the ride cymbal and adding a few small fills.

Rob with Andrea Capozzoli, Maggie Scott and Dmitry Ishenko in Boston, MA

STUFF YOU CAN USE

Groove #27: Half-Time Shuffle

TIP JAR:

- This type of half-time R&B shuffle was popularized by legendary soul drummer Bernard Purdie along with Toto drummer Jeff Porcaro. The key is to lay back on the beat and (again) create a big gap between the volume of your accented and non-accented notes.
- Use the "slap-tap" technique on the hi-hat to make it funky. The underlying triplet feel happens throughout, but the snare hit on beat 3 creates the feeling of a half-time backbeat.
- It should feel relaxed and a little behind the beat. Variation B turns it into a 2-bar phrase with a couple extra embellishments, however it should still be light and bouncy.
- From Dmitry: "I'm listening to the triplets to keep the rhythm because my part is quite sparse. I don't mark that many beats except for the downbeat, so those triplets help me out a lot."

Photo by Thomas Mester

Groove Workshop 3: R&B, Funk & Soul

Groove #28: Slow & Sparse

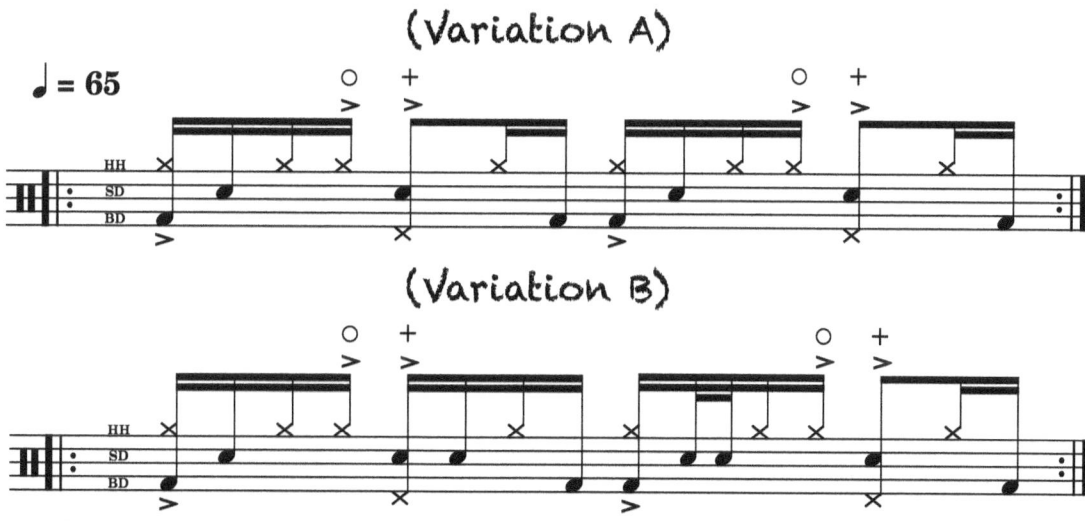

TIP JAR:

- I *love* this groove. The slow tempo makes it challenging to get in the pocket, and opening the hi-hat on the "a" of beats 1 and 3 gives it great shape and definition.
- This one should be played far behind the beat and your bass drum should lock in with the bass player.
- Variation B adds a few ghost notes, but the key is to keep popping those hi-hat and snare accents to make it feel good.

Groove #29: 6/8 Gospel/R&B Ballad

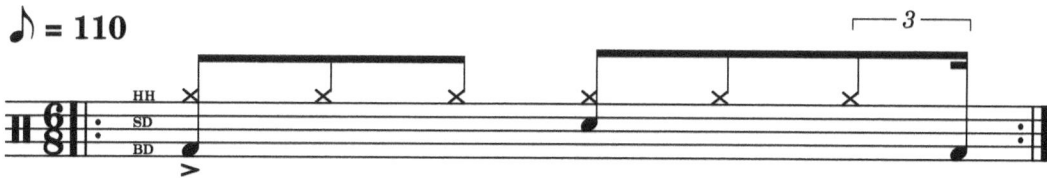

TIP JAR:

- You can find this pattern in everything from Aretha Franklin to Alicia Keys. It looks easy, but can be a bit tricky to get the feel just right. It should be played a little behind the beat, but it's important not to let it drag.
- The last bass drum note is the secret sauce to making it funky, so getting the note placement right is critical.
- You could theoretically use this hi-hat groove for the verse of a tune and then switch over to the ride cymbal for the chorus.

STUFF YOU CAN USE

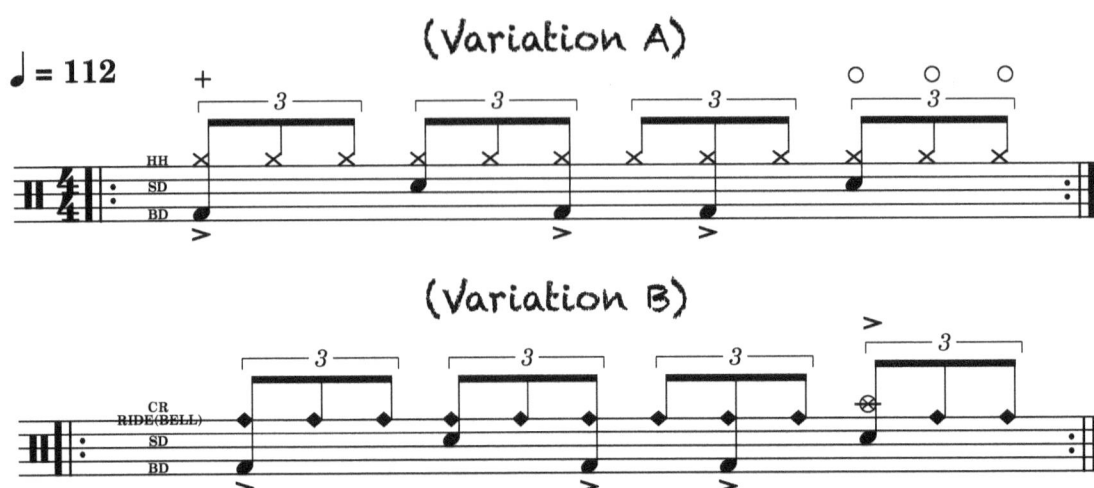

Groove #30: Gospel Trips

(Variation A)

(Variation B)

TIP JAR:

- This triplet-style groove (which was inspired by gospel artist Fred Hammond) has some interesting syncopations that make it funky and fun to play.
- The first two beats are very straightforward, while beats 3 and 4 are more chopped up. This creates a "call-and-response" effect between the two parts of this groove.
- Stay on top of the beat and keep driving forward with the hi-hat while you lock in the bass drum with the bass player.
- Variation B moves it over to the ride cymbal bell and adds a crash on beat 4. You could conceivably use A on the verse of a tune and switch to B for the chorus to create a texture change without deviating from the main rhythm.
- From Dmitry: "This is a really cool syncopated beat and I'm definitely working off the bass drum the whole time. Those syncopations are like a series of little hiccups that drive the groove forward."

Groove Workshop 4: World Music

GROOVE WORKSHOP 4: WORLD MUSIC

This next set features a variety of grooves from around the world adapted for the drum set. These beats provide a brief glance at each style, and I hope they'll help you in the event someone asks you to play one of them in a rehearsal or onstage. There are whole books that delve deeply into the history of these rhythms and if something piques your interest, I hope you'll take the opportunity to explore it further. In the meantime, here's some *Stuff You Can Use*.

Groove #31: Irish Jig

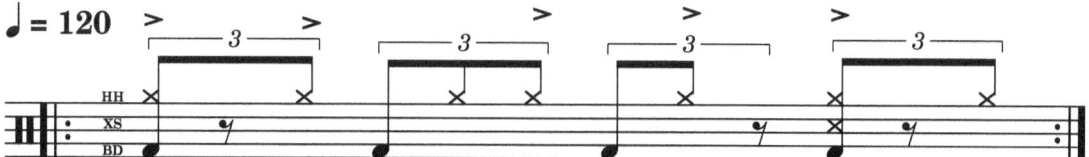

TIP JAR:

- The two main types of Irish music patterns you might encounter are a jig, which is subdivided into 3s and a reel, which is subdivided into 4s. I've written this jig pattern as triplets in 4/4 to make it easy to read.
- The hi-hat provides the syncopation and accents, while the bass drum plays quarter notes and the cross-stick has a single hit on beat 4.
- The drummer and bass player hit the first and third triplets of beat 1 together every time. Once you get comfortable with the basic pattern, explore a little bit and try out some variations. You can move to the ride cymbal bell or add some more cross-stick and a crash or two. Have fun with it!

Rob playing the bodhran @ The Iridium in NYC. Photo by Sean Harkness.

STUFF YOU CAN USE

Groove #32: Irish Reel

(Variation A)

♩ = 130

(Variation B)

TIP JAR:

- This one is a little faster and has a looser hi-hat sound. Imagine you're at an Irish pub and the fiddle player is ripping a solo while everyone's drinking a pint and having a rollicking good time. That ought to set the mood!
- The key to this one is the 2-beat feel where the bass drum plays the downbeats and the snare plays the upbeats. Those snare doubles give the pattern a nice little bounce. Try to stay relaxed and don't hit too hard.
- The role of the bass and drums is to be really clear and lay it down with the downbeats locking in together. Irish music features percussive instruments like the fiddle, bodhran and acoustic guitar, so there is always a lot of rhythm happening on top of this groove. It's best to keep it simple so the music doesn't get too cluttered.

Photo by Yana Davydova

Groove Workshop 4: World Music

Groove #33: Soca

(Variation A)

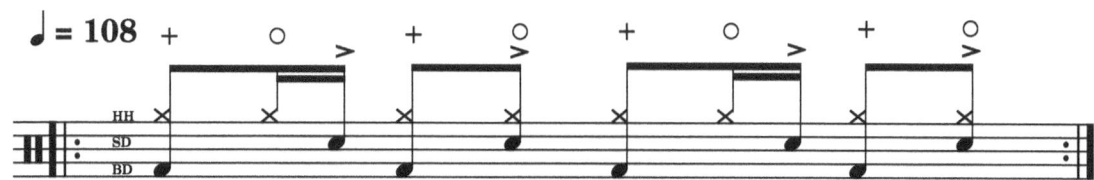

(Variation B)

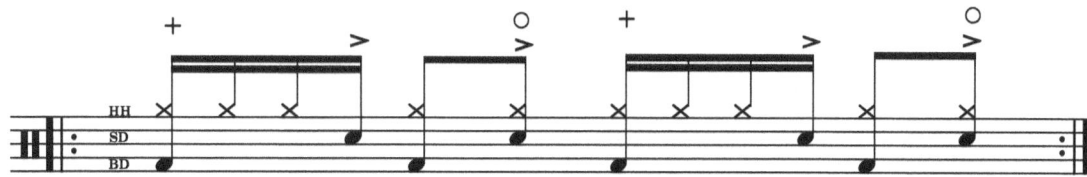

TIP JAR:

- A soca is a Caribbean dance groove. Its defining rhythm is the combination of a 4-on-the-floor bass drum pattern and a syncopated snare part. The bass and drums play this rhythm together to give it a fun, bouncy feel.
- Variation B is a little tighter and busier, but the underlying rhythm on the bass drum and snare stays the same. As you get comfortable, trying varying the hi-hat or adding some crashes and short fills.
- This is rhythmically similar to a calypso groove, which is usually a bit slower and has a less heavy quarter-note pulse. But if someone asks for either, you can use this!

Photo by Thomas Mester

STUFF YOU CAN USE

Groove #34: Jazzy Bossa Nova

(Variation A)

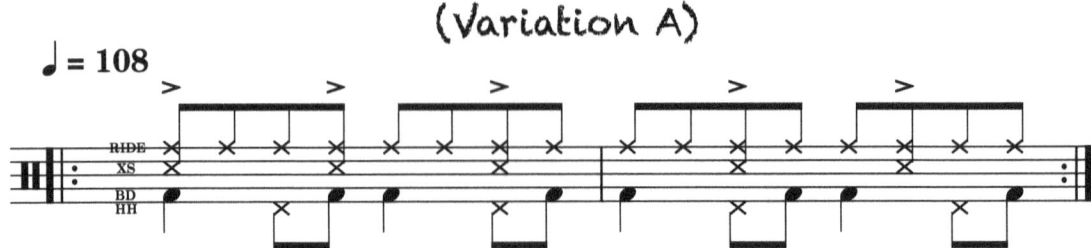

(Variation B)

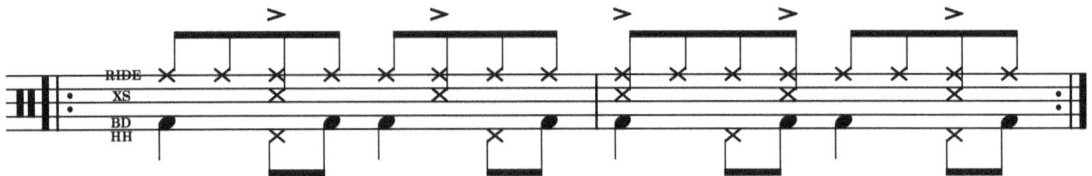

 **TIP JAR:**

- A bossa nova is a Brazilian groove built around a repeating rhythmic figure called a clavé, which in this case is played by the cross-stick. You'll notice there are 2 types here, and the difference between them is important to understand. A 3/2 clavé means that there are three notes in the first measure (beat 1, the "and" of 2 and beat 4) and two in the second measure (beat 2 and the "and" of 3). A 2/3 clavé is exactly the reverse, with the second measure coming first.

- This type of pattern is used in both traditional Brazilian music and jazz and should be played with a relaxed, gentle feel. Bossa novas are usually medium to slow tempos.

- Getting your foot pattern organized so it lines up with your hands is deceptively hard. Practice the feet alone at first, then try adding just the cross-stick. When you've got that together, add your right hand.

Rob and Vern Woodhead braving the elements after a show at The Mercury Lounge in NYC.

Groove Workshop 4: World Music

Groove #35: Samba

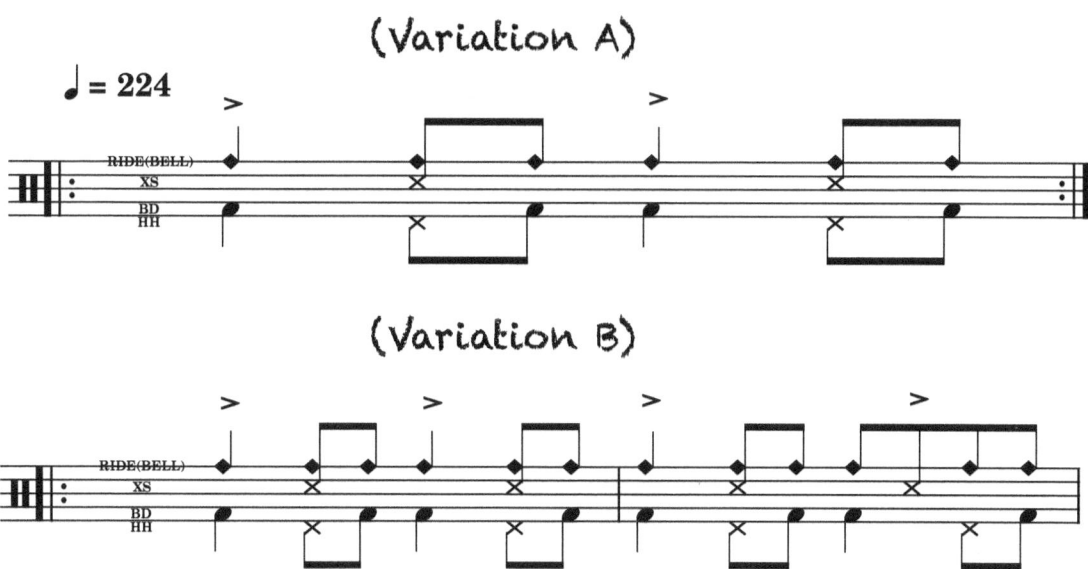

TIP JAR:

- This is another Brazilian rhythm, and it has the same foot pattern as the bossa nova. But sambas are faster and have more bounce and rhythmic attack. Think of the festive dancing atmosphere of Carnivál!
- This one should be very light and buoyant. It can be hard to play fast, busy patterns without getting too loud, and sambas require a lot of touch. The key to getting a good sound is for all your limbs to blend and balance the separate parts.
- Play beats 1 and 3 on the bass drum a little more firmly to give the pattern some shape and articulation. This also lines up with what the bass player is doing.
- From Dmitry: "This one is busy, but the lightness of the feel is what really makes it work."

Hand-crafted plywood Ashikos from White Raven Drumworks in Bridgewater, VT

STUFF YOU CAN USE

Groove #36: Rhumba

TIP JAR:

- A rhumba is an Afro-Cuban ballroom dance rhythm characterized by its graceful and delicate vibe. Rhumbas can also be found in pop and jazz, so it's great to have one in your pocket if someone asks for it. Here's the one my first drum teacher Steve Larrance taught me.
- This groove is played with the snares turned off. Your left hand plays the cross-stick and tom-tom notes, while the right hand stays on the open snare.
- The feel should be light and relaxed, but without getting sloppy. Practice the feet alone at first, then add the hands. Work on the left hand on its own so you can move effortlessly between the cross-stick and tom.
- Variation B adds a triplet embellishment in the first measure. Try to make that as crisp as possible.

Groove Workshop 4: World Music

Groove #37: Baião

(Variation A)

♩ = 216

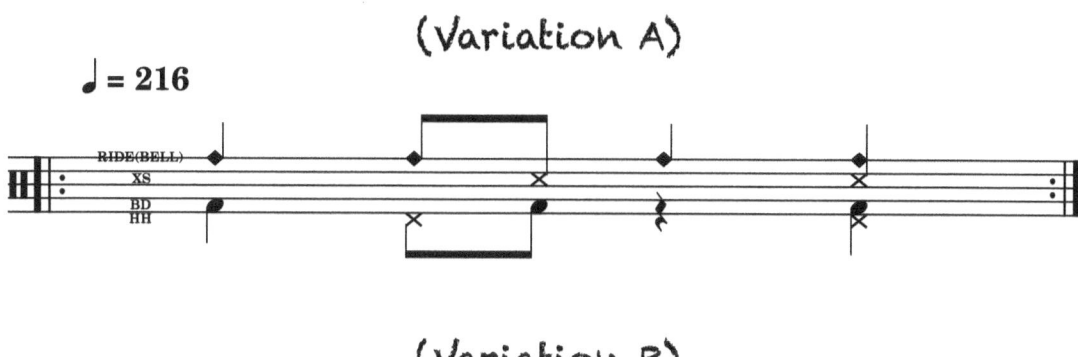

(Variation B)

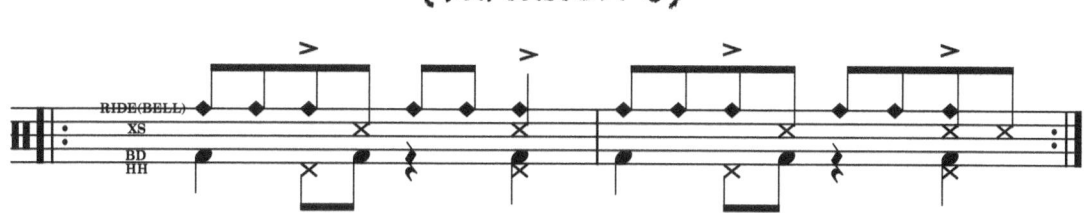

TIP JAR:

- The Baião is another upbeat Brazilian rhythm that has a distinctive foot pattern. Practice that on its own first, then add the hands.
- Like many of the others, this groove works best if you try to play lightly and with touch. The foot pattern is the foundation, while you can think of the hands almost as an accompaniment.
- Lock it in with Dmitry: "I'm playing exactly those three notes with the bass drum and really nothing else."

Photo by Thomas Mester

STUFF YOU CAN USE

GROOVE WORKSHOP 5: ROOTS

Groove #38: Country/Bluegrass Train

(Variation A: Brushes)

(Variation B: Sticks)

(Bonus: Ending Fill)

TIP JAR:

- This is a great one to have in the bag and there are a few different ways to play it. You can find variations of this groove in everything from traditional bluegrass to Dolly Parton or Mumford & Sons, and we'll be using it in a tune from the second half of the book. It's called a train groove because the snare part sounds like it's chugging right down the tracks.

- Hitting those snare accents on beats 2 and 4 along with the "and" of beat 3 will give it a nice bouncy feel. The first groove should be played with brushes, while variation B is a sticks version that also adds a triplet for flavor (use that sticking to make it smooth). I've also included an often-played ending to many songs in this genre *(Stuff You Can Use!)*.

- Lock in the bass drum quarter notes with the bass player.

- From Dmitry: "I'm connecting to those bass drum notes as assertively as I can. This groove is ever-so-subtly pushing and it's not too far behind the beat."

Groove Workshop 5: Roots

Groove #39: New Orleans Second Line

(Variation A)

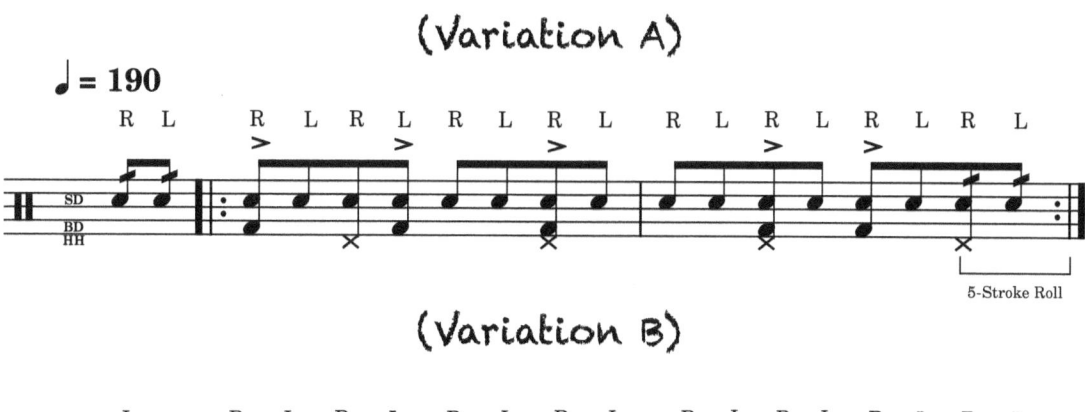

(Variation B)

TIP JAR:

- This funky marching-style groove is one of my all-time favorites. It gets its name from traditional parades in New Orleans where the band is called the "main line," while the "second line" is everyone who follows dancing and partying. Attending one of these parades is one of the most fun experiences you can ever have.
- The bass drum part is the key, and it's best to start out by clapping the rhythm slowly along with a metronome.
- Play way behind the beat and swing the 8th notes really hard. Variation B adds a bass drum note and a longer roll in the second measure, and it's fun to play loosely and experiment as long as the main bass drum figure stays constant. That's the second line mojo!
- On the play-along track, play 16 measures of groove, then 16 measures of solo over the bass line, then 16 more bars of time.
- From Dmitry: "Swampy! I'm locking in with the accents on the snare drum. It's almost like a clavé similar to Afro-Cuban music with the 3/2 or the cross-stick from a bossa nova. It's kind of a universal, cross-cultural figure and it's very prominent in New Orleans music."

Rob with engineer Charles Burst @ The Seaside Lounge Studios in Brooklyn, NY

STUFF YOU CAN USE

Groove #40: New Orleans Funk

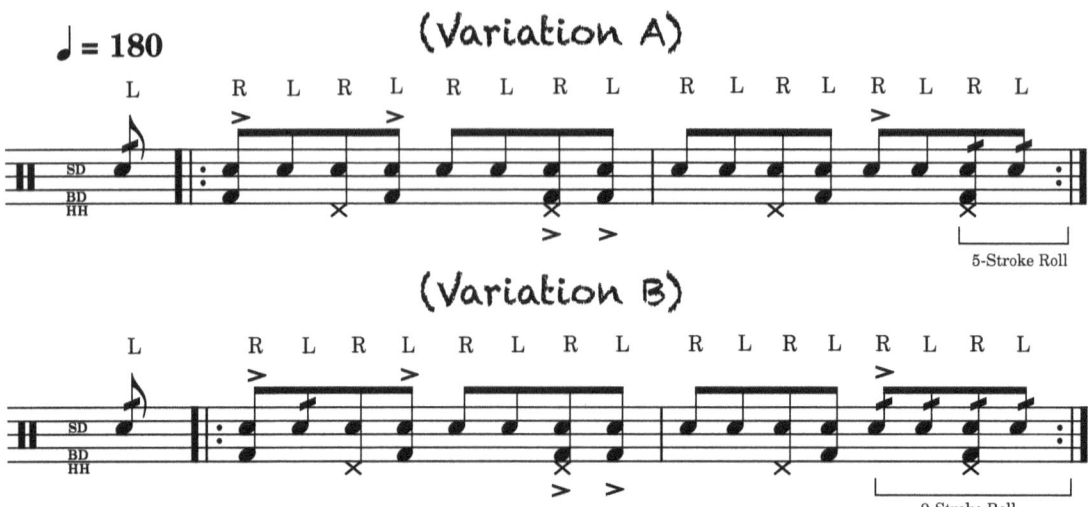

TIP JAR:

- This variation on the second line groove is associated with New Orleans bands like The Meters, who took that traditional beat and combined it with funk. Check out their drummer Zigaboo Modeliste for some awesome examples.
- This groove is still based around the snare, but there is more of a backbeat feel subtlely implied. Once you get comfortable, try moving around the kit to create different sounds and try out textural changes (the hi-hat, ride, rims of the drums...try it all!).
- From Dmitry: "I'm hearing both the backbeat and the second line rhythm and bringing them out at different times. I feel free to go either this way or that way, but they're both very present and I'm aware of them at all times."

Groove #41: Boogaloo

TIP JAR:

- This is a straight 8th-note pattern that combines elements of funk, jazz, rock and Latin. That sounds like a lot for just one measure of groove, but it's tons of fun to play. Check out the Eddie Harris tune "Cold Duck Time" with Donald Dean on drums for a good example.
- The bass drum and bass player lock up on the "and" of beat 2 to give it a little syncopation and bounce. You can also give it more flavor by added buzzed notes like that snare on beat 4.
- Keep the backbeat light and ride cymbal loose and relaxed. This beat should be groovy and propulsive even though it has a laid-back vibe.

Groove Workshop 5: Roots

Groove #42: Slow 12/8 Blues

TIP JAR:

- This basic blues groove looks super-easy, right? However, I think it's actually one of the toughest ones to get perfectly in the pocket and lock in with the rest of the band. It's tempting to get excited and play lots of fills, or get bored and start dragging at such a slow tempo. It's written here in 12/8, but you can also count it as triplets in 4/4.

- The role of the drums in this type of music is to lock in with the bass player and be supportive. Embrace the simplicity and have fun!

- From Dmitry: "It should be behind the beat and not too tense for this style of music. Playing simply is best. This is one of the first grooves I learned on the bass."

Photo by Dmitri Levitas

STUFF YOU CAN USE

GROOVE WORKSHOP 6: JAZZ

Groove #43: Brushes Medium Swing

(Variation A)

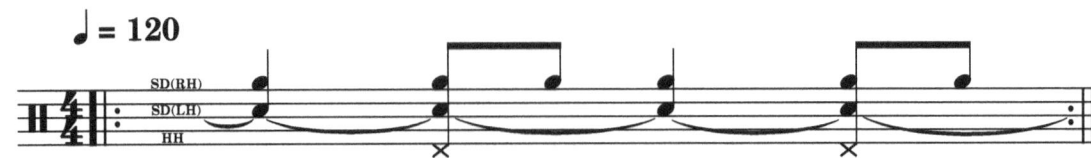

(Variation B)

TIP JAR:

- Use your left hand to stir in a clockwise circle around the outer edge of the snare head while your right hand plays the basic swing rhythm. Imagine the snare as a clock and hit beats 2 and 4 at 11:00, with the rest of the notes over near 3:00 (check out the video for a demonstration). Cross your right hand over your left so they come together when you hit beats 2 and 4. This is the same pattern you would play with sticks on the ride cymbal, just on different parts of the snare. The key is to get your left hand to make that circle at just the right speed so everything lines up.

- This one should be smooth and relaxed. Variation B has a little accent on the "and" of beat 3 that you can pop with your left hand as it circles around. These types of subtle accents give the pattern some flavor, and you can try adding them on other beats as well.

- From Dmitry: "I'm playing quarter notes [which is called 'walking'] and listening to the hi-hat on 2 and 4 to give me a sense of the pulse. The hi-hat is really the metronome for me and has to be crisp and in the pocket. Sometimes if you're on a gig and there is a lot going on, the brushes can get a little lost but that hi-hat always cuts through."

Groove Workshop 6: Jazz

Groove #44: Brushes 2-Feel

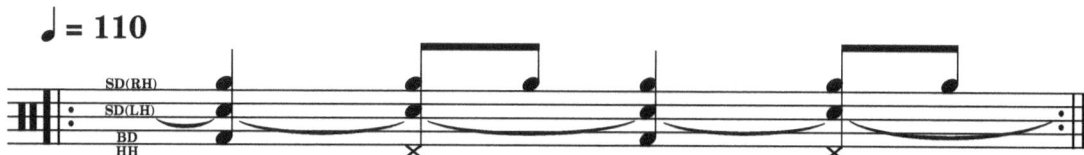

TIP JAR:

- This one is called a "2-feel" because we're emphasizing beats 1 and 3 instead of every quarter note (i.e., 2 notes per measure instead of 4). It has the same snare stirring pattern as the previous one, but adds some very light bass drum notes on 1 and 3.
- Playing your bass drum in this way is a concept from the big-band era called "feathering" (light as a feather). It's almost as if you can feel the vibration of the drum even more than hearing it. This level of touch can be hard to achieve and takes some practice.
- You can also emphasize beats 2 and 4 on the snare just a little more, but not so much that it turns into a polka. This one should have a nice, easy bounce to it.
- Side note: I first learned how to play a 2-feel from legendary jazz bassist Rufus Reid. He would do a little dance with the bass and move his shoulders on 1 and 3. It was so funky, but understated and smooth as silk.
- From Dmitry: "I'm feeling that 1 and 3 in my body almost. It's very subtle, but very grooving."

Rob, Dmitry Ishenko & Steve Fell @ The Bohemian Caverns in Washington D.C.
Photo by Marjorie Mitzner

STUFF YOU CAN USE

Groove #45: Brushes Waltz

(Variation A)

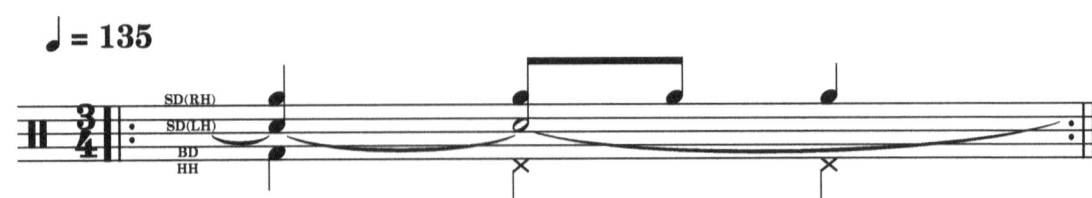

(Variation B)

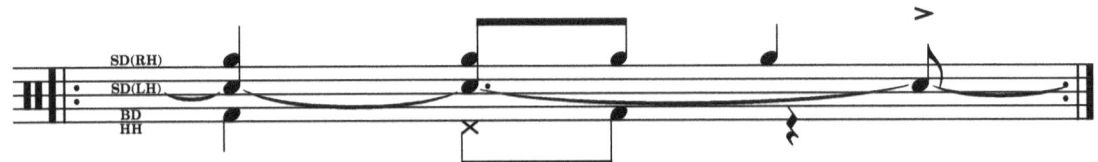

TIP JAR:

- This is a similar groove, but in 3/4 time. My method for playing this pattern may be different than you'll see in other places, but the end result is really what matters *(Stuff You Can Use)*. You'll still be stirring in a clockwise motion, but instead of moving your left hand in large circles around the outer edge, make two smaller circles on the left side and keep the right around 2:00 as it plays the swing pattern.

- Sometimes I play the hi-hat on beats 2 and 3 like in variation A, while B has a dotted quarter-note rhythm in the bass drum to give it a polyrhythmic "3 over 4" feel.

- As you get comfortable, add some left hand accents or other embellishments. Playing these grooves with the rest of the rhythm section is like making soup. You don't just want to dump all the ingredients in the pot at once. Add a little bit at a time and keep sampling it as you go along. Eventually you'll end up with something that tastes great.

- From Dmitry: "I'm hooking up with beat 2 on the hi-hat as well as the 'swoosh' the drums play on beat 1. This groove is very flexible from a bass perspective because there are many different ways you can chop up that beat as long as you don't make it too repetitive. It's always changing around and growing spontaneously."

Groove Workshop 6: Jazz

Groove #46: Brushes Ballad

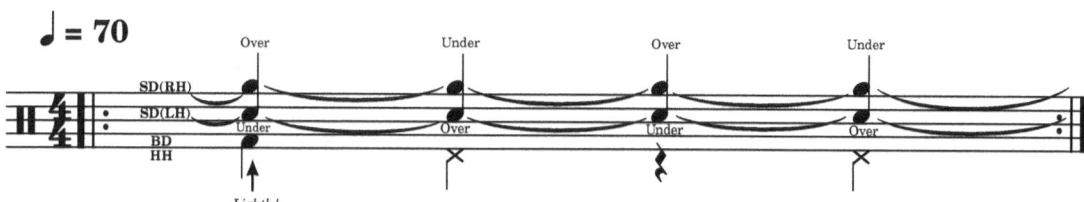

TIP JAR:

- It's really challenging to play a slow ballad with brushes and make it groove. There are a number of different stirring patterns you can use, and I like this one because it has a nice shape to it. Alternate between crossing your hands over and under each other on every beat to arrive at the shape of an X. Start the right hand at 1:00 and the left at 7:00, then move them around their respective edges until they reverse positions.
- This track is called a "walking" ballad since the bassist is playing every quarter note. The other common type is a "straight" ballad feel, where he would be playing more on beats 1 and 3 and filling the spaces in-between. The good news is, aside from the feel difference, this stirring pattern will work for both types! You're not really playing all the notes of the swing pattern like the previous grooves, but they are implied within your stirring.
- Resist the undeniable urge to add a lot of extra notes or make it too active. Keep it simple and smooth.
- From Dmitry: "In this case, I'm really listening to the snare drum brush pattern. If I feel it rushing, I might switch to half notes and add a little 8th-note pickup to try to pull it back."

Groove #47: Jazz Shuffle (Art Blakey)

TIP JAR:

- Popularized by legendary drummer Art Blakey, this pattern is different from the rock shuffles we covered earlier since the left hand plays every 8th note on the snare. The trick is to accent beats 2 and 4 just enough to get that bluesy, funky feel while keeping it swinging. That backbeat along with the 4-on-the-floor bass drum pattern are what makes this a shuffle instead of a swing pattern.
- Practice the left hand by itself at first to get the technique down, and then fit that together with the right.
- This one should be really driving and push ahead.
- From Dmitry: "I'm walking quarter notes just like on a regular swing feel, but the snare is what gives it that funky shuffle feel, and that's what I'm listening to."

STUFF YOU CAN USE

Groove #48: Afro-Cuban Jazz

Like many of the other patterns we've explored, this Afro-Cuban jazz beat has a clavé, or strong underlying rhythm. Start by clapping it slowly with a metronome, and then play it on the bell of the ride.

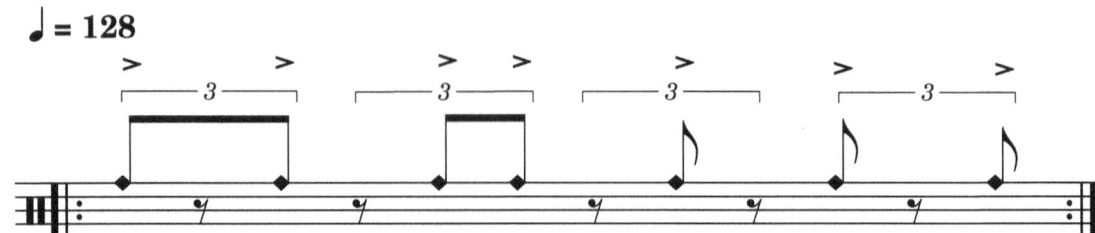

Once you're comfortable, add the feet and the left hand.

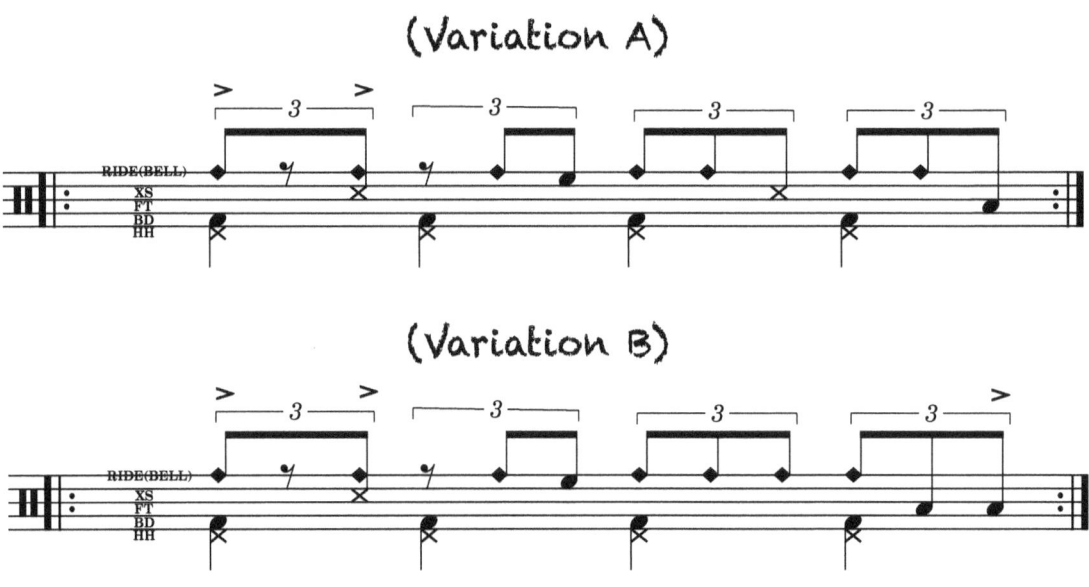

TIP JAR:

- The key to this one is to move smoothly between the tom, cross-stick and floor tom with your left hand.
- This is a very active groove with a lot going on in the hands. Try moving it around the kit to create different tones and textures while keeping the foot pattern steady. On the play-along track, you'll groove with the bassist for 16 measures, and then play a solo while he plays underneath. For the solo, try starting with some simple ideas based on the groove and expand upon them. Let the solo develop organically and don't start shredding right away. Save some good stuff for the end!
- From Dmitry: "This is one of my personal favorite rhythms to play. There's so much in there polyrhythmically. You can think in 4, you can feel the fast triplets, or you can do quarter-note triplets against that, which I do a lot in my bass line. You can bring all these possibilities in and out whenever you want and it's so much fun."

Groove Workshop 6: Jazz

Groove #49: Elvin

(Variation A)

(Variation B)

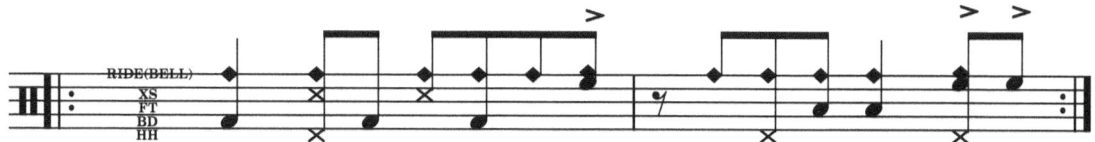

TIP JAR:

- Named for legendary drummer Elvin Jones, this groove is a hybrid between a jazz swing pattern and a straight 8th-note Latin feel. You can most famously hear him play it on the song "Passion Dance" by pianist McCoy Tyner.

- Start by practicing the left hand by itself to get comfortable with the movement pattern around the kit. Then add the right hand and the feet.

- Just like the last one, there are many polyrhythms going on underneath the main groove and lots of possibilities to stretch out and have fun. There is always a strong undercurrent of triplets beneath the 4/4 feel which is a hallmark of the "Elvin" style. On the play-along, groove with the bassist until you're comfortable, then solo over his bass line.

- From Dmitry: "That tom pattern is definitely derived from Afro-Cuban music. I try to hang on to the downbeats along with the 'a' of beat 1 as my main notes. Everything else is up to me in the moment. This one has a nice loose feel."

Performing @ Rockwood Music Hall in NYC
Photo by Michael Gallant

STUFF YOU CAN USE

GROOVE WORKSHOP 7: ODD TIME SIGNATURES, SOLOING, BACKING A SOLOIST

Odd time signature grooves are some of the most fun and challenging patterns you can play on drums. To make them easier to count, it helps to subdivide the measure into smaller groups of beats. In this section, we'll cover a few of the most common subdivisions and go over tips and tricks for tackling more complex meters from tunes in the second half of the book.

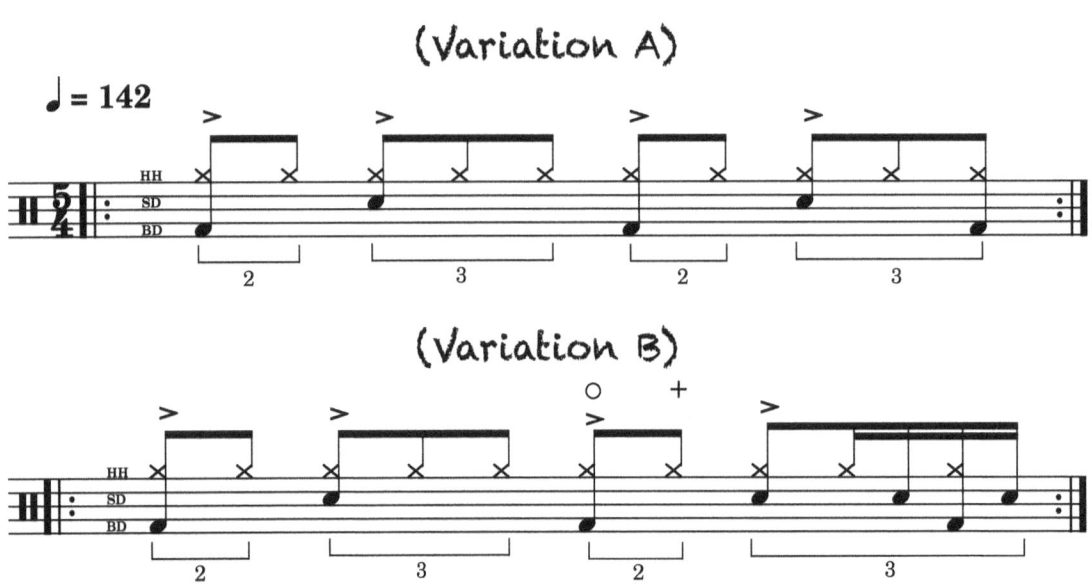

Groove #50: 5/4 (2-3 Subdivision)

(Variation A)

(Variation B)

TIP JAR:

- 5/4 is a meter you'll encounter in genres such as rock, jazz, R&B, metal and many other styles. In this set, we'll refer to the "Big 5," which is a whole measure of 5 quarter notes, as well as the "Little 5," which is the division of 8th notes into groups of 2 and 3 which occurs twice per measure.
- Check out the Soundgarden tune "My Wave" for an example of a 2-3 groove with the "Big 5." You can also hear it on the Tool song "Vicarious" from their *10,000 Waves* album and "Question Myself" on the Woodhead record *Cabezazo*.
- If you listen to the bass on the play-along track, you will hear this 2-3 subdivision of 8th notes ("Little 5"). Start by clapping the rhythm alone (repeat counting 1, 2, 1, 2, 3) and then play variations A and B along with the track.
- Once you're feeling good about the groove, try soloing while the bass plays that rhythm underneath.

Groove Workshop 7: Odd Time Signatures, Soloing, Backing a Soloist

Groove #51: 5/4 (3-2 Subdivision)

TIP JAR:

- This one subdivides the measure into 3 and 2 beats using the "Big 5" (quarter notes). This is how Dave Brubeck's famous jazz tune "Take Five" is phrased with Joe Morello on drums. You can also hear it on Radiohead's "15 Step" from their *In Rainbows* album.
- Use the same process as the last one: clap and count (1, 2, 3, 1, 2), play the pattern with the bassist, then try soloing along.
- From Dmitry: "I'm interacting with the drums a little bit during the solo, but mostly I'm trying to keep a solid foundation and simplify my line."

Recording @ The Seaside Lounge Studios in Brooklyn, NY
Photo by Dmitry Ishenko

STUFF YOU CAN USE

Groove #52: 7/4 (4-3 Subdivision)

(Variation A)

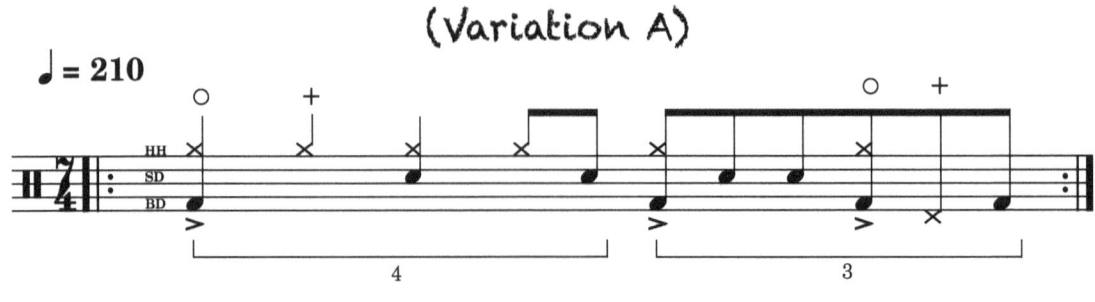

(Variation B)

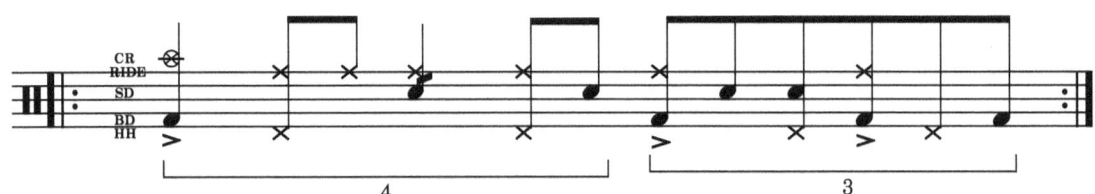

TIP JAR:

- 7/4 is another very common time signature across all styles. "Solsbury Hill" by Peter Gabriel, "Money" by Pink Floyd and the verses of "All You Need is Love" by the Beatles are just a few of the most famous examples.
- This groove uses a "Big 7" to subdivide the measure into phrases of 4 and 3 beats.
- This is a great pattern to practice soloing over. On the play-along track, the bass and drums take turns playing 8-measure solos separated by 8 bars of groove. This is called "Trading 8s." Make sure to keep track of the form in your head while you play along.

8 bars groove together

8 bars bass solo, drums accompany

8 bars groove together

8 bars drums solo, bass accompanies

Repeat

- **WHEN THE BASSIST IS SOLOING,** move over to the hi-hat and keep your volume lower. It's important to play solid time to support the solo and avoid using too many toms or other low frequencies that could get in the way of what they are playing. It can be tricky to decide how much to interact with the soloist. You don't necessarily want to parrot or mimic them, but it can be cool to hook up rhythmically on a few small figures. You want them to feel like you're listening to what they're doing and being supportive. We'll discuss this in more detail when we tackle the full band play-alongs in the second half of the book.
- From Dmitry: "When I'm playing under the drum solo, I'm thinking about holding down the most important accents, which for this particular time signature are beats 1, 3, 5 and the 'and' of 6. That rhythm really drives this one. I'm trying to just hold that down and let the drummer do their thing. If you play too much behind a solo it can get a bit hectic. One slip of an 8th note and you could be on a different part of the beat. Especially with odd time signatures, it's really hard to get back on track if that happens, so in this case, simple is good."

Groove Workshop 7: Odd Time Signatures, Soloing, Backing a Soloist

TIP JAR: CONTINUED

- **WHEN THE DRUMS ARE SOLOING,** try to keep those important accents in mind and start by developing some ideas based on that rhythm. You don't necessarily want to just repeat that over and over, but if you can play some things outside the rhythm while still keeping it in mind, you'll end up with a much more interesting solo.
- From Dmitry: "Very often when I solo, I try not to play any downbeats because it's so easy to fall in the trap of repeating this pattern. If you can start a phrase on different parts of the measure, like beat 3 or beat 5, you'll be able to leave some space and it won't always be this obvious thing. Repeating that too much can make you sound like you're not feeling secure in the time signature or just holding on for dear life. You don't really want to create that impression!"
- *Final Hint: This type of experimentation is great for when you're practicing, however when you perform live, just make sure you know where you are at all times.*

Groove #53: 7/4 (3-4 Subdivision)

(Variation A)

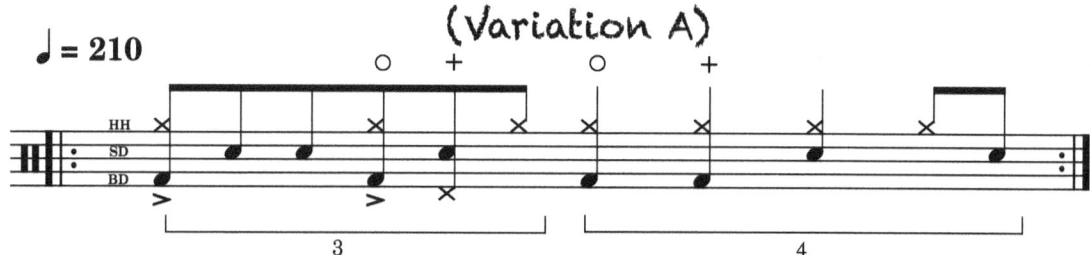

(Variation B)

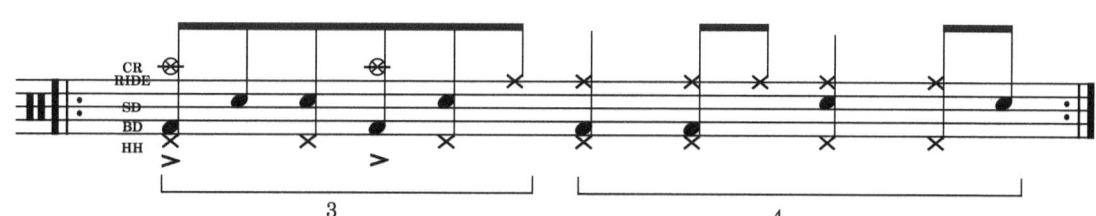

TIP JAR:

- This 3-4 subdivision is another common way to phrase a 7/4 groove. It's really just a reverse of the 4-3, with the second phrase being played first.
- It can be a real challenge to get comfortable with this one since as Dmitry puts it, "beat 4 shows up sooner then you expect! I usually play dotted quarter notes over the '3' part of the 3-4, but you have to be right on it for beat 4."
- While the 4-3 and 3-4 are similar, it's important to stick with one or the other when you're playing them in a song. It can get really chaotic if the drums and bass are lapsing back and forth, so it's best to agree in advance on how to divide the groove. That consistency will make the music sound better and you'll be able to play confidently knowing exactly how to divide the 7.

STUFF YOU CAN USE

Now that we've added a whole bunch of patterns to the bag, it's time to head out for a drive and play some tunes! But first, we'll need to get some directions…

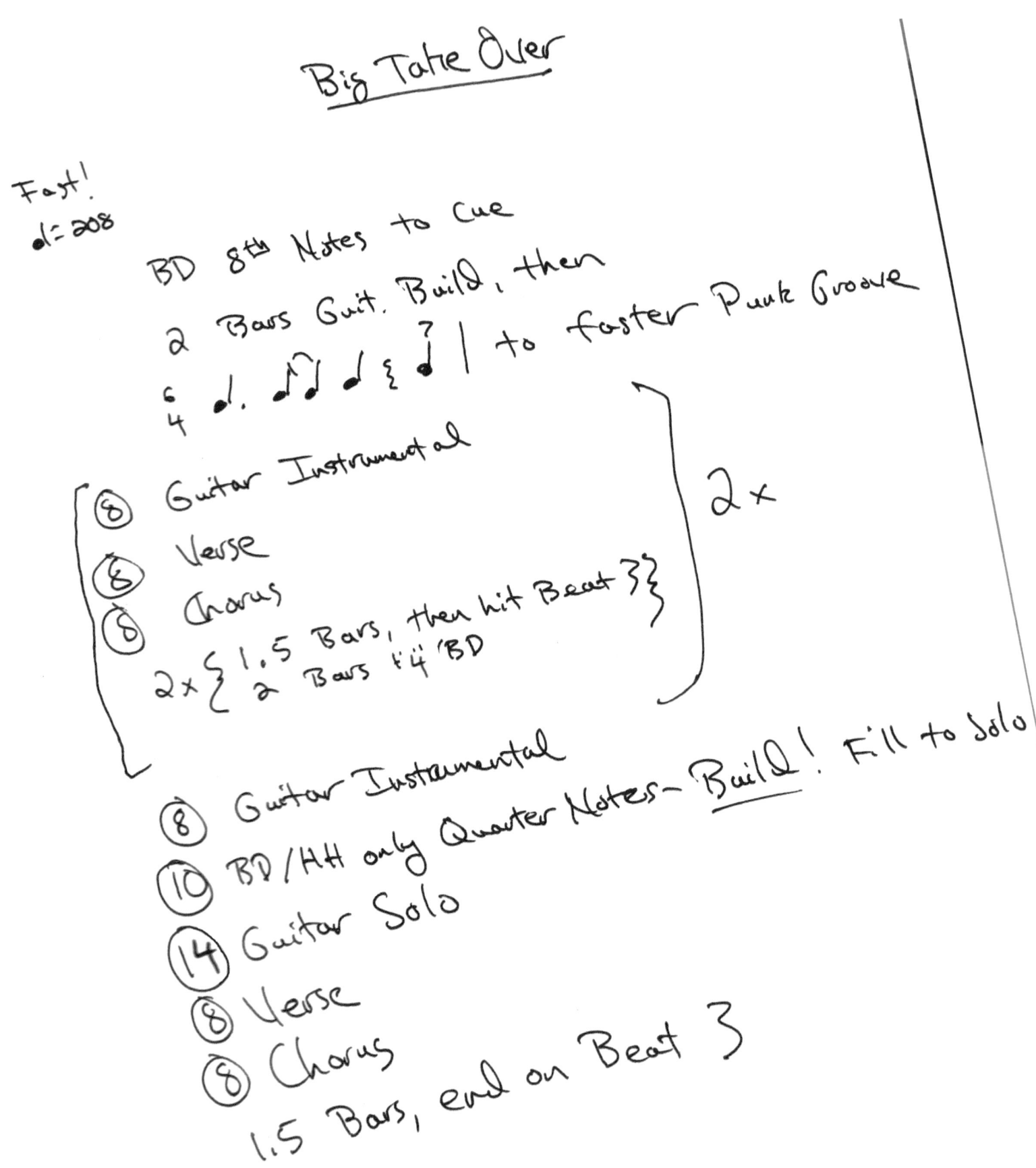

CHARTS, LEAD SHEETS & ROAD MAPS

The purpose of written charts is to help artists communicate important information about how they want their music to be played. Sometimes I hear folks refer to a chart as "the music." This isn't exactly right. A chart is just a way to lay out the form, hits and dynamics to help you *play* the actual music. The best tool you have is your ears, however learning how to read and write different types of charts will only make you a better drummer.

Written charts come in all shapes and sizes, and this section includes a wide variety. There are a few note-for-note transcriptions of what I played, but it's rare for an artist to hand you one of those for their tune unless you're playing certain specific styles (for example, musical theater, classical and certain types of progressive rock...think Zappa). Often the composer will create a "lead sheet" that serves as a guide, but also leaves room for you put your own stamp on the music. Sometimes lead sheets are written specifically for the drums, but often everyone in the band gets the same chart and has to interpret what to play using the written information along with their ear, intuition and creativity. I've included both of these types of lead sheets for you to work with on different tunes. But even more frequently, folks just send a recording and say "learn this!"

Here's how I do it: if they don't provide a chart, I listen to the song and write out a "road map" that outlines the form, hits and length of each section. These maps are what I use to learn most of the material I play around town and on tour. I've made thousands over the years, and I'm excited to share my method with you since I've found that it's the quickest and easiest way to learn tunes on the fly. Most importantly, I've found that going through the process of mapping out a tune helps me memorize it. Often, I'll make them and then not use them onstage because my brain and hands have absorbed the material as I listened to it and wrote it out. Writing these maps will help you identify small details in the music that you might otherwise miss. Catching these details can be the difference between a good performance and a great one. I even hear professional drummers who are fabulous players who don't take the time to really learn the minor ins and outs of a tune. I've occasionally learned this the hard way myself over the years, and being fired or let go from a band will get your attention pretty quickly! One thing I know for sure: the other band members will love you if you get the small bits right. As the drummer, you need to know the form of the tune better than anyone else in the band, even the person that wrote it.

STUFF YOU CAN USE

I can't tell you how many times someone has thrown a song at me at the last minute and I've huddled backstage in the dark with my phone, headphones and a pencil. Though I usually transfer the maps to my iPad for a cleaner look onstage, I'm old-school at heart. So grab a pencil and let's check out some maps!

Think of these road maps as your driving directions for the tune. Each part of the song is like a different street, and the number of measures in each section represents the mileage you'll travel before moving to the next part. The tempo in the upper left-hand corner is your speed limit. Your map should be detailed but easy to read, and I always add plenty of landmarks that help me stay on track. For example, "turn left at the ugly red barn after the big tree" equals "go back to the hi-hat when the vocals drop out after the bridge." I usually write out basic kick/snare patterns for each section, and sometimes I'll scribble out the whole groove. You don't really need staff paper, although it is helpful if you're writing out a lot of grooves to go with your text. Lined or unlined white paper does the trick, but so does a cocktail napkin (as long as it's not a super-long tune)! Each song requires different information and it's important to avoid cluttering the page with stuff you don't need. Just try to make your maps clear and easy to read if you're in a dark club or a crowded practice space. You might remember everything perfectly an hour before you play and then, boom! Your mind goes blank and you're screwed…until that prep you did on your road map kicks in and saves the day.

BBQ from Green Mesquite in Austin, TX

Charts, Lead Sheets & Road Maps

SONG WORKSHOP #1: "CLASSIC BREAKDOWN"
BY WOODHEAD

This first tune is a rocker called "Classic Breakdown" by the band Woodhead. I've been a member of this group for almost ten years, and their influences include artists like David Bowie, Talking Heads and Radiohead. Woodhead is the brainchild of composer, singer and guitarist Vern Woodhead, and also features guitarist Yana Davydova and Dmitry Ishenko (whom you've already met) on bass.

This song starts with two bars of drums alone, followed by entrances from the bass, guitar and vocals. Having everyone come in one at a time allows the groove to percolate and intensify. The form of this tune is pretty standard: intro/verse/pre-chorus/chorus, then repeat and solo. The real secret sauce to making it sound great is the intensity and texture changes that happen in different parts of the tune. The most unusual element of this song is that the chorus sections are actually quieter than the verses. As Dmitry says, "it's the anti-chorus."

Let's start by checking out the individual grooves for each section. The intro/verse groove has a floor tom on beat 3, which you should play with your right hand. This is tougher than it looks since you'll have to cross over from the hi-hat and back every time!

Intro/Verse

When we get to the pre-chorus the feel opens up a bit, alternating between a loose hi-hat backbeat and the tighter verse groove for 2 bars each. Dmitry says, "I actually tighten up my sound and mute the bass a little on this section, which is in contrast with the drums."

Pre-Chorus

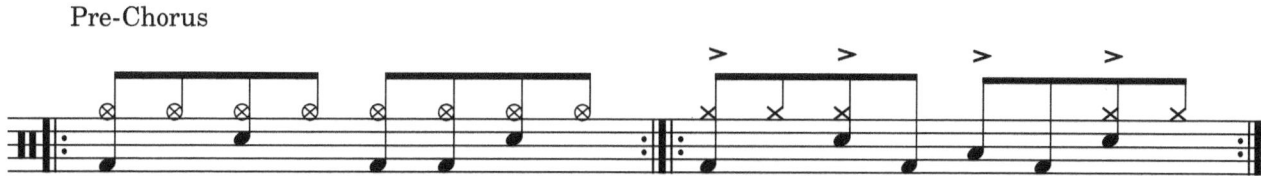

Then the first chorus comes and instead of exploding, everything contracts. Keep the pattern crisp and smoldering without playing too loud. Playing quietly, but with great intensity is one of the most important things a drummer can do to make the music feel good. Dmitry adds, "I'm actually keeping my sound kind of open and ringing in the chorus, so I feel I'm still carrying this intensity while the drum part shrinks in a little bit. I think there is still a lot of momentum, it's just that the dynamics are way down."

When I first got a rough demo recording of this tune from Vern, the composer, this quieter chorus stuck out to me right away. Vern plays a bit of drums himself and his demos always contain good ideas. However, I was curious about why he decided to write the chorus that way…so I asked him!

STUFF YOU CAN USE

He answered, "this idea came from the lyrics. The song is about a car driving through a storm and then breaking down. It's actually a metaphor for the human condition. The verse talks about 'wet winds, storms and lighting,' so it's pretty aggressive. And in the chorus, the car [or person] breaks down (the 'Classic Breakdown')."

Interesting! But you might be wondering, "what does this have to do with the drum part?" Here's what he said: "I think it's really helpful for the drummer to be aware of lyrical changes in the music. Many songwriters are consciously or subconsciously doing 'word painting' with their lyrics, and maybe you can find something in there that affects the intensity or vibe of what you play. Or even if it's nothing specific, maybe there's something in there to guide you or provide general inspiration."

The takeaway for me is that every bit of information you can gather about a song can be helpful, even if it might not seem like it relates directly to your part.

After the chorus, there is a short re-intro section with a slight open hi-hat variation in the pattern.

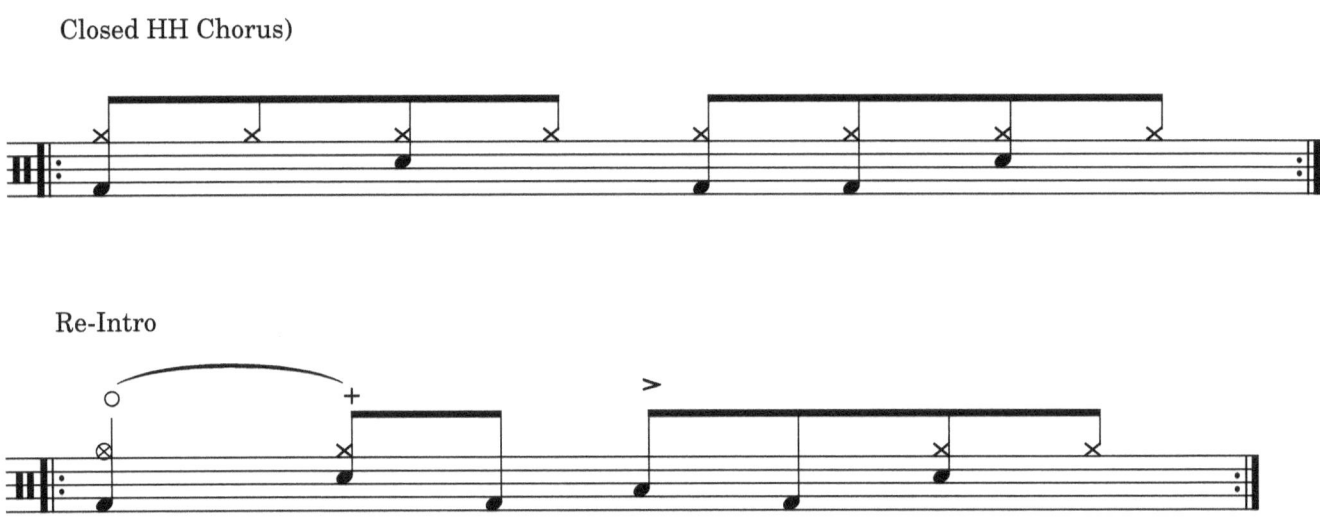

Then we play the same verse, pre-chorus, chorus form over again followed by 16 measures of a "build" section based on the chorus backbeat groove. Vern says, "the drums are essential for this dynamic build-up into the solo because the guitar part is a really simple ascending 8th-note figure." Gradually get louder and open the hi-hat until you reach the crazy guitar solo outro section. This part is very simple and high-energy. It should be loud, but try to avoid bashing so hard that your technique falls apart and you lose clarity and precision in your playing.

As guitarist Yana Davydova explains, "the drums should be pushing energetically and building this section with some intention that it's going somewhere. It's a simple, repetitive part, but it grows and you have to have energy and stamina all the way to the end. I love these kinds of repetitive parts when they're played by a good drummer who doesn't do too many fills. They have a hypnotic quality and the other musicians feed off that. It's all about the attitude."

Now that we've gone through the different sections and learned a bit about the lyrics, it's time to take this one for a spin! Here are some driving directions.

Charts, Lead Sheets & Road Maps

♩ = 120
Medium Rock, 2 Bars Count-in

"Classic Breakdown"

By Vern Woodhead

[2] Drums Only

[8] Intro (Add Bass & Guitar, Same Groove)

[8] Verse 1 (Same)

[8] Pre-Chorus 1 (Build Slightly) (2 Bars Open HH, 2 Bars Verse Groove) x2

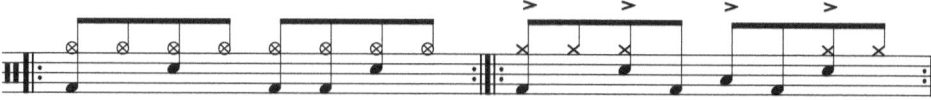

[16] Chorus 1 (Closed HH Backbeat, Quieter but intense)

[8] Re-Intro (Variation of Verse Groove)

[8] Verse 2 (Original Verse Groove)

[8] Pre-Chorus 2 (Build Slightly) (2 Bars Open HH, 2 Bars Verse Groove) x2

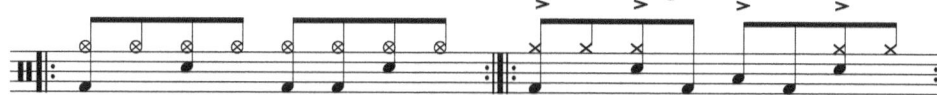

[8] Chorus 2 (Quieter but intense)

[16] Guitars Build, Start opening HH

[16] Outro: To Crash- LOUD!

End Bar 17, Beat 1 (Long)

STUFF YOU CAN USE

SONG WORKSHOP #2: "THE CONJURATION"
BY WOODHEAD

This is another Woodhead tune with a lot of subtle changes in texture and intensity. Playing through the different patterns in this tune is like building a house. You add a couple bricks at a time and keep enhancing it, but the foundation remains solid. There's a short drum fill pickup at the top followed by the intro groove, which is a medium 6/8 played on the ride cymbal. Play those hi-hat accents with your left hand while the right stays on the ride.

When Vern Woodhead (the composer) sent me his demo for this one, I noticed those accents right away in his programmed drum beat. He explains, "the way I write drum parts is entirely intuitive. I usually put something on there and if I don't like how it sounds, I move the accents around. I always try to give the drummer a demo since it's a great place to start and you're in the songwriter's head. That way they can learn that part, and if they're feeling different things with the patterns and fills, they can add them from a much more informed perspective. And by adding your own parts, you're going to bring the song to life. That's the sh*t right there."

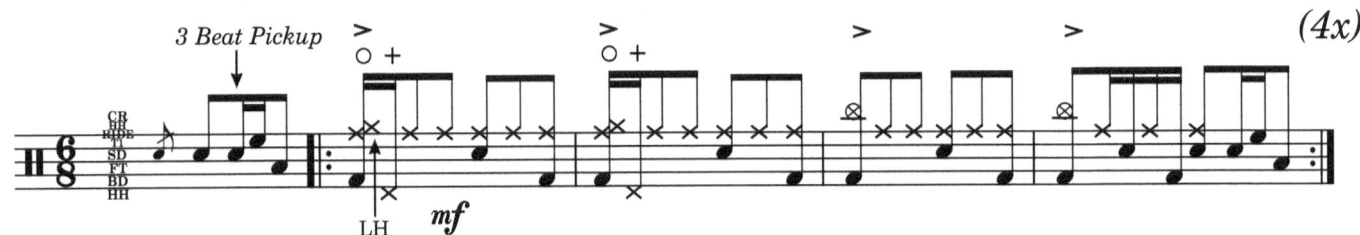

Next is a section we're calling the "pre-verse." This is really just a mellow interlude before the vocals come in at the top of the first verse.

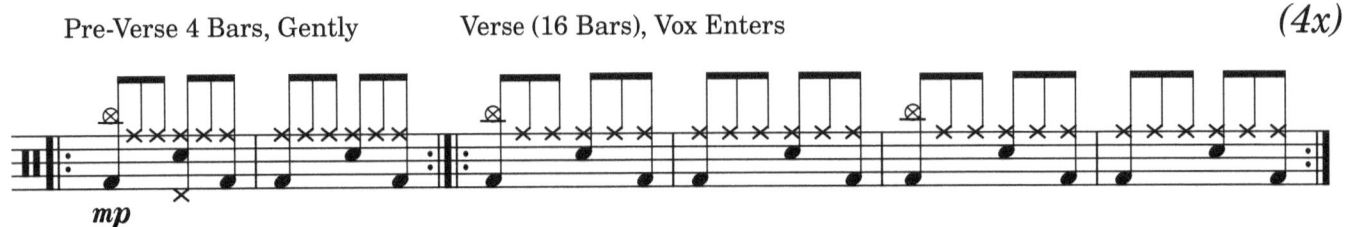

Then we hit the pre-chorus and gradually increase the volume as the groove becomes more active. Guitarist Yana Davydova explains, "when a song has a specific character or tone color, it's great when the drummer matches that with their part. The guitar is doing more in this section and my tone is really dry. When a drummer has this connection to the vibe of a song, their part blends harmoniously into the whole band. It's really amazing when I hear the music as a cohesive whole and it's all in balance."

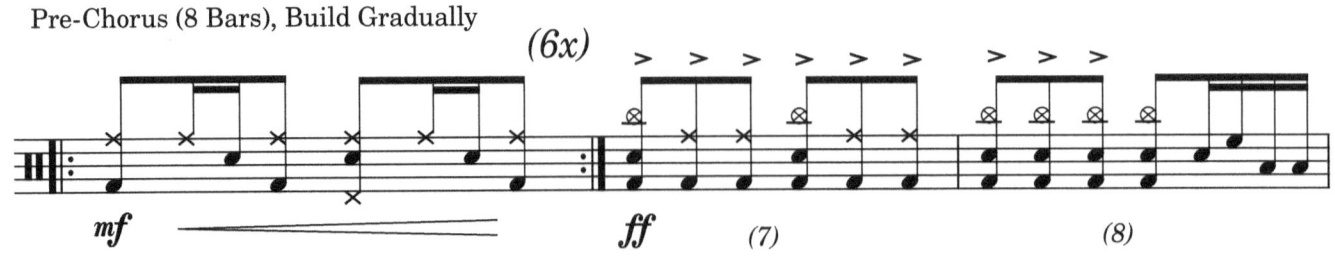

Charts, Lead Sheets & Road Maps

Dmitry says, "I feel like we've already built it up, and now we need to build it even further. I'm playing staccato 8th notes in those last 2 bars of the pre-chorus leading into the chorus, and sometimes just pounding out those obvious 8th notes is the way to go."

Once the chorus comes in, we're rocking out on the open hi-hat and adding fills at the end of each 4-bar phrase.

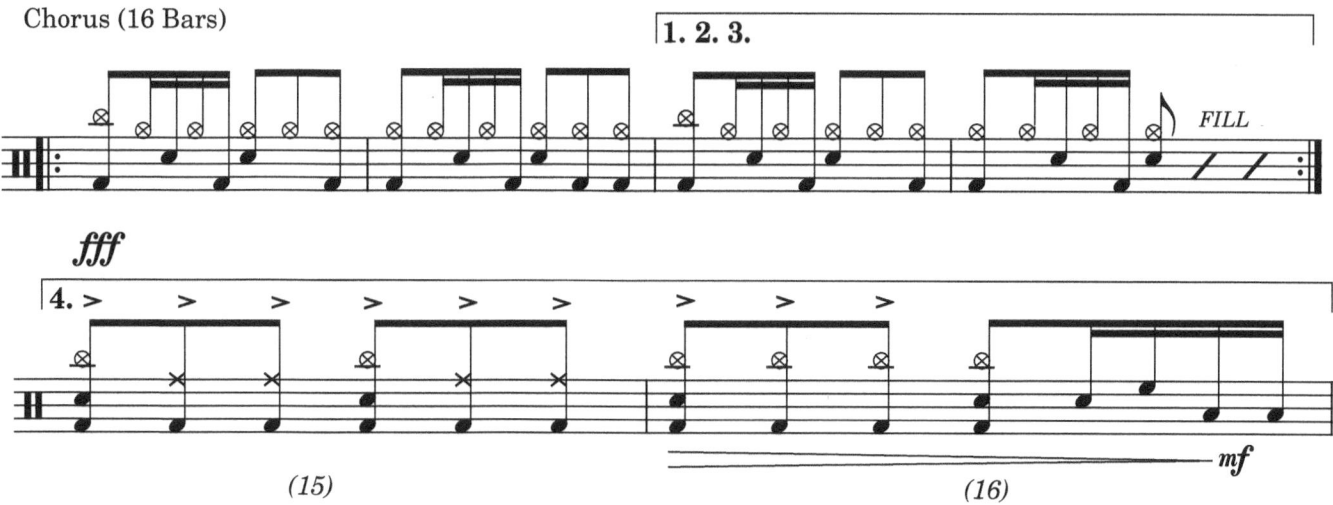

After the chorus, we go back to the top of the form and play the whole thing again. In this style of music, *it's important to try to play the same beat every time a section of the tune comes around.* This gives the song structure and creates the impression that you're making intentional musical choices rather than aimlessly wandering about. There are always exceptions to this, and they can work well as long as they are done on purpose. But keeping your parts well-organized and uniform is a good place to start.

Along with a road map, I've also included a more detailed drum chart. Different songs require different types of charts, and it's important to be able to read and create them in a variety of formats. This ability to adjust will help you in the real world, since no two musical situations are exactly the same!

Photo by Sonia Goydenko

STUFF YOU CAN USE

Recording for the book @ C-Room Studio

Woodhead Live @ Pianos in NYC

Charts, Lead Sheets & Road Maps

"The Conjuration"

By Vern Woodhead

♪ = 192

6/8 Rock, 2 Bar Count-in
Drums ½ bar pickup fill

16 Intro, w/HH hits at start of each 4-bar phrase

4 Pre-Verse (Gently)

16 Verse 1 (Vox enter, Same groove)

8 Pre-Chorus, Bars 7 & 8: 8th-note build and fill

16 Chorus 1 (Open HH)

8 Re-intro (Same as Intro)

4 Pre-Verse (Gently)

16 Verse 2

8 Pre-Chorus 2, Build Bars 7 & 8

16 Chorus 2

End hits Bar 16, Beats 1 and 2 (long)

STUFF YOU CAN USE

"The Conjuration"

by Vern Woodhead

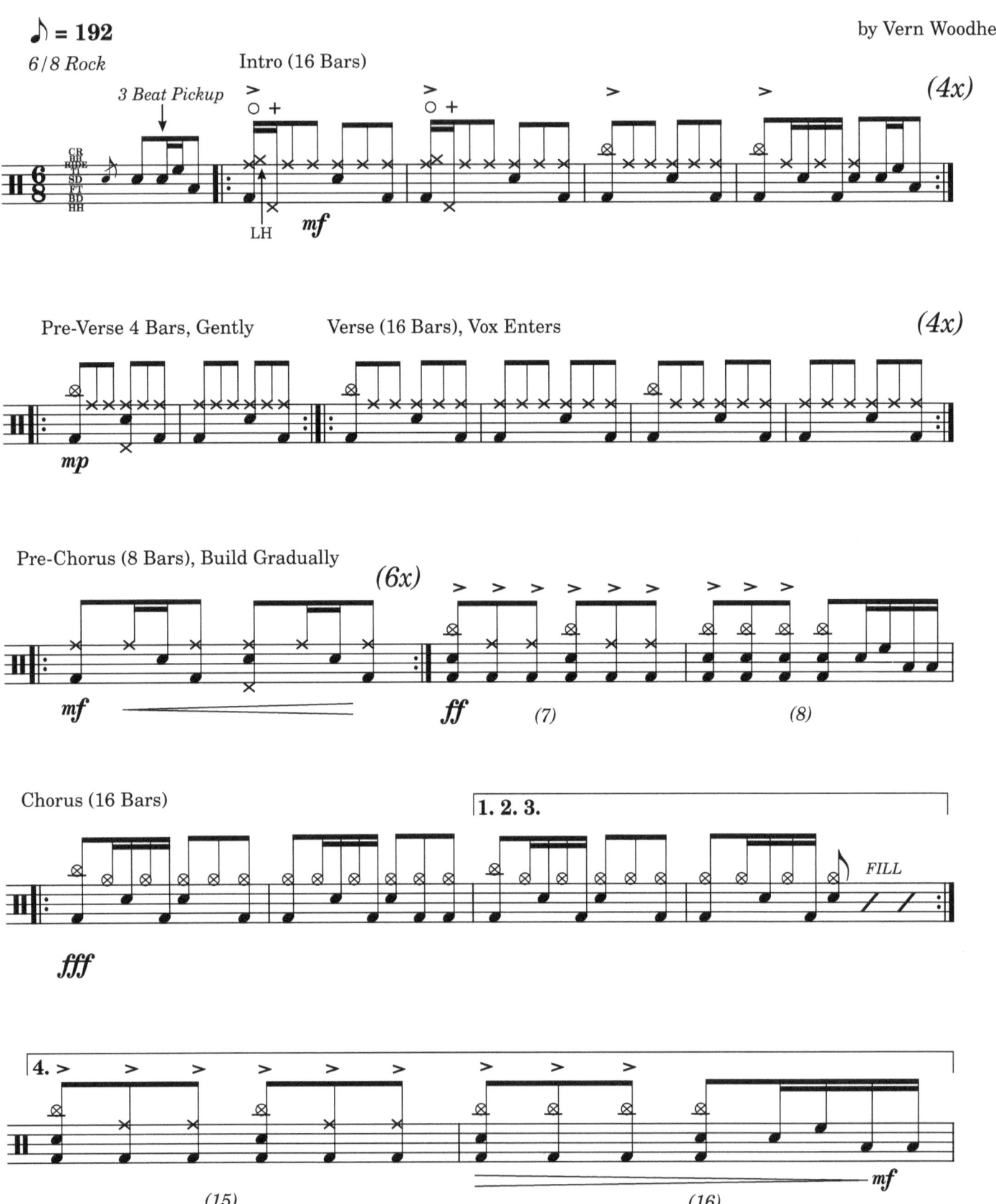

Charts, Lead Sheets & Road Maps

Re-Intro (8 Bars)

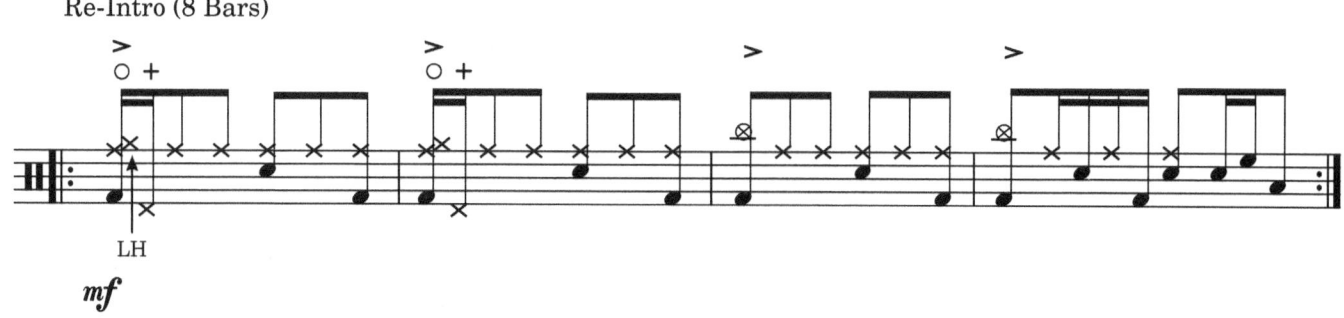

Pre-Verse 4 Bars, Gently   Verse (16 Bars), Vox Enters   (4x)

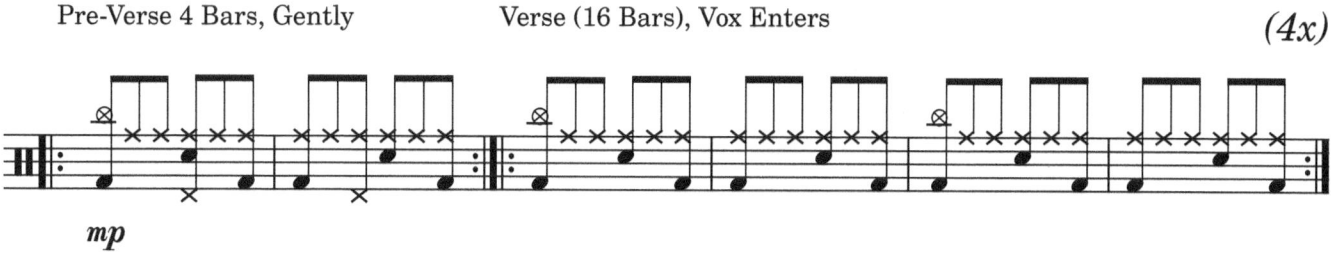

Pre-Chorus (8 Bars), Build Gradually

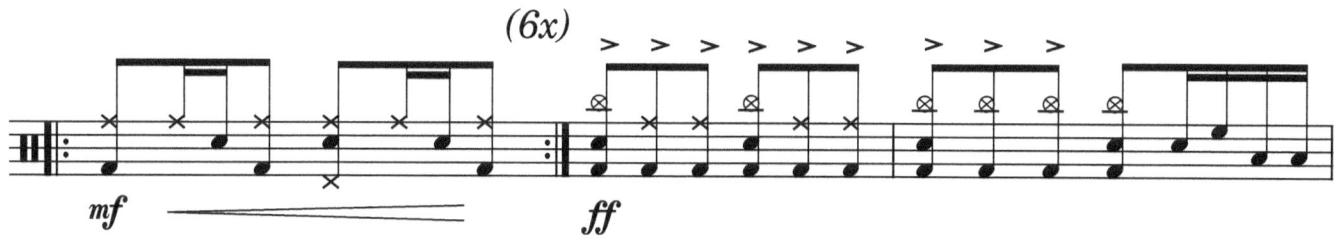

Chorus (16 Bars)

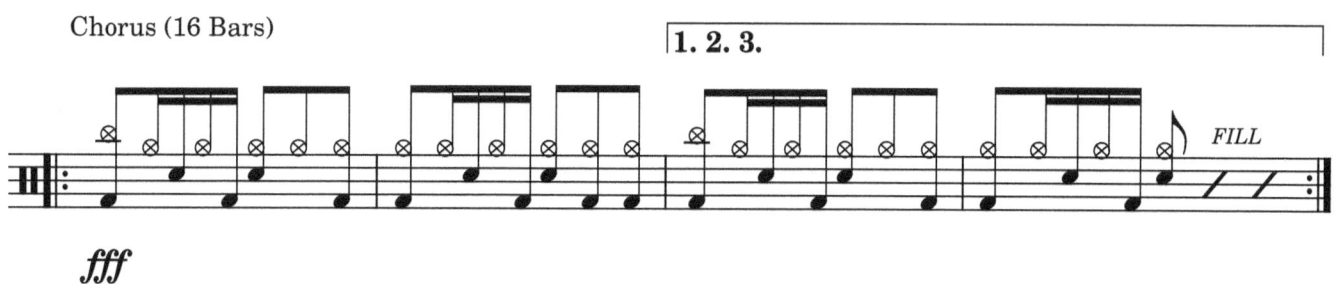

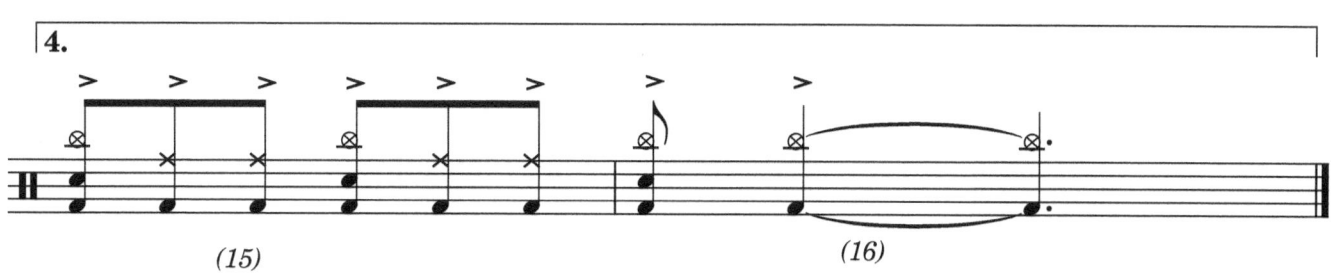

STUFF YOU CAN USE

SONG WORKSHOP #3: "JULY 1"
BY WOODHEAD

This is another Woodhead offering that switches back and forth from a 9/8 time signature to 4/4. Transitioning smoothly between these sections without any moments of uncertainty can be a real challenge.

Let's work on the two sections on their own. The 9/8 pattern is subdivided into phrases of 4+5 beats (you can also think of it as 2+2+2+3). Play beats 8 and 9 on the toms with your right hand, and try to make your motion smooth around the kit. The tune begins with 2 measures of drums only, followed by 4 of drums and bass before the vocals enter for a 16-measure verse. Guitarist Yana Davydova says, "I feel that rhythm from the bass and drums. That descending tom part has a nice tone color and complements the guitar part well. It's the blending of two colors."

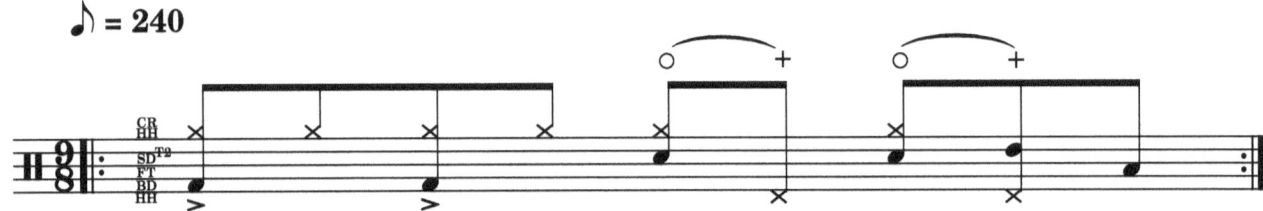

As we prepare to make the switch to 4/4, start imagining how the new time signature will sound in your head, even as you're still in 9/8. Two 8th notes will now equal one quarter note, a concept called "metric modulation." It's a bit like converting inches into centimeters, or ounces to grams. The pulse stays the same and the only thing that changes is how we're counting it. The drums will play an important role in making this a clean switch for everyone. This first transition is a bit abrupt, and it's critical to land on that first downbeat all together.

This 4/4 section is an 8-measure musical phrase with a broken-up half-time feel that repeats twice. You may look at this and think, "this is not a pattern…what do I play?" These hits are played together with the band and there's a lot of space between them. It can be tempting to fill it all up, but according to Vern, there's actually more going on here than meets the eye. "Those hits are part of the melody. While the melody is moving, the drums should reinforce it and make it stronger without filling over top of it. The spot for a fill is during the last two bars where the melody stops. It's like a call-and-response."

After we play the 8-measure 4/4 section twice, it's time to switch back to the 9/8 feel. The key to a smooth transition is to clearly telegraph to everyone that it's coming.

Charts, Lead Sheets & Road Maps

Dmitry says, "I'm usually listening for a little set-up from the drums. If I know something big is changing and there's a metric modulation where two 8th notes become a quarter note from 9/8 into 4/4, this can be hard to do. Especially if the music is new to me, there's a chance I may not be able to nail that change, so a little setup or obvious fill is what I'm listening for. Sometimes obvious fills are great! They need to happen." Yana adds, "I don't get lost in the form because the drum part prepares me for that change. It's a very cool thing to do and it makes the whole band sound better."

In this case, playing a couple 8th notes during the last bar of the 4/4 will help everyone hear the new time signature. It's like sending a big smoke signal that says "here we go!" Once we get back into the 9/8, make sure to count carefully, as verse 2 is 12 bars instead of 16 like verse 1. After we transition back to the 4/4 again, note that the last chorus is twice as long (32 bars). The tune ends on the last hit of the phase.

Dmitry Ishenko, Yana Davydova, Rob & Vern Woodhead

On Tour

Vern @ C-Room Studio

STUFF YOU CAN USE

"July 1"

♪ = 240

By Vern Woodhead

[2] Drums Only, 9/8 Groove

[4] Drums/Bass

[16] Verse 1 (Vox enter, Same groove)

[16] Modulate to 4/4 for Chorus 1, pulse stays the same

Play hits, fill in-between w/1/2x Feel

Modulate to 9/8 for:

[12] Verse 2 (Vox enters, same groove)

[32] Modulate to 4/4 for double-length Chorus, pulse stays the same

Play Hits, fill in-between w/1/2x Feel

End Bar 31, Beat 1 (Long)

Charts, Lead Sheets & Road Maps

SONG WORKSHOP #4: "GOWANUS MASH"
BY WOODHEAD

This last one from Woodhead is actually a medley of 3 different songwriting ideas designed to help you practice transitioning quickly and smoothly between unrelated tempos and feels. This is an awesome thing to work on since it will prepare you for so many real-life musical situations. This concept grew out of the composer Vern Woodhead's yearly practice of writing and recording one new song or musical idea every day in the month of July. Listen to all the different sections ahead of time and try to internalize the tempos so you aren't surprised by the transitions. As Dmitry puts it, "this one requires one-hundred percent focus and rhythmic awareness. Stay with the click track and it will guide you right through."

Vern adds, "if there are a few tempo and groove changes within one piece of music, it's not enough to just count along. Sometimes in that first bar or two, you're still finding the pulse. You need to know firmly what to expect in that new tempo. Even a good musician can have a little awkwardness in the first couple bars on this kind of thing."

So with that in mind, let's go through the sections step-by-step. We begin with 2 bars of drums playing this groove on the ride cymbal. Use your right hand to play the toms on beat 4 while keeping your left on the snare. We'll call this Song 1.

After those 2 bars, the rest of the band enters and plays this groove for 9 bars. This is an unusual length for a verse, so make sure to keep counting! In the 10th bar, the drums play these hits together with the band and we get ready to move to the next tempo and feel.

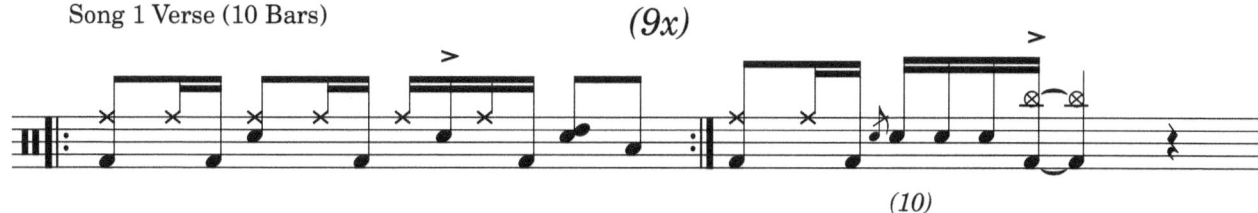

After the last hit on the "a" of beat 2, you'll hear the click track complete the measure at this tempo (80 bpm, or beats per minute) and then switch to 67 bpm for the start of the next bar. However, the drums and bass have a rest in this spot so you don't have to come back in right away! As Dmitry points out, "we at least get a little break between songs 1 and 2 to recalibrate quickly."

After the tempo change, the first thing you'll hear is guitarist Yana Davydova's riff in the first half of the measure which signals the start of Song 2. This is a bit like a "call," and you'll play the "response" along with the bass starting on the "a" of beat 3. She says, "I really try to internalize the new tempo and listen to the drums. It happens in a split-second and we all need to be on the same page."

Also, we've switched from a straight to a swing feel. Not easy! Use your ears and try to lock in this transition with the band.

STUFF YOU CAN USE

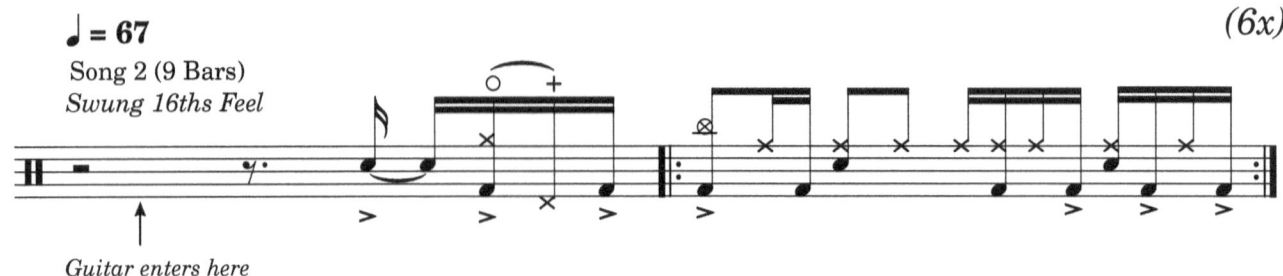

Guitar enters here

The groove should be super-relaxed and behind the beat. This section is 9 bars long, and there are some full-band hits in bars 8 and 9 that will lead us into the third song.

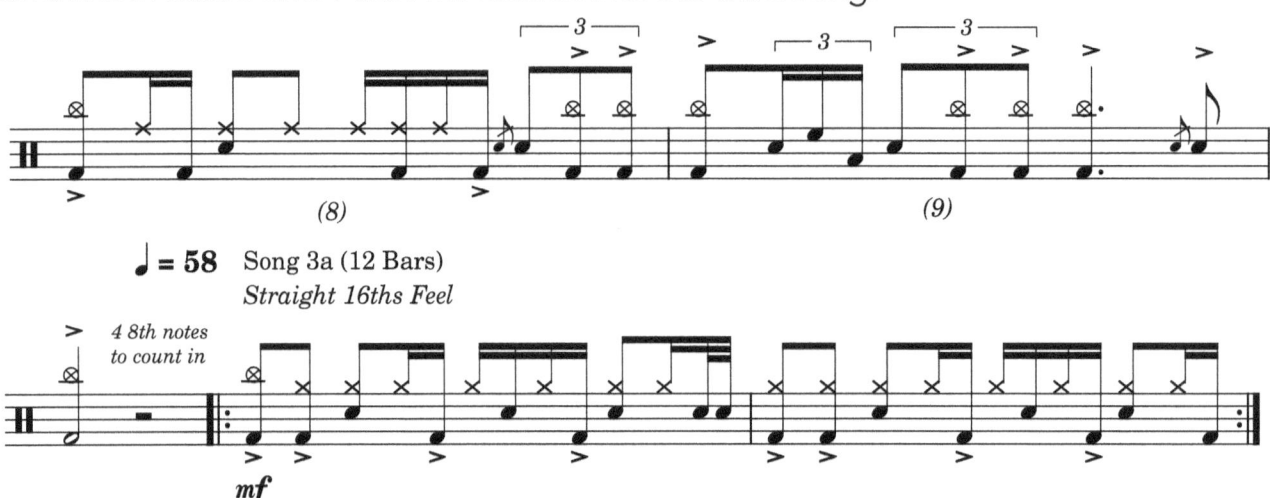

After you play the last hit on beat 1, the tempo will slow to 58 bpm for Song 3a. As Dmitry says, "just stay on that click and get ready for the downbeat." Just like last time, you'll have some time to hear the new tempo before 4 8th-note clicks bring you in. Good news! This song has two separate sections and the first is 12 measures long. The groove is a straight-16ths feel and it's a little heavier than the previous songs, but still relaxed. The most important thing is to lock in your first two bass drum notes of each bar with the bass player. Also note that the vocals don't enter until bar 5.

As we reach the end of the section, get ready for the next change. This time the tempo will remain the same but the feel is different. Play the hits in bar 12 and rest on beat 4 before you crash hard into Song 3b.

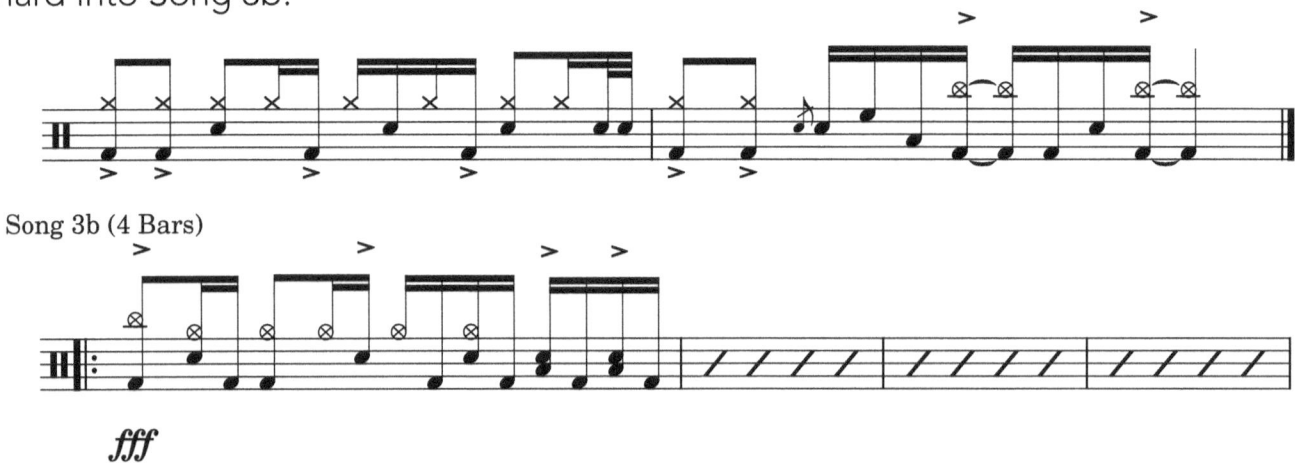

Vern explains, "this part is deceptive since it's so chill and slow and then really surprises you with the energy of the second part." The texture changes to the open hi-hat, and the dynamics and intensity increase.

Charts, Lead Sheets & Road Maps

Yana adds, "I like heavy, low-end EQ from the drums. Jazz drummers are more in the treble range, while rock drummers are bottom-heavy. In this style, I appreciate a nice, solid, heavy thumping accent coming from the drums which really grounds the whole band and gives it a wider sonic range. Sometimes crash cymbals are in the same range as my parts. It's important to have a good sense of separation. It's good to use a lot of deeper sounds and not overuse the crash cymbals while the guitars are doing their thing."

After 4 bars, it gets quieter and more relaxed as we switch back into Song 3a. Play that groove for another 4 bars and then play the ending hits with the band in bar 4.

That's a lot of changes! But having those tempos and feels stored in your brain ahead of time will help you navigate through. As Vern puts it, "this is almost like a short version of a four-movement symphony. I think there is a deliberate arc to it. The first movement is strong, while the second one tends to be a very different feel but without a drop in energy. The third tends to be lower and slower. The fourth movement has more 16th notes and is more bombastic even though we're at the same tempo. Beethoven's 9th is a prime example. A lot of rock musicians should try to understand Beethoven since his music starts with the simplest short motif and builds from that."

(Note: this is a concept called "motivic development" which is very useful when you explore solo ideas. More on this later.)

STUFF YOU CAN USE

"Gowanus Mash"

♩ = 80
2 Bars Count-in

by Vern Woodhead

Song 1 (Intro- 2 Bars Drums Only)
Straight 16ths Feel

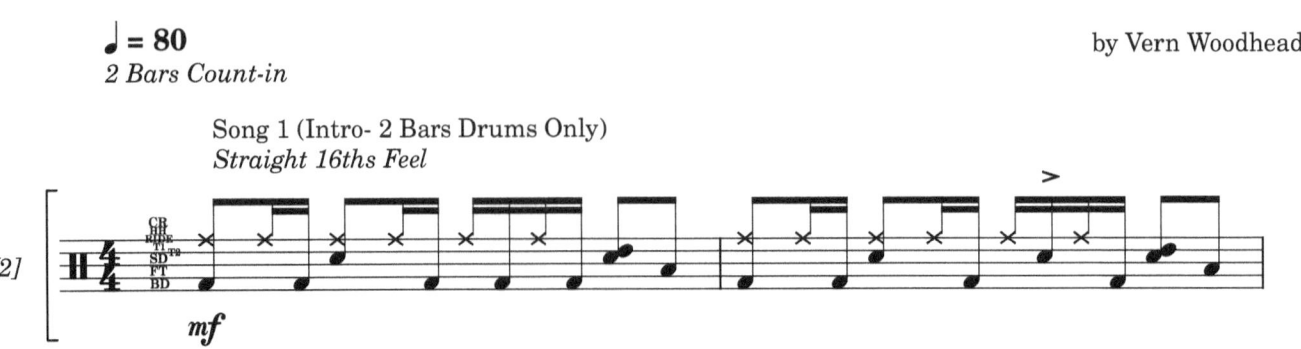

Song 1 Verse (10 Bars)   (9x)

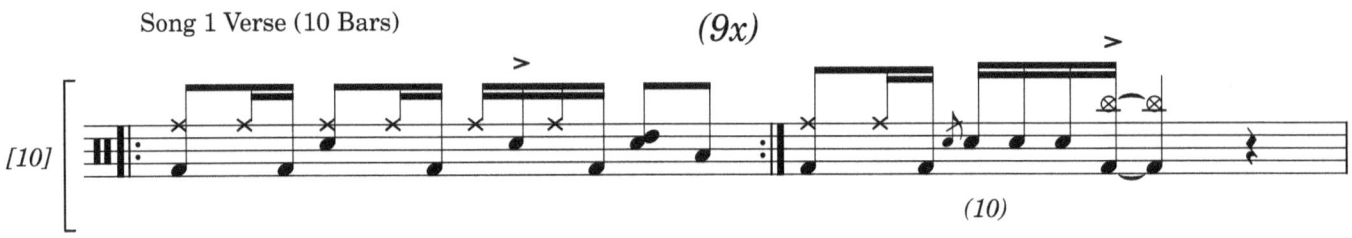

♩ = 67   (6x)
Song 2 (9 Bars)
Swung 16ths Feel

Guitar enters here

Charts, Lead Sheets & Road Maps

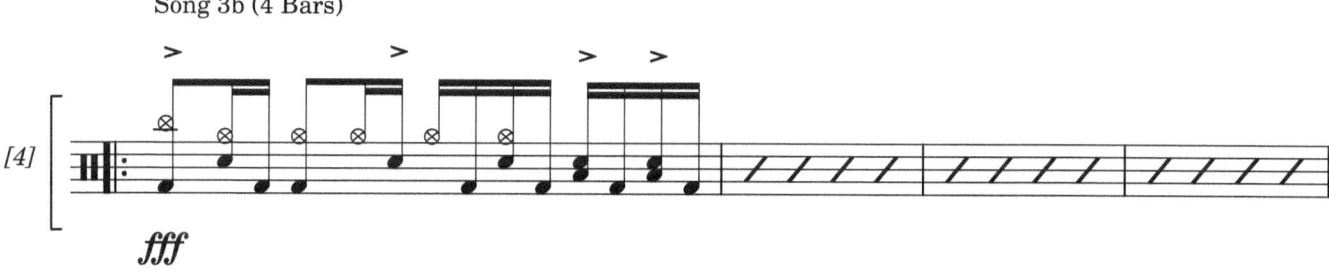

75

STUFF YOU CAN USE

SONG WORKSHOP #5: "OUR FUNERAL"
BY SIMON GARRETT

These next couple of tunes feature British rocker Simon Garrett. His music combines the grungy feel of artists like Iggy Pop and Thin Lizzy with funkier elements like Prince, Daft Punk and David Bowie. Simon is also a solid drummer and able to clearly explain what he's hearing from the drums in his music. He sends demos, but also gives me a lot of leeway to come up with my own parts and ideas.

This first tune is called "Our Funeral" and also features Matthew Milligan on bass. Matthew is the bassist for the band Wheatus (of "Teenage Dirtbag" fame) and also tours with Mike Doughty from Soul Coughing. He lays down a fat pocket on this one, and I hope you enjoy playing with him as much as I do.

"Our Funeral" is an up-tempo and energetic rock tune with a half-time feel on the first part of each chorus. A few of the sections have an odd number of measures, and there are some important accents within the main groove that the band plays together throughout the tune.

It begins with a short drum fill that resolves on the "and" of beat 4 when the bass and guitar enter. It's important to try to nail this and get off to a good start. You can use the written sticking or simplify the fill a little. As long as you start on beat 3 and hit that "and" of 4 with the band, you're all good!

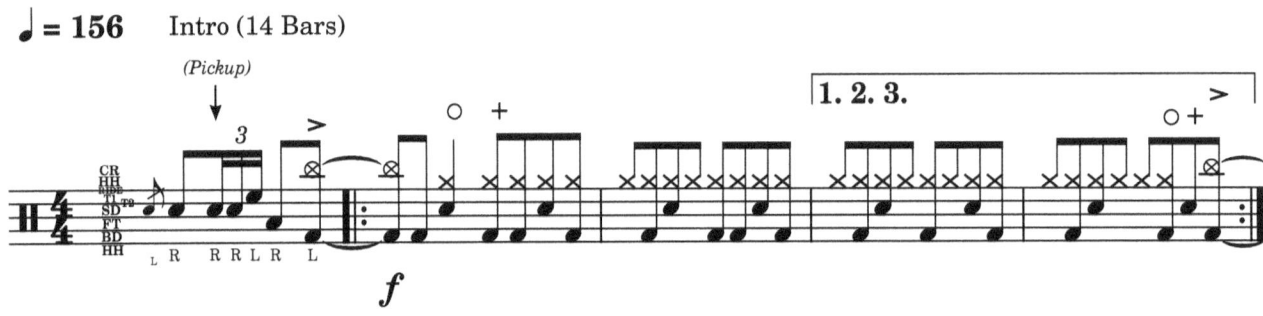

This intro is 14 bars long, so make sure to keep track of where you are. Much like the opening fill, the main underlying rhythm of this tune is the hookup between the bass and drums on the "and" of beat 4, which is a rhythmic anticipation we call a "push." You don't necessarily need to play huge crashes on these beats every time, but try to lock in your bass drum with the bass player and crash at the end of each 4-measure phrase. Matthew explains, "it's really important that the bass and drums are on the same page. If I push and the drummer is on the downbeat, it turns into slop city."

Simon adds, "I love those pushes. I have them in almost every one of my songs. It adds a bit more energy and momentum to it. This song has almost a disco thing going on underneath the rock. It's like a Larry Graham bass thing where he's playing octaves. It's good when the drummer really chunks out 2 and 4 on the snare since that allows the bass to position itself sonically around that. A big thing of mine is that I don't want everything to be on the downbeats. I think that's terribly boring."

Charts, Lead Sheets & Road Maps

Verse 1 is the same groove and also 14 bars, while verse 2 is 16 bars. When you get to the last two measures of each verse, start loosening the hi-hat a little to build into the next section.

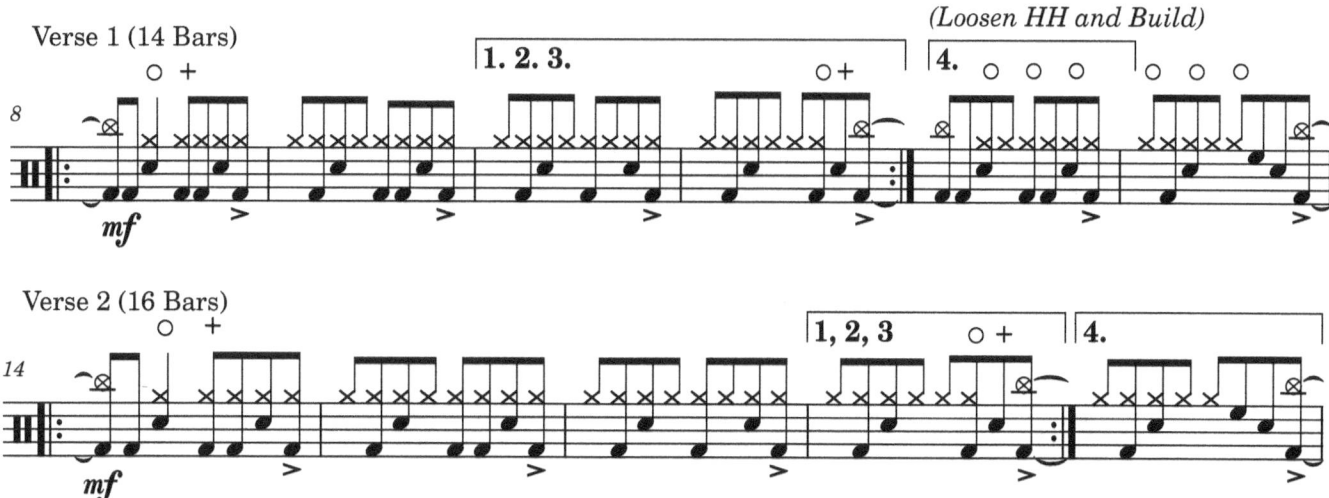

The pre-chorus groove is a bit different since the open hi-hats give it a little bounce and we're not accenting the "and" of 4 except in measure 8. Keep it simple and stick with Matthew. He points out, "this part of the song is the most verbose and has loads of lyrics, so our role is to provide a solid foundation for Simon and stay out of the way." Simon continues, "this section is like an intermediary between the verse and the chorus. I'm really trying to flesh out what the lyrics are doing."

As I was working out my drum part, I began thinking…"well, what *are* the lyrics doing and how can I apply that to what I'm playing?"

Simon explains, "this tune is actually about a relationship that is dying. That's 'Our Funeral.' The verse talks about 'the sweetest of times' and all the good things, then in the pre-chorus 'something dumb breaks and gets bent out of shape.' It's like, 'hang on a minute, this is all going to sh*t.' And the chorus is the death of it."

So think of the pre-chorus as a beginning of this unraveling and the increased activity in the drum part as a way to show that uneasiness. Once we get to the last 4 bars, loosen the hi-hat and start building up for the chorus. When we hit bar 16, there is a hard stop on the "and" of beat 4 and a short rest.

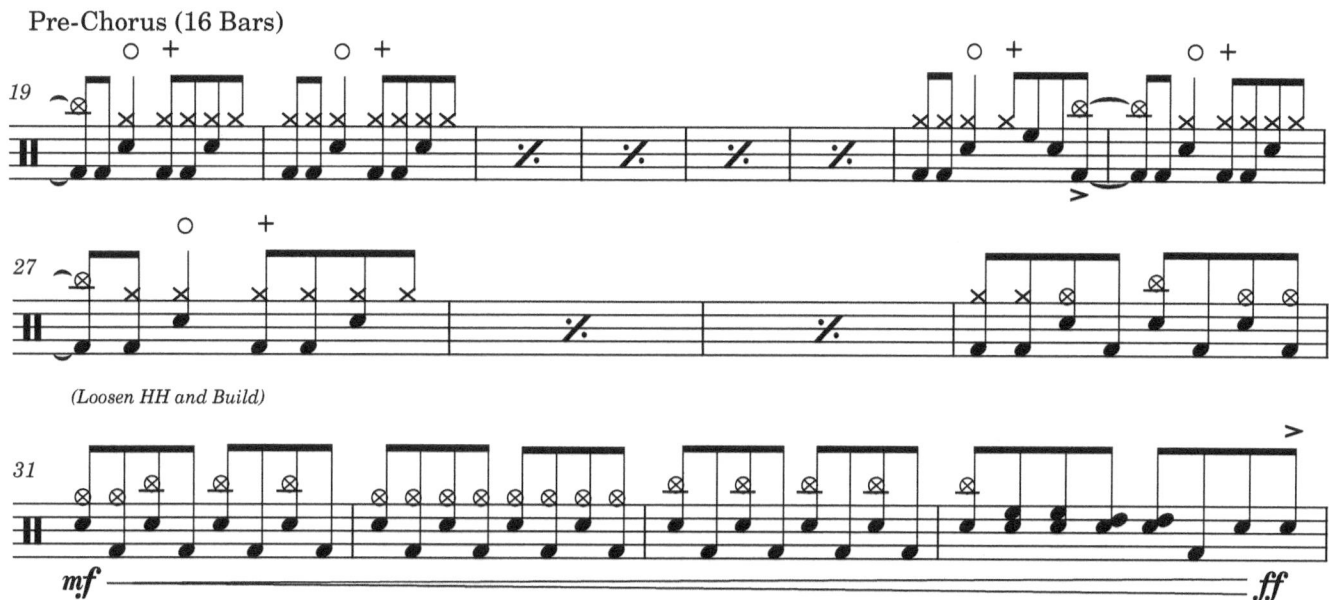

77

STUFF YOU CAN USE

After the rest, fill into the "and" of beat 4 again and play this half-time groove for the first 8 measures of the chorus (and keep the hits going underneath). Simon describes this feel difference, saying "sometimes it's nice just to have a breather and change it up."

Chorus 1 Part 1 (1/2x Feel, 8 Bars)

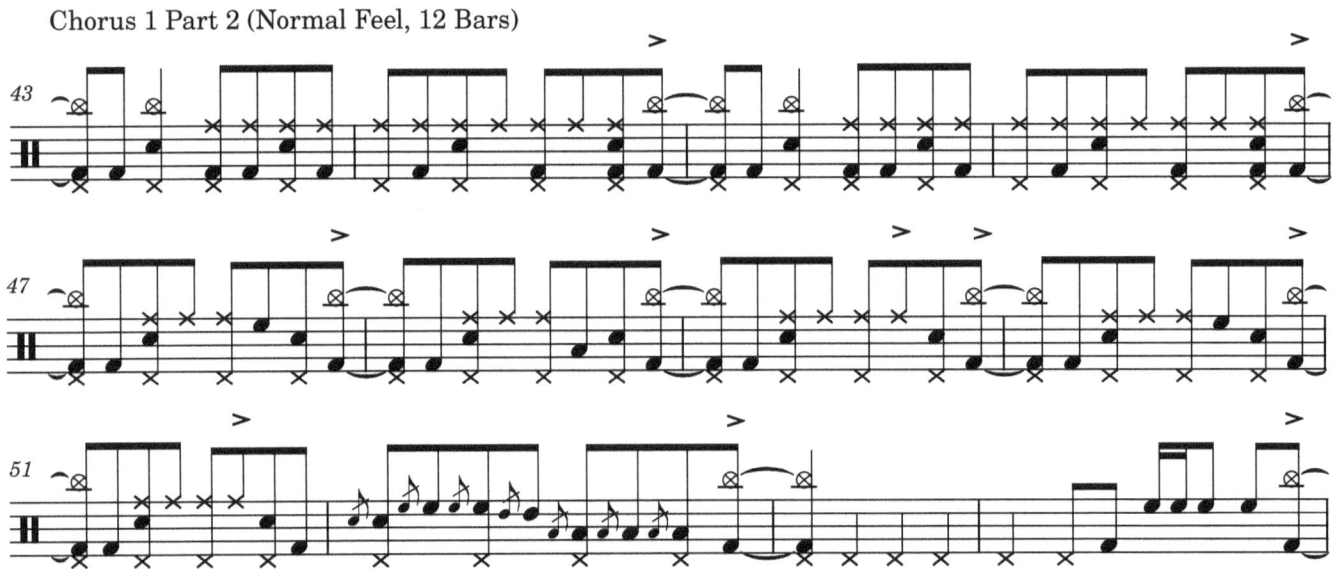

Play those 8 measures, then go back to the original feel for the final 12 bars of the chorus. It's hard to avoid getting excited and rushing when you make that switch. Watch out for the lift in Bar 10!

Chorus 1 Part 2 (Normal Feel, 12 Bars)

Then we play the verse, another pre-chorus and chorus exactly like before, and we're off to the 12-bar guitar solo. Switch to the ride and keep building intensity without getting too far away from those hits with the bass.

Guitar Solo (12 Bars)   (Repeat 3x)

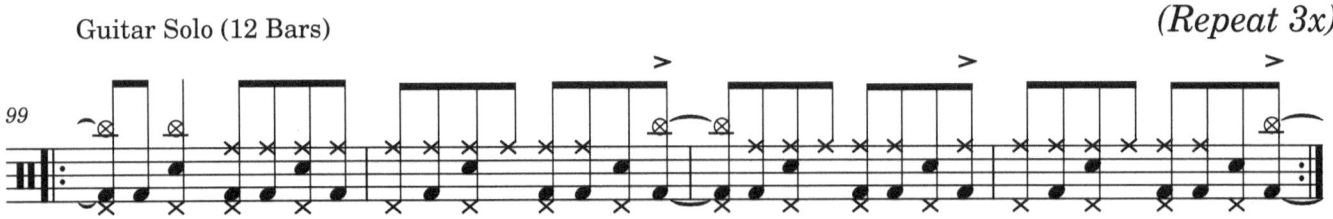

As the guitar solo wraps up, we arrive at the outro, which is 10 bars and has some hits with the band. Make sure to play all the written accents and build into a crisp and short ending on (you guessed it), the "and" of beat 4. Matthew concludes, "it's fun when you have an artist who has a clear idea of what they want from the bass and drums, but also gives you room to make it your own."

Charts, Lead Sheets & Road Maps

Outro (10 Bars)

Here's a road map to get you started, and I've also included a note-for-note transcription so you can dive even deeper into the details.

Simon Garrett in Brooklyn, NY
Photo by Alison Schopmeyer

Matthew Milligan & Rob onstage

STUFF YOU CAN USE

The Seaside Lounge Studios in Brooklyn, NY
Photo by Thomas Mester

Rob @ C-Room Studio
Photo by Thomas Mester

Charts, Lead Sheets & Road Maps

"Our Funeral"

♩ = 156
Medium/Fast Rock, 2 bars count-in

By Simon Garrett

|14| Fill beats 3 & 4 into Intro Groove w/hits

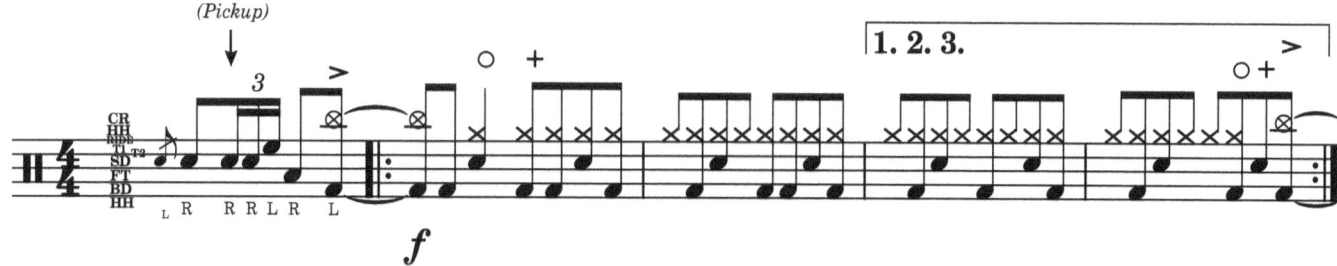

|14| Verse 1 (Same HH groove/hits build bars 13 & 14)

|16| Verse 2 (Same HH groove/hits)

|16| Pre-Ch. Open HH sparsely & build to stop Bar 16, Beat 4+

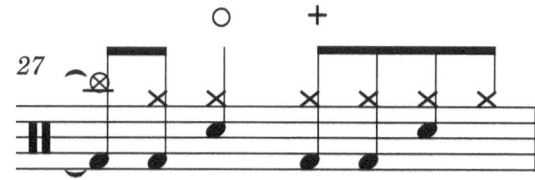

|8| Chorus 1a (Ride 1/2x Feel), Rest Bar 1 Beats 1 & 2 Fill Beats 3 & 4

|12| Chorus 1b (Normal Feel- Ride) Lift Bar 10, Beat 4+
Rest Bar 11, Fill Bar 12

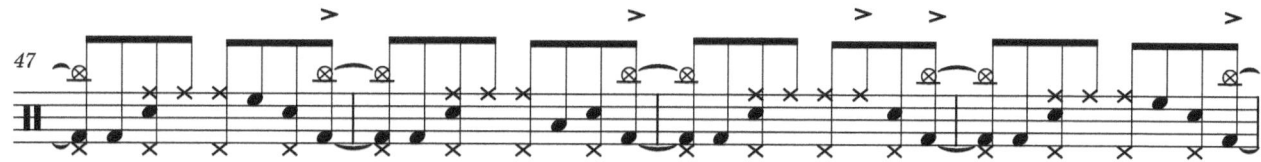

|16| Verse 3 (Same HH groove/hits)

|16| Pre-Ch., Build to stop on Bar 16, Beat 4+

|8| Chorus 2a (1/2x Feel), Rest Bar 1 Beats 1 & 2, Fill Beats 3 & 4

|12| Chorus 2b (Normal Feel- Ride), Fill Bar 12 to Solo

|12| Guitar Solo (Ride, Same Groove)

|10| Outro w/same hits, Fill to End Bar 10, Beat 4 +

STUFF YOU CAN USE

"Our Funeral"

by Simon Garrett

Charts, Lead Sheets & Road Maps

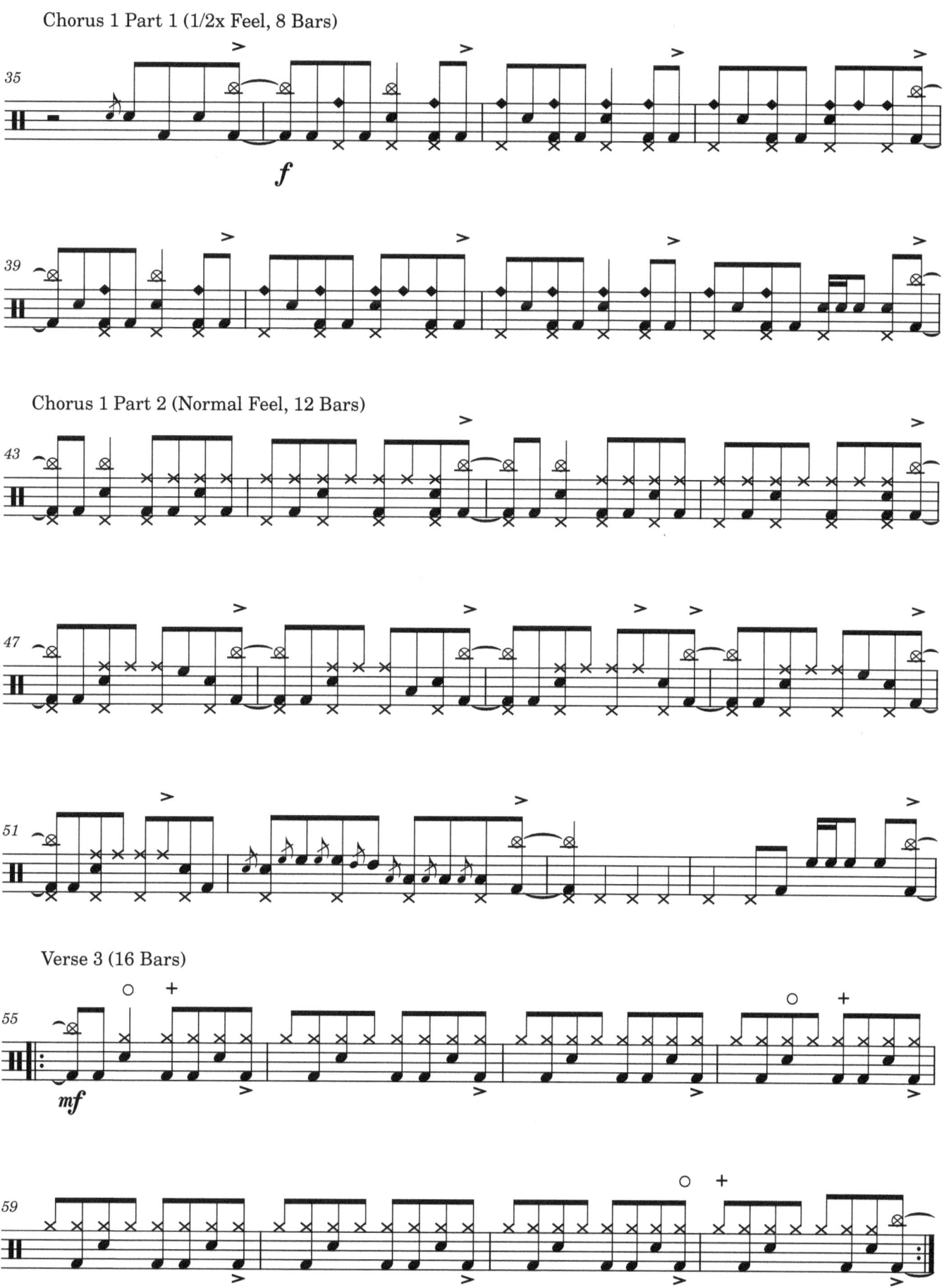

STUFF YOU CAN USE

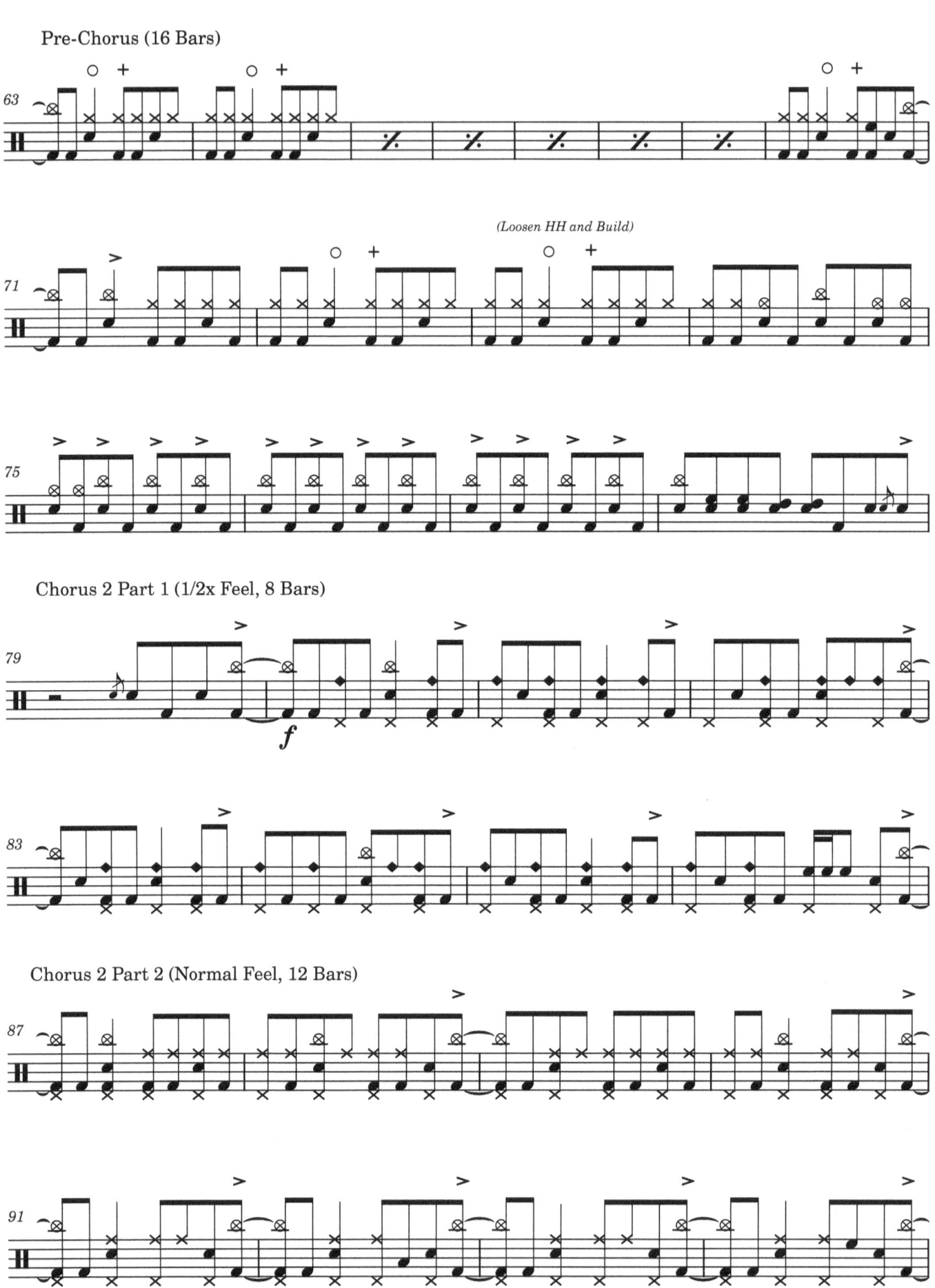

84

Charts, Lead Sheets & Road Maps

Guitar Solo (12 Bars) *(Repeat 3x)*

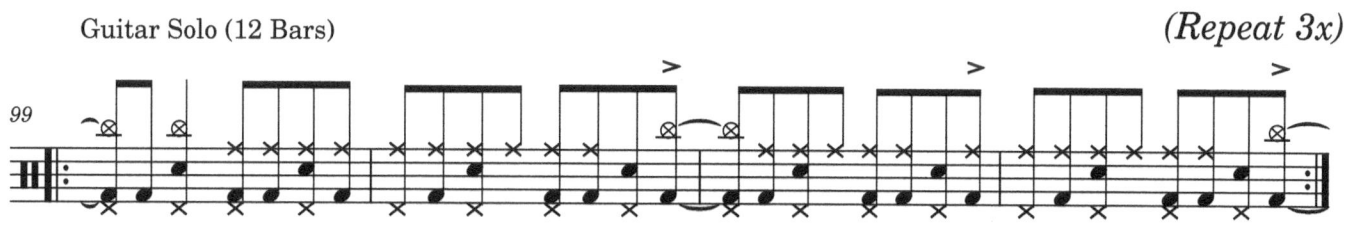

Outro (10 Bars)

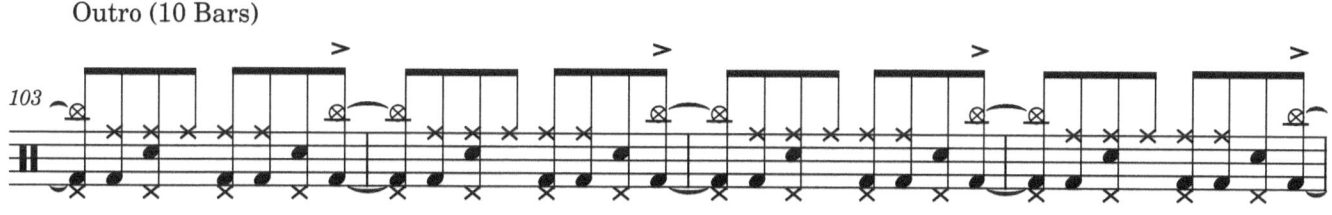

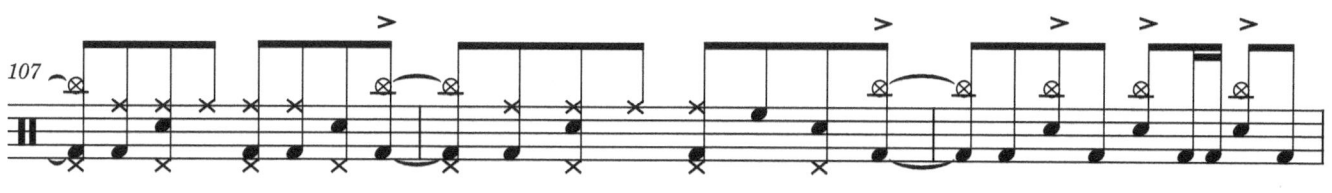

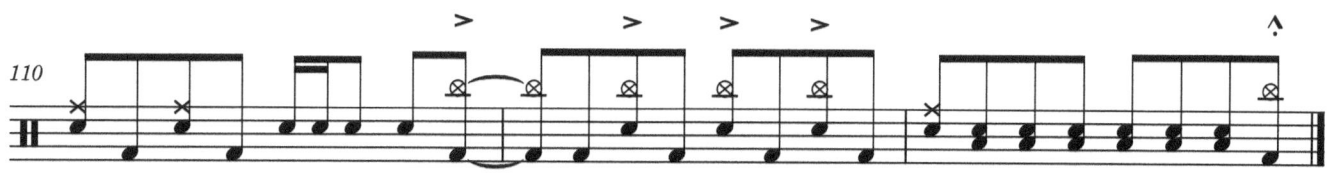

STUFF YOU CAN USE

SONG WORKSHOP #6: "ESCAPE"
BY SIMON GARRETT

Simon explains, "this tune is all about the different grooves. I was trying to get outside of my normal creative process and make something totally unique using loops in Ableton. It has almost a cinematic quality to it. I had all these funky bass lines and this really nasty synth part. And I had this massive, great big chunky groove that took up a lot of space. I wanted to get away from this being a rock song."

"Escape" actually begins with the chorus, which is a bit unconventional (although The Beatles did it a lot).

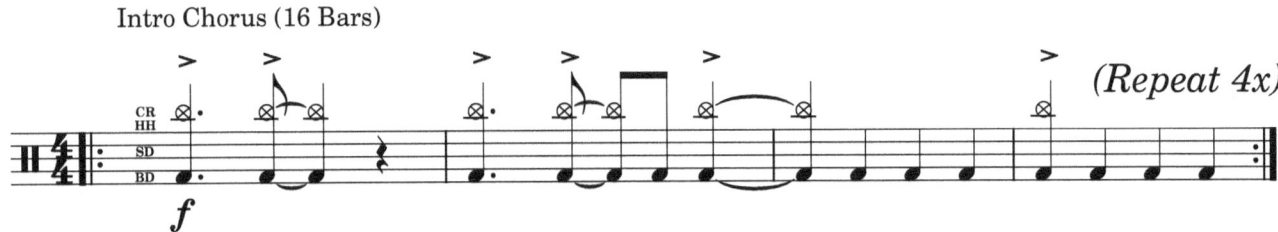

Since this written part is not really a groove, *the trick with the chorus is knowing when to fill and when to chill.* The hits in the first 2 measures of the phrase reinforce the melody, while the last 2 have space for you to fill in a bit while keeping the bass drum steady. Simon adds, "I like this idea of having a very rigid motif with all these big things happening over top of it. You can either pick up the accents or be intuitive with it and give some space."

The next section is called the pre-verse, and it's super-funky and tight. It's essentially just a version of the verse groove that occurs before the vocals enter.

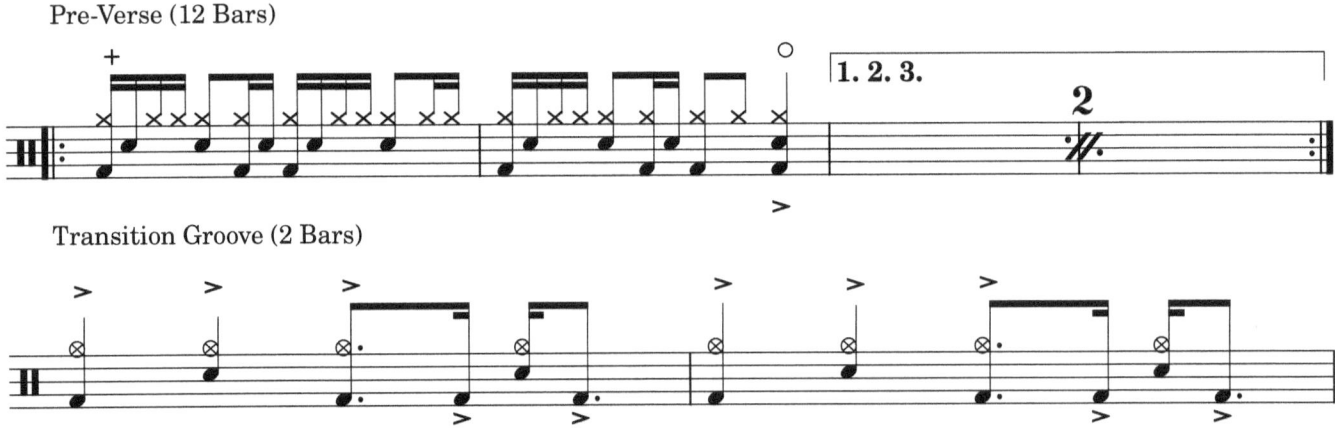

The verse groove is similar to the pre-verse, but a little simpler so it doesn't get in the way of the lyrics. Between each verse there is a brief loose hi-hat pattern we'll call the "transition groove" that leads us into the next section.

Charts, Lead Sheets & Road Maps

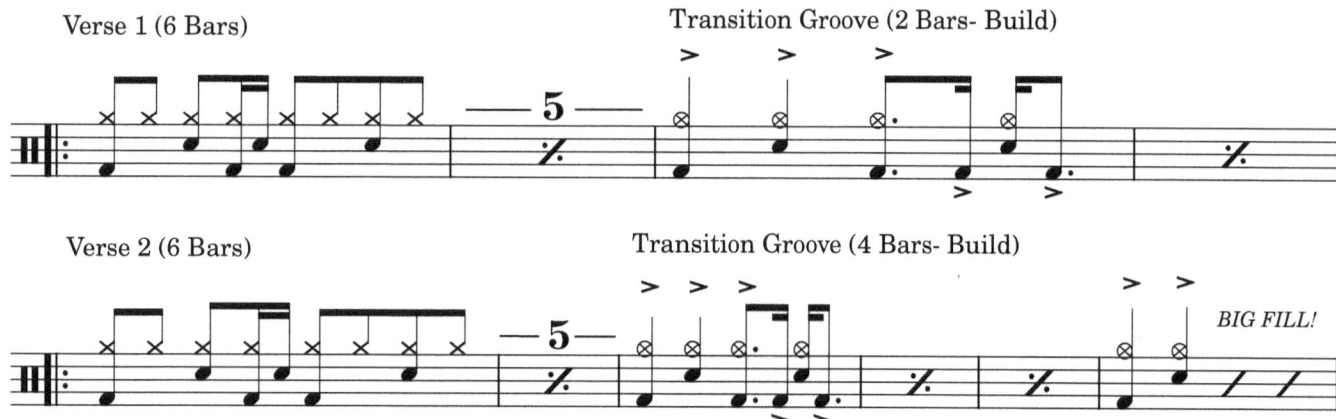

The transition groove after verse 2 is 4 measures long, and then we're back to the totally epic chorus.

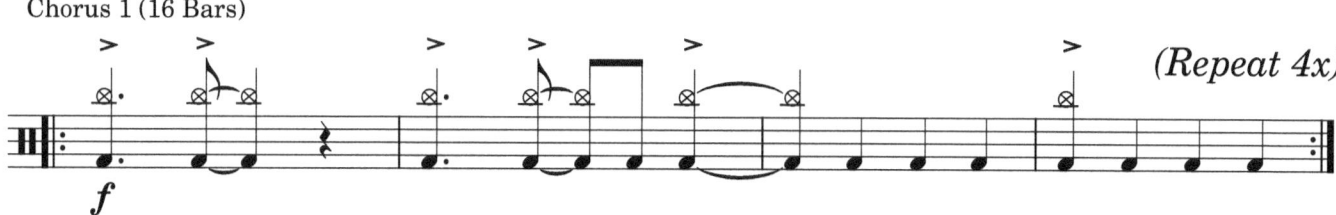

Simon explains, "it's really about having an 'A' and a 'B' part. A funky, stompy disco beat in the verse and a transition groove with a little space. When the big thing hits, it's really a case of what we want to do with it since it's so powerful on its own. I like to hear some fills around those accents. It's almost a bit proggy in those moments."

After that second chorus, we're back to the busier pre-verse groove for 8 bars, followed by verses 3 and 4 with the transition groove wedged in-between. Take note that verse 3 is 8 measures instead of 6. Also, the transition groove after verse 4 is 6 measures. Stay on your toes and keep counting!

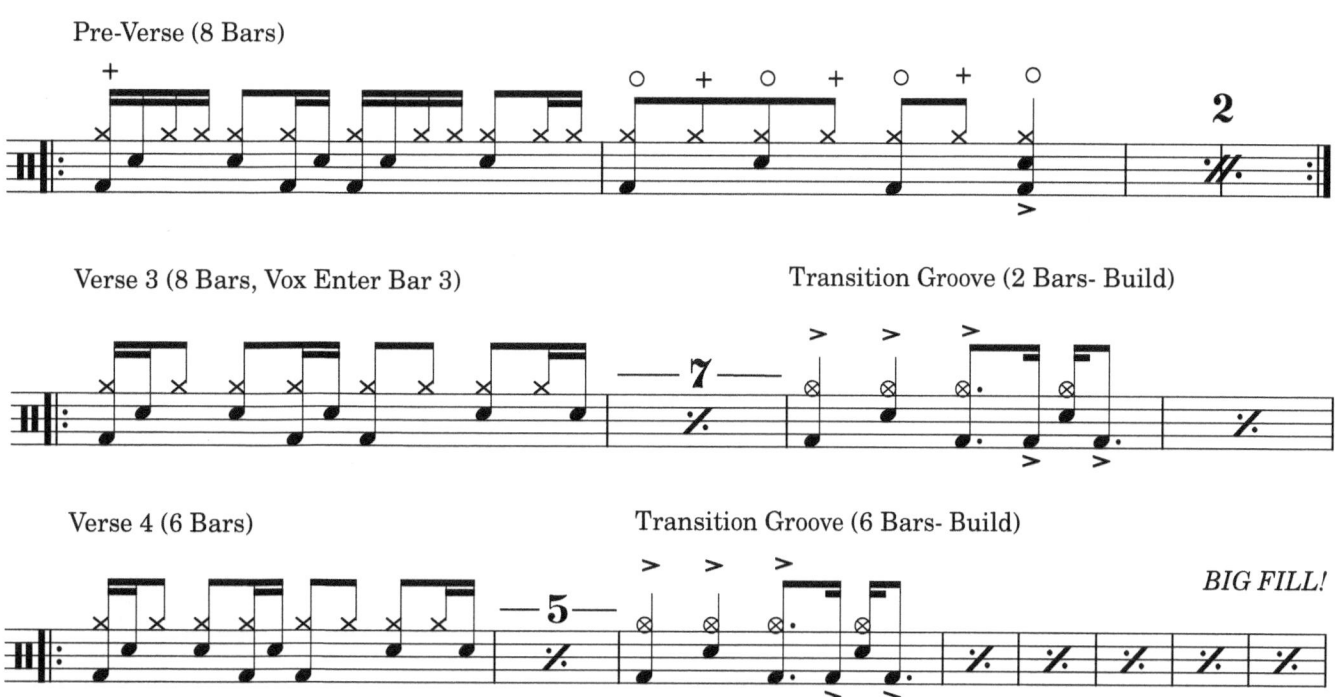

STUFF YOU CAN USE

Fill into the chorus and then play the outro, which has a similar feel to the verses. Make sure to play the last note short and tight with the rest of the band.

Simon concludes, "this song is about fighting against nihilism and lack of meaning in life. It almost has an allusion to the novel *The Neverending Story* where there's a creeping evil in the kingdom. Can you feel it holding you down? It's that sort of fight that all creative people have against not knowing if anything they do is ever any good."

Simon Garrett &
Rob @ Sunnyvale in
Brooklyn, NY
Photo by Alison
Schopmeyer

Charts, Lead Sheets & Road Maps

Matthew Milligan & Simon
Photo by Alison Schopmeyer

Matthew, Simon & Rob @ C-Room Studio

STUFF YOU CAN USE

"Escape"

♩ = 120

By Simon Garrett

Charts, Lead Sheets & Road Maps

Pre-Verse (8 Bars)

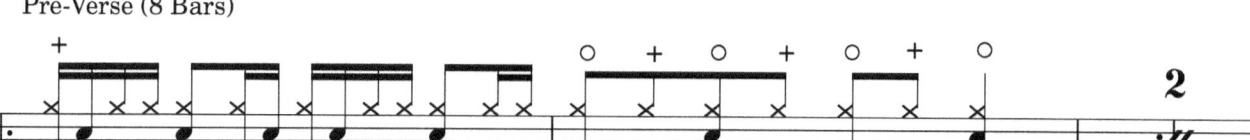

Verse 3 (8 Bars, Vox Enter Bar 3)   Transition Groove (2 Bars- Build)

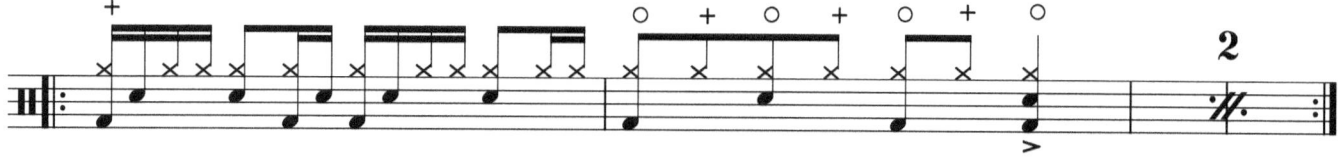

Verse 4 (6 Bars)   Transition Groove (6 Bars- Build)

BIG FILL!

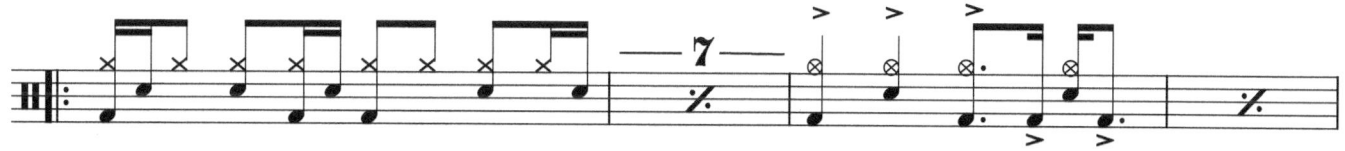

Chorus 2 (16 Bars)

(Repeat 4x)

Outro (Verse Groove, 12 Bars)

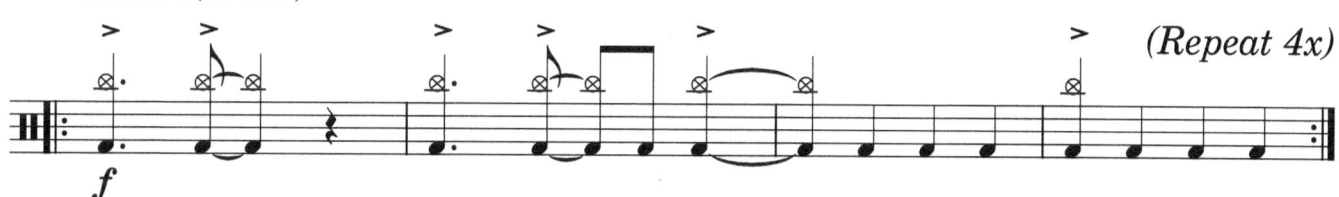

STUFF YOU CAN USE

SONG WORKSHOP #7: "SLEEP"
BY DAVE ROSS

This next set features ace guitarist and singer Dave Ross, along with Dmitry Ishenko on bass. Dave's biggest songwriting influences include Afrobeat legend Fela Kuti, Seal and Stevie Wonder, and his music is always challenging and fun to play. He often has very specific groove ideas for the drums, but also provides a lot freedom to develop the nuances of the part.

In this first tune "Sleep," the main groove has an important snare accent that happens throughout most of the song. This hit lines up with the bass line and gives the groove an angular and funky Latin-ish feel. Dmitry says, "the most important thing is the downbeat, and that's where we really need to lock. The second bass note is on the 'a' of beat 1, and that's the most forceful note that the bass and drums need to nail together without flamming."

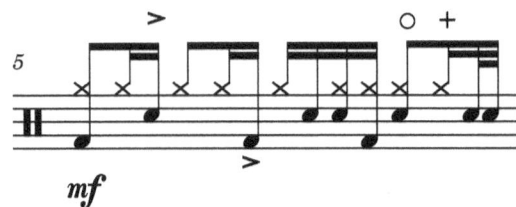

Dave explains, "I never say to the drummer, 'just play.' There are always going to be certain accents in the songs I write, and this one has that kick and snare pattern. So I lay out the specific things that go into each composition and the imagination of the drummer takes over after that."

The song begins with 4 measures of bass and guitar with a little drum fill in bar 2 that punctuates the riff. Once we hit measure 4, play a short fill to get into the main groove.

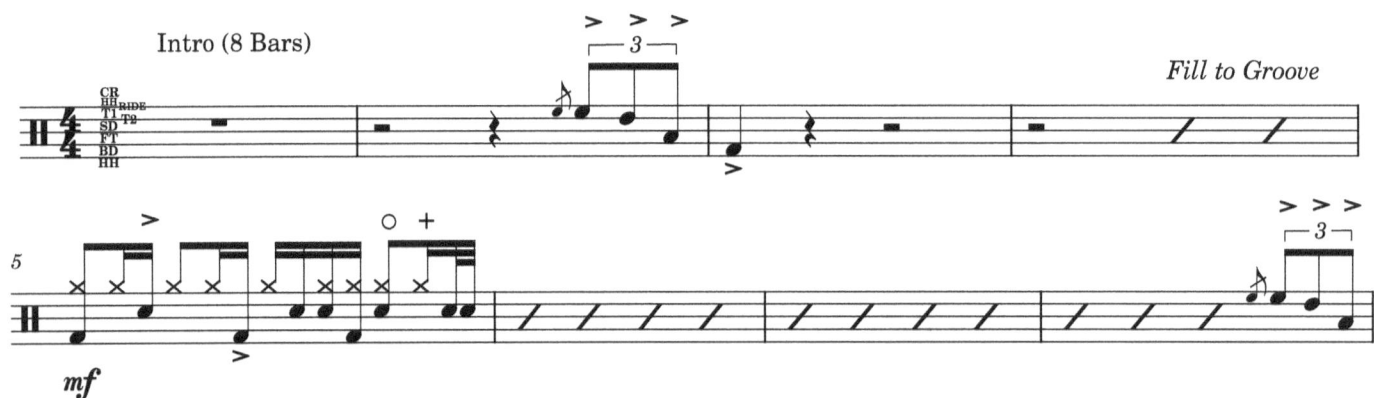

After 4 bars of groove with the band, the vocals enter for the first 8-bar chorus, followed by an 8-bar verse and another chorus. In this tune, the chorus and verse have the same groove, so it's important to keep building the intensity without interfering with the vocals. That bass and guitar riff is happening pretty consistently throughout the tune as well, so once you're comfortable hearing it, you can allude to that rhythm without mimicking it the whole time. These short fills written at the end of certain 4 and 8-bar phrases are a perfect example.

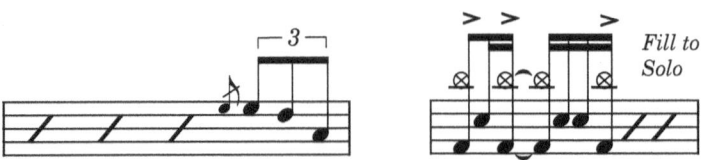

Charts, Lead Sheets & Road Maps

After the second chorus, switch to the ride for a short 8-measure guitar solo. Dave says, "during the guitar solo, the main parts are the kick and snare. They have to be strong and create momentum. And of course, try not to play too busy during anyone's solo. The drums are really important in moving the song in this section."

Following the guitar solo, we have a double-length chorus of 16 bars followed by the bridge. This is the only section of the tune where the rhythm changes to a backbeat with the right hand on the ride. Also notice the difference in the guitar part, which has a less syncopated strumming pattern. Dmitry explains, "I would call this a Latin rock groove, but it has elements of Brazilian and Afro-Cuban rhythms too. I'm really listening for the bass drum on the 'a' of beat 2. That's the note I'm really looking for."

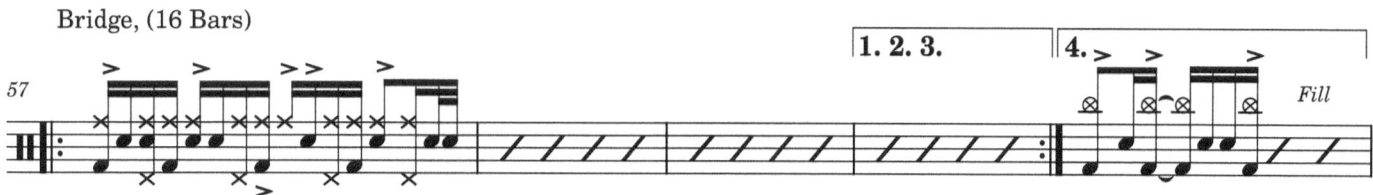

After the bridge, we've got a 4-bar interlude, one more big chorus (back to the original groove) and a short 4-bar outro.

Since this song is really just a long, slow build from beginning to end, I decided to ask Dave what his inspiration was when he wrote it.

"The lyrics tell a story of this crazy dream I had in a hotel in Nashville that used to be a Civil War hospital. I was in this giant space with spirits everywhere telling me 'sleep, it will take you somewhere. If you're not scared, come and you'll be enlightened.' And then I found myself inside a huge drum and the spirits were beating a rhythm on it. The drum part in this song is literally a transcription of what the spirits were playing in my dream. So the drum part was written by ghosts, really. I transcribed it from them. That's the link in this song. You're literally playing the spell."

STUFF YOU CAN USE

"Sleep"

by Dave Ross

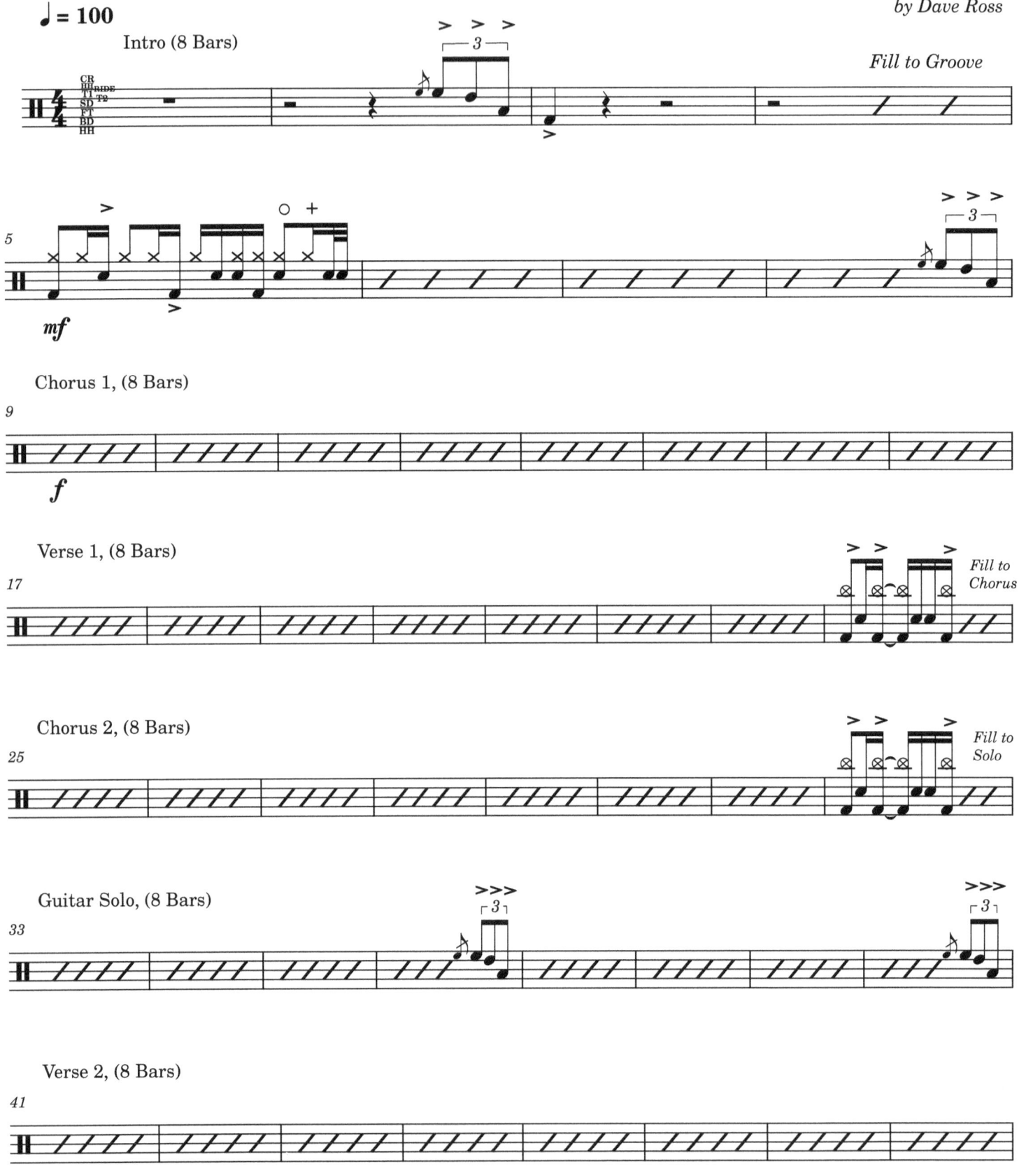

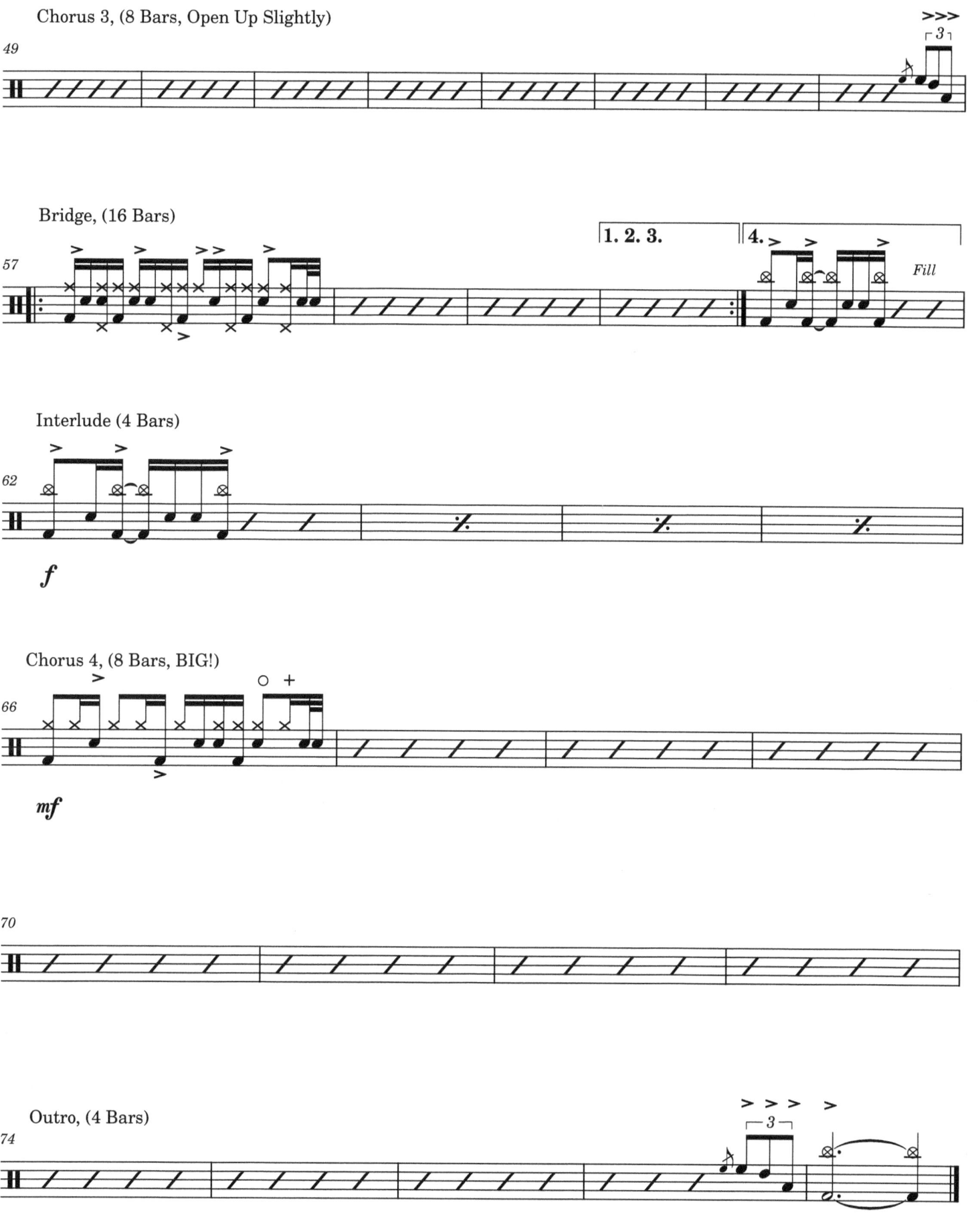

STUFF YOU CAN USE

Schnitzel in rural Illinois

Dave Ross, Rob & Dmitry Ishenko @ The Williamsburg Library in Brooklyn, NY

Charts, Lead Sheets & Road Maps

SONG WORKSHOP #8: "WORN AWAY"
BY DAVE ROSS

This next one features some complicated odd time signatures, so we'll break down the sections step by step. The pre-chorus and chorus sections are in 15/4, while the verses are in 29/4. This may seem daunting at first, but the key is to subdivide the groove into smaller bits that make it easier to count and feel. As bassist Dmitry Ishenko says, "I can't really count past 17 when I'm playing, so we have to chop it up."

Dave adds, "I didn't sit down to try to write a song in 29. I started out with this 7 groove and I was digging it. Once I got to 28/4, I realized it wasn't locking right and I added an extra beat. Once I had the 3 measures of 7 and the one measure of 8, the clavé was apparent. It was very organized and natural and I really didn't put forth a lot of effort once that 29 pattern was set. It's just based on a Brazilian clavé style."

The first step is to count and clap the clavé for each section. The intro, choruses and drum solo are all felt in groups of 15 beats, (subdivided 3-4-3-5).

The verses are in groups of 29 beats, (subdivided 3-4-3-4-3-4-3-5). As Dave explains again, "it's really just 4 bars of 7 with an extra beat added at the end."

STUFF YOU CAN USE

The pre-chorus is also in 29, but the rhythm of the clavé is a bit different.

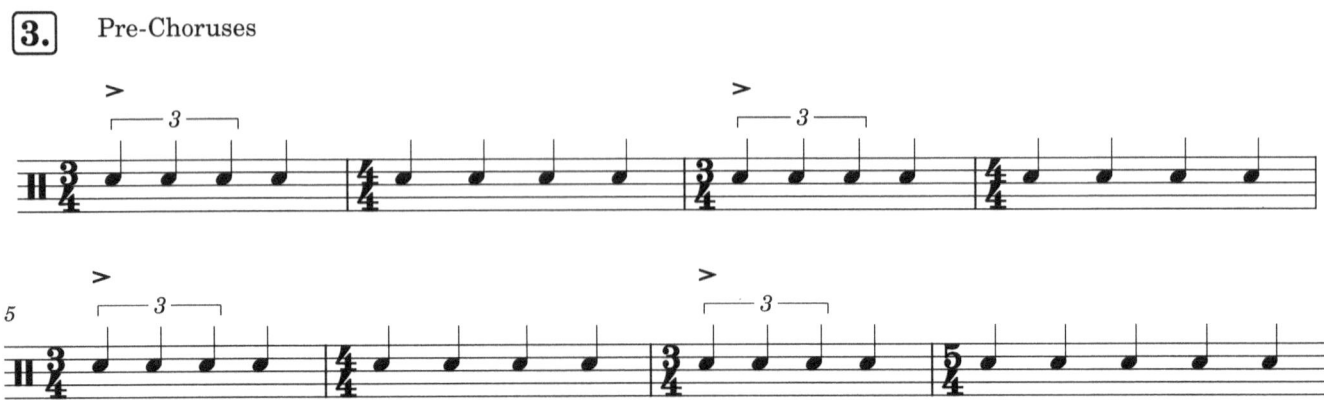

After you've gotten comfortable clapping these along with a metronome at 120 bpm, it's time to start working on the full kit patterns. One thing that remains constant throughout all of them is the bass drum quarter notes, which Dave calls the "heartbeat" of the song. Work on these grooves slowly and isolate the hands and feet at first.

The tune begins with an intro in 15. This groove returns in the choruses on the ride cymbal and you'll also play over it for the drum solo at the end.

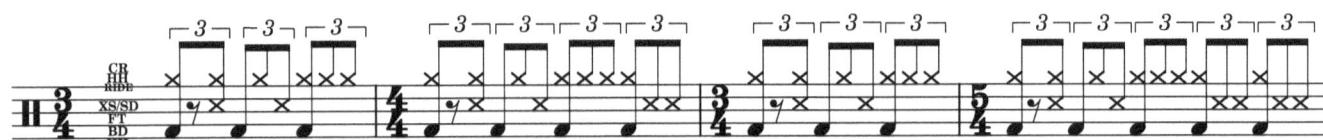

Then we're onto verse 1 in 29:

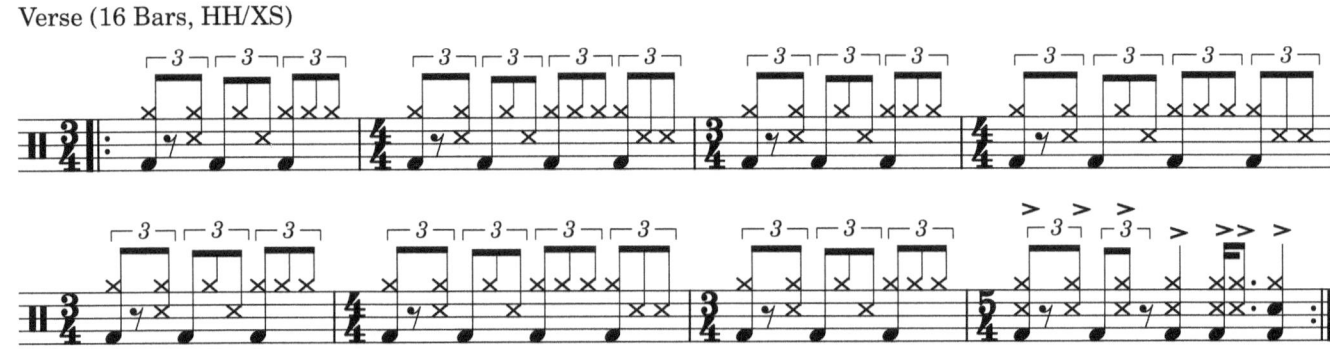

After this verse, the first pre-chorus comes in and has a very specific snare hit on beat 1 of the first, third, fifth and seventh measures of the phrase (or, all the bars of 3/4 time). Dave says, "that accent happens to frame the lyrics. It acts as a jumping-off point since it's followed immediately by the words."

Charts, Lead Sheets & Road Maps

Pre-Chorus (8 Bars, SD/Crashes)

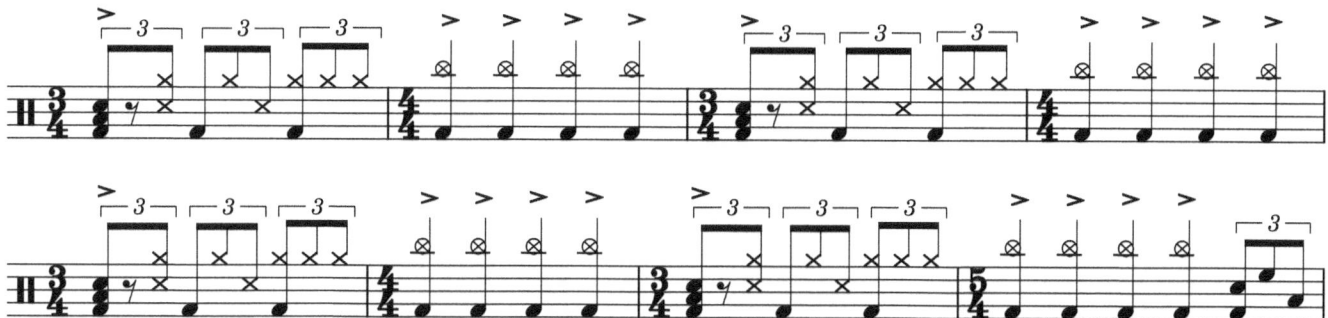

Next comes the chorus where we go to the ride for a more open texture, followed by a re-intro on the closed hi-hats. These are both felt in 15/4 like the intro at the top of the tune.

Chorus (8 Bars, Ride Bell/SD)

Then we do the whole thing all over again, with verse 2, pre-chorus 2 and chorus 2 happening exactly like before.

Now we're on to the guitar solo, which is over the 29 groove from the verse. Keep the groove solid under the solos and clearly mark the top of the phrase each time it comes back around.

Guitar Solo (16 Bars)

The tune concludes with a drum solo over the 15/4 groove from the verses.

Drum Solo Over Vamp (24 Bars- Build!)   (Repeat 6x)

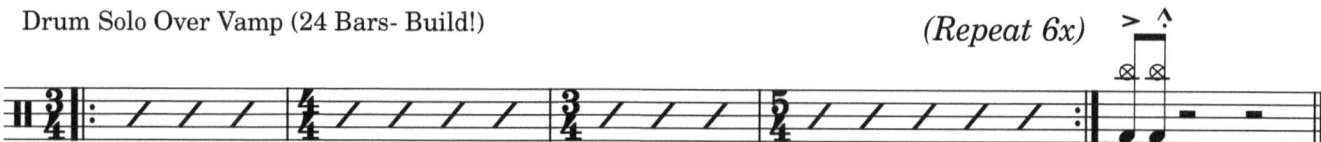

The guitar and bass are playing a vamp underneath the solo which you can use as a starting point to come up with some ideas. Dave suggests, "during the drum solo it's good for the bass and guitar to play the riff without much embellishment. I'm just looking for the drums to play some interesting ideas while creating the emphasis and feel of the 7 and 8 happening over and over. There are those pivotal accents in the solo at the beginning of each measure."

Start with a simple idea from the vamp and build the intensity and dynamics slowly. You don't need to blow all your chops right at the start since you'll have time to develop some ideas naturally. Most of all, have fun with it and don't get discouraged if you fall off the beat the first few times you practice this. I didn't nail it the first time myself!

STUFF YOU CAN USE

Rob, Dmitry Ishenko & Dave Ross @ The Parkside Lounge in NYC

Dave conjuring up the spirit world.

"Worn Away"

♩ = 120

By Dave Ross

4	Intro (3/4/3/5)
16	Verse 1 (3/4/3/4/3/4/3/5) x2
8	Pre-Chorus 1 (Same, SD on beat 1 of all bars of 3)
8	Chorus 1 (3/4/3/5) x2 (Ride)
8	Re-intro (Same)
16	Verse 2 (3/4/3/4/3/4/3/5) x2
8	Pre-Chorus 2 (Same, SD on beat 1 of all Bars of 3)
8	Chorus 2 (3/4/3/5) x2 (Ride)
16	Guitar Solo (Like Verses - 3/4/3/4/3/4/3/5) x2
24	Drum Solo (3/4/3/5) x6

End Hits Bar 25, Beat 1, +

STUFF YOU CAN USE

"Worn Away"

♩ = 120

by Dave Ross

Intro (4 Bars, HH/XS)

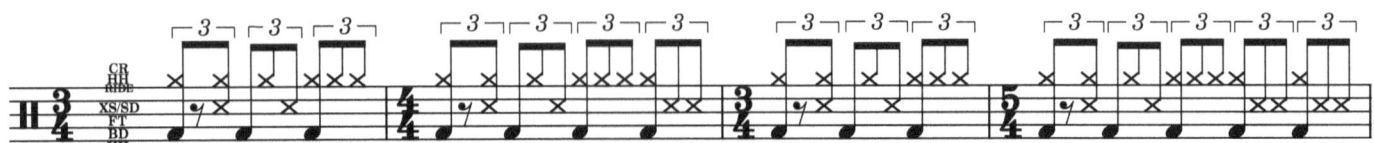

Verse (16 Bars, HH/XS)

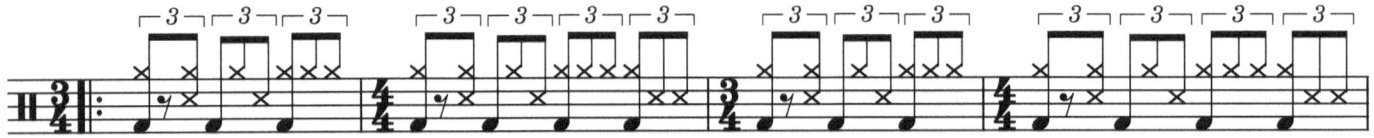

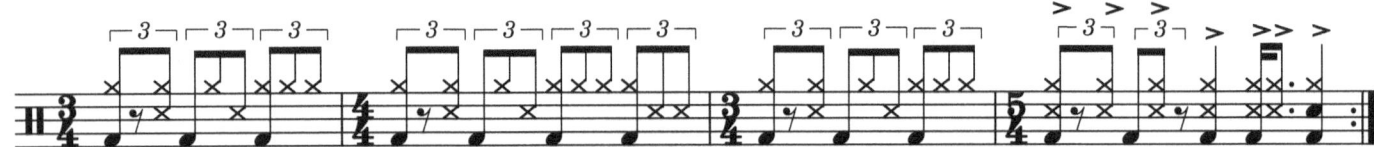

Pre-Chorus (8 Bars, SD/Crashes)

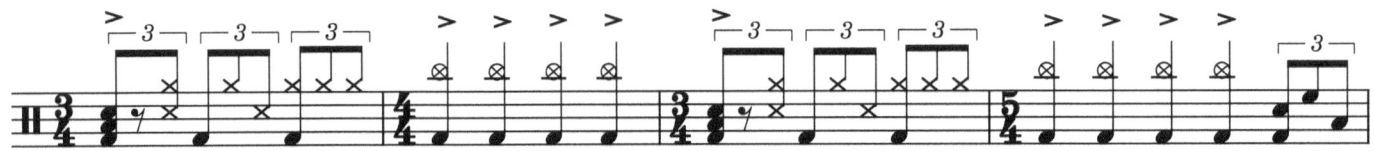

Chorus (8 Bars, Ride Bell/SD)

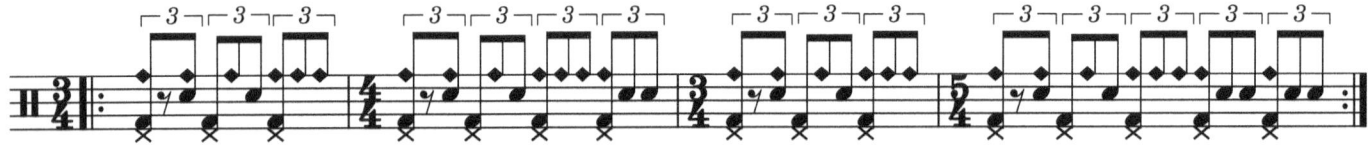

Re-intro (8 Bars, HH/SD)

Charts, Lead Sheets & Road Maps

103

STUFF YOU CAN USE

SONG WORKSHOP #9: "FAMOUS"
BY LUKE BUCK

These next two tunes feature singer-songwriter/guitarist Luke Buck along with Matthew Milligan on bass. Luke's favorite band is Radiohead, and he's also heavily influenced by Counting Crows and Muse. I've worked with him for a number of years and though he doesn't play drums, he's good at communicating ideas about the feeling he's trying to capture in different parts of his songs. He says, "I'm comfortable trying to explain what I want using hand movements and singing the parts. I really want to capture the vibe that the drums have in each section."

"Famous" is a straightforward rock tune, but there are a lot of subtle groove changes that are really important. To use this metaphor again, it's like making a pot of soup and sprinkling in one new ingredient at a time as you stir it all up. Matthew says, "when you're playing in the rhythm section for a singer-songwriter, one hundred percent of your job is to support that person and give them a solid foundation to do their thing."

The tune begins with 8 measures of guitar and vocals before the bass and drums kick in with a tight 16th-note backbeat. Use the "slap-tap" technique to get a nice funky feel on the hi-hat.

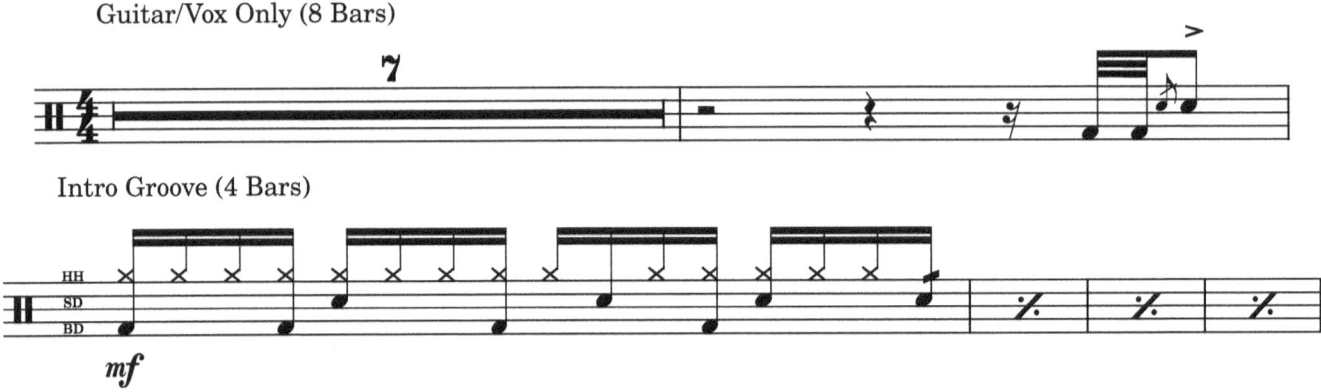

After 4 bars, the vocals re-enter and the bass drum pattern changes by one 16th note. That seems like no big deal, right? Even though it's a very small change, it's an important signal that we're in a new section. Luke says, "this whole song is a gradual build. It starts with guitar and vocals, then the bass comes in, then the drums inch it along and give it this feeling of growth so it's not the same thing. It's a simple song and it's easy to want to make it complicated. But I feel like when you stick to the basics, it comes out a little easier and can feel more authentic."

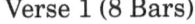

After 8 measures, we're on to the first chorus and the pattern changes again by a single note.

Charts, Lead Sheets & Road Maps

This open hi-hat on the "and" of beat 1 allows the groove to breathe a little bit. The first chorus is not much louder than the verse, but we'll get there in later choruses.

Next is an 8-measure re-intro that is exactly the same as the beginning. Then verse 2 happens and we have our first big change. Luke wanted a different texture on this part and suggested some tom-toms. The rhythm of this groove is actually similar to what we were playing before, we've just moved the hands around the kit to create a different sound. He explains, "when I wrote this, Muse had just come out with a new album and there was one track that sounded like a pop-punk type of thing. I loved it and that's where I got the idea to work in the toms. I wanted something to separate this part so it didn't get too monotonous." Check out Groove #'s 5 and 6 from the first half of the book for more examples of this type of pattern.

Verse 2 (8 Bars Tom Groove)

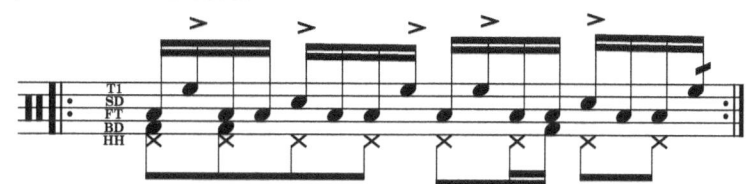

Then, we get to the *big* chorus. This one is longer, louder and represents the most energetic part of the song. You're actually riding on a crash cymbal for this part, but it's important to try to stay under control. This is a modern rock vibe and you should totally "go for it", but make sure your technique doesn't break down. Matthew explains, "as we're ending verse 2, we build up with 8th notes and the drums switch to that crash cymbal. It's all about the dynamics. We're embracing this big openness that has finally arrived after what's been simmering underneath."

Luke adds, "we hit this wall of guitars which hopefully brings people to the next level. It's total '90s guitar, something you would listen to driving with the top down." After 12 measures, the tom-tom part from the second verse makes a brief return for 4 more bars. This provides a nice little interlude where the texture changes again. Matthew explains, "it's almost like a verse moment has been inserted smack into the middle of the chorus to return to that feeling."

Chorus 2 (12 Bars BIG!)

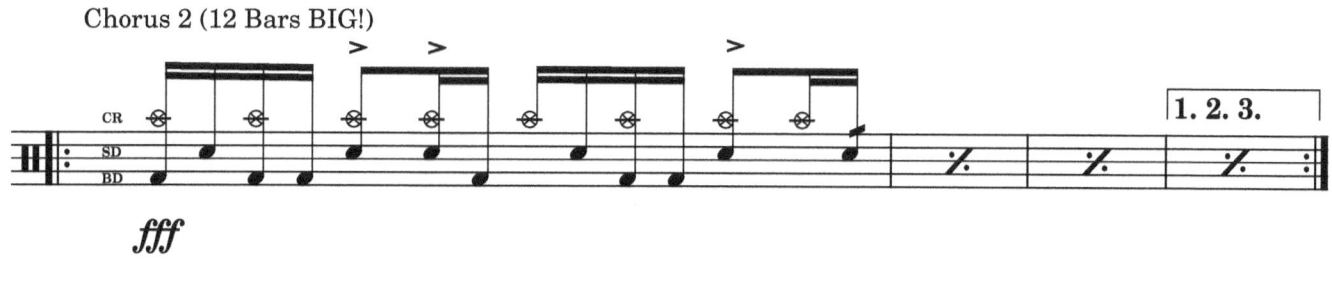

Chorus 2 Interlude (2 Bars Toms)

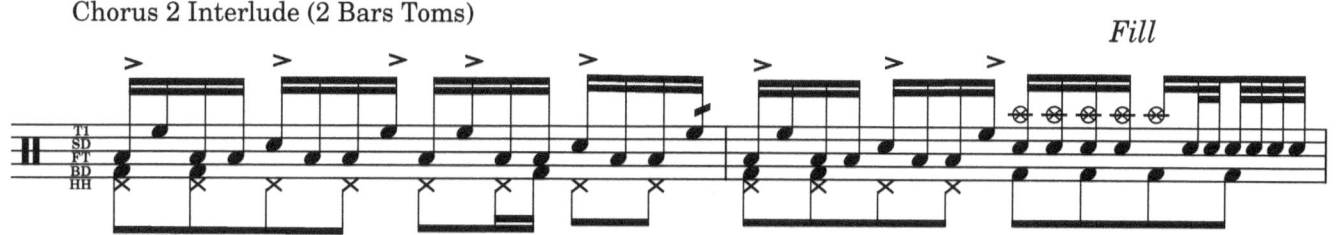

STUFF YOU CAN USE

Then we rock out on the chorus for another 5 measures, followed by a bar of hits that the whole band plays together. These hits reinforce the vocal melody and again break up the chorus with a subtle, but important texture change.

Chorus 2 Continued (5 Bars)

Chorus 2 Hits (1 Bar)

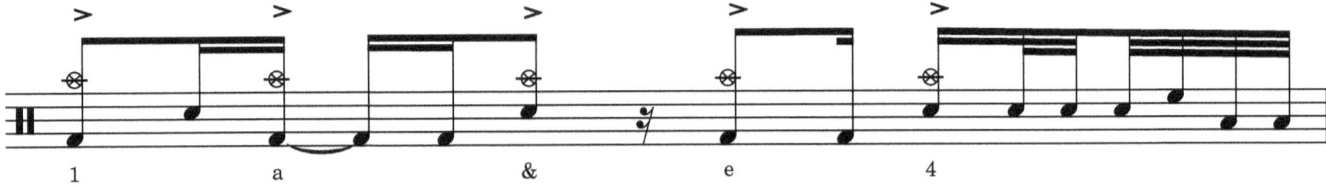

Then we play 8 more bars of chorus, followed by a switch back to the tight hi-hat groove for the outro. End with a crash on beat 1 of the 5th bar of that section.

Outro (4 Bars, End Bar 5 Beat 1)

Luke concludes, "I wrote this song about being ignored and feeling like I wasn't worth anything to someone specific. The first lyrics are, 'if I left now, would you even notice?' The idea behind the big moment where we hit the second chorus so loudly is that it's me screaming that I can't be ignored and I'm fine without you. That's where the catharsis and energy come from at the end of the tune. When we play this, it can have some rough edges. That's music. It can sound a little gritty. The last thing I want is for people to get bored…'cause if you're bored, why are you listening to me? I want you to be part of the music."

Charts, Lead Sheets & Road Maps

Luke Buck, Matthew Milligan & Rob @ Rockwood Music Hall in NYC
Photo by Nicole Mago

Luke @ City Winery in NYC
Photo by Tiff Rex

STUFF YOU CAN USE

"Famous"

♪ = 165
Straight 16ths Rock

by Luke Buck

Guitar/Vox Only (8 Bars)

Intro Groove (4 Bars)

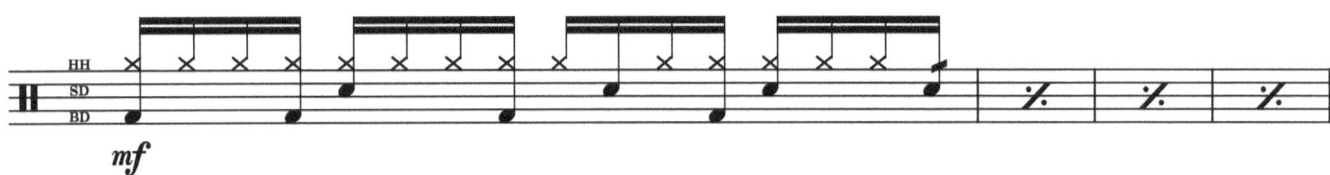

Verse 1 (8 Bars)

Chorus 1 (8 Bars- Not much louder)

Reintro (8 Bars, Same as Intro)

Verse 2 (8 Bars Tom Groove)

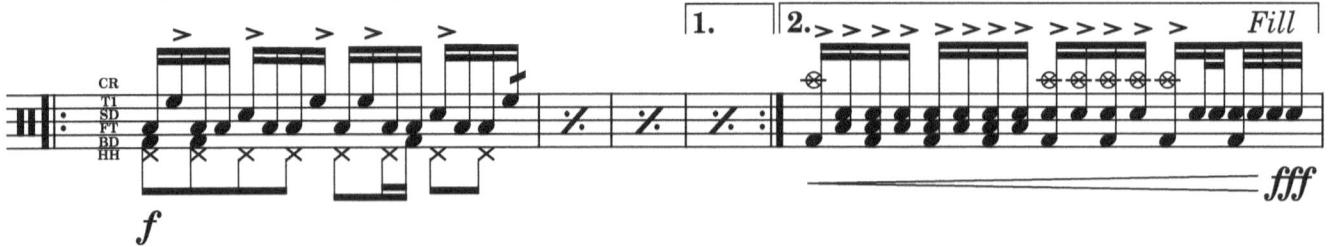

Charts, Lead Sheets & Road Maps

Chorus 2 (12 Bars BIG!)

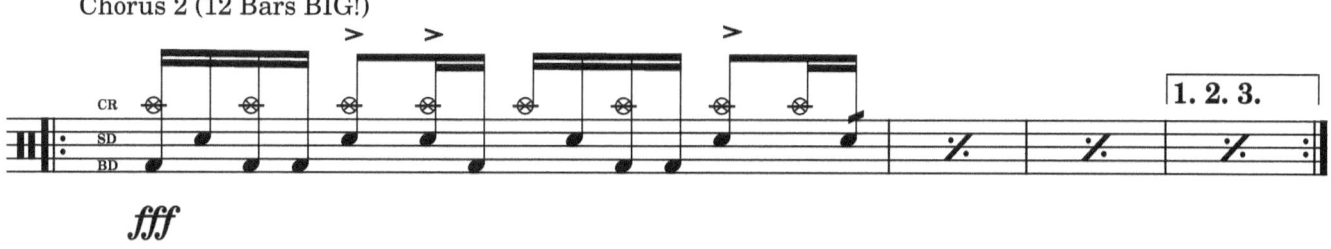

fff

Chorus 2 Interlude (2 Bars Toms)

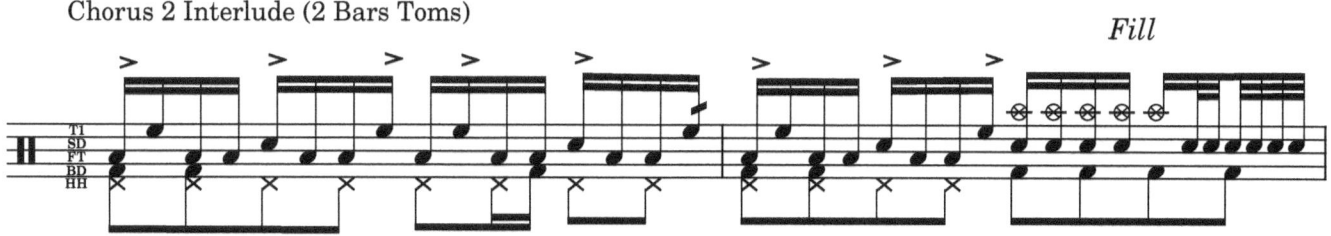

Chorus 2 Continued (5 Bars)

Chorus 2 Hits (1 Bar)

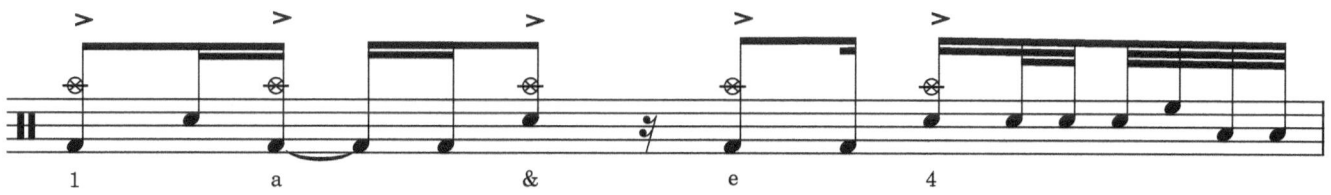

Chorus 2 Continued (8 Bars)

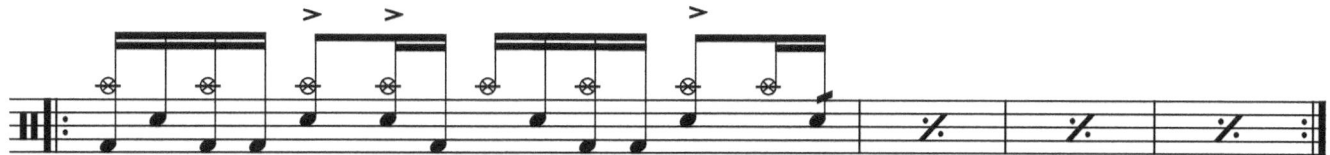

Outro (4 Bars, End Bar 5 Beat 1)

STUFF YOU CAN USE

SONG WORKSHOP #10: "WITHOUT YOU"
BY LUKE BUCK

This one has a rockabilly, country/pop, Mumford & Sons vibe to it. The main pattern is a train groove on the snare (which we covered in Groove #38 earlier in the book). We call it a train because it sounds like your snare is rolling right down the tracks. It also has a thumping quarter-note bass drum pattern that provides a lot of drive and propels the beat forward. Bassist Matthew Milligan says, "even a simple pattern where you're hitting quarter notes can have a huge impact. Luke really wants it to kick some butt."

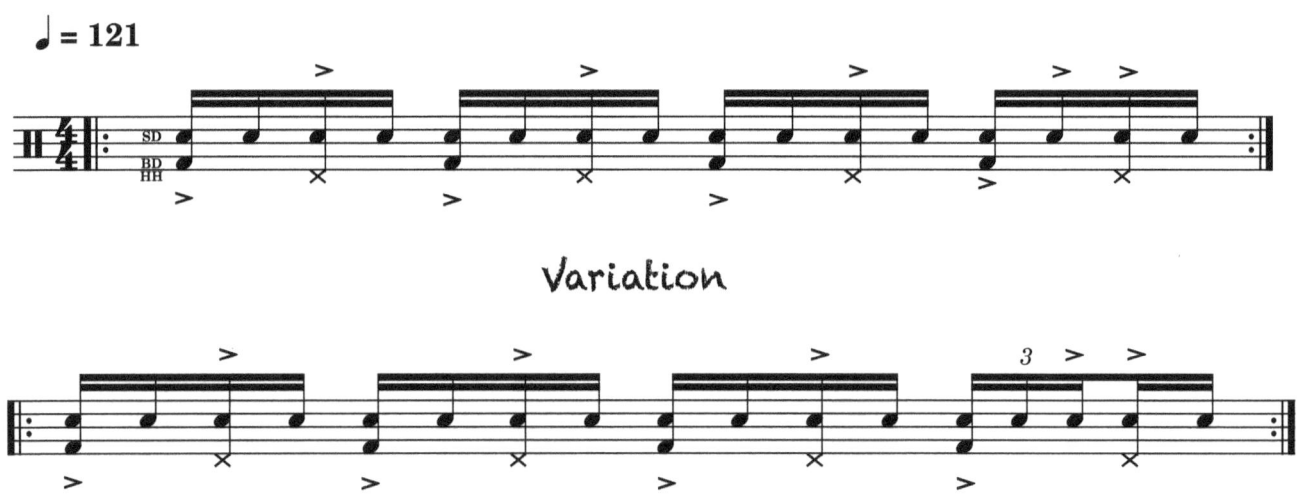

Since this groove and the variation listed below pretty much cover the whole tune, most of the important details revolve around the road map. There are a ton of extra measures, pauses and other small bits that make this one deceptively hard to play. You really have to keep counting!

The drums start alone for 4 bars (with the usual 2 bars of click track count-in). Luke will count the rest of the band in! Then we play an 8-bar intro, followed by 16 bars of the verse. The groove remains the same, but when the vocals enter make sure to get a little quieter while holding the intensity.

As we hit the first 9-bar chorus, the feel opens up a bit and builds along with the band. Keep it steady, lock in with the bass player and watch out for the extra measure at the end. On bar 9, beat 3 there is a "lift," which is a short pause or rest that the band plays all together. Think of it as a stop sign, and make sure not to blow through it. Luke will give you a ticket!

He says, "I think it's really important for the drummer to listen to all the non-drum parts of the song, especially the vocal cues. If you do, adding in those extra measures and lifts will make perfect sense."

This lift is 2 beats long, and then we're back into the groove for 8 measures of the re-intro. Then we play another verse and another 9-measure chorus, but this time there is no lift and we go straight through to the bridge.

Charts, Lead Sheets & Road Maps

This 11-bar section is a little louder, and you can add some occasional crashes on beats 1 and 3 to kick up the energy even more. When we reach the downbeat of measure 11, there's a lift for the remainder of that bar. There's a lot of tension released in that spot, and when we hit verse 3 the bass player drops out and everything contracts. Matthew says, "this part is all about changing the momentum of the song and moving it forward."

The first 8 bars of verse 3 have only quarter notes on the bass drum as Luke sings. When we hit bar 9, come back in energetically with the pattern and build into the next chorus. The juxtaposition between these two sections is another classic example of tension and release, as the first 8 bars of chorus 3 just have crashes on beat 1 of each measure. This gives the vocals room to breathe and when you hit the 8th bar, fill back into the groove and keep it percolating. Luke explains, "I think of a song as a wave where it'll build up and come back down. You go up and down, and maybe you do a twisty or a little spiral that keeps it interesting and fresh."

Chorus 4 keeps building even more, and watch out for the extra measure since this section is 9 bars long. Once we hit the 12-bar outro, we're at a fever pitch in intensity but still not too loud. Fill into bar 11 and lift on beat 1 before ending on the downbeat of bar 12. Matthew points out, "the last thing you want is for the final notes of the song to not be perfect. Every song should have a clear-cut ending. It's easy to overlook, but ending a song sharply makes everyone sound so much better."

This one is all about the road map, but as long as you keeping counting and don't miss your turns, you'll arrive right on time. Luke concludes, "this is one of those songs where if you're not listening, you're lost and your snare drum train will turn into a trainwreck."

Luke Buck, Rob & Matthew Milligan @ The Knitting Factory in Brooklyn, NY
Photo by Tiff Rex

Luke carved these himself!

STUFF YOU CAN USE

"Without You"

♩ = 121
2 Bars Count-in

By Luke Buck

| 4 | Drums only (SD Train Groove) |

| 8 | Intro (Bass & Guitar enter, Same groove) |

| 16 | Verse 1 (Same) |

| 9 | Chorus 1, Lift Bar 9, Beat 3 |

| 8 | Re-intro |

| 16 | Verse 2 |

| 9 | Chorus 2 |

| 11 | Bridge (Add crashes & build) Lift Bar 11, Beat 1 |

| 16 | Verse 3 (BD only first 8 bars, then full groove) |

| 8 | Chorus 3, Hit on only Beat 1 of each bar, fill Bar 8 |

| 9 | Chorus 4 Groove! |

| 11 | Outro, Stop Bar 11, Beat 1 |

End Bar 12, Beat 1

Charts, Lead Sheets & Road Maps

SONG WORKSHOP #11: "ALWAYS LEAVE ME WANTING MORE"
BY ANDREA CAPOZZOLI

Andrea is a multi-talented singer, trumpet player, pianist and songwriter who I've had the pleasure of working with for over 15 years. She teaches at Berklee College of Music and has a strong sense of rhythm and an incredibly funky feel. Her main influences are artists like Chaka Khan, Aretha Franklin and Whitney Houston. This track also features Dmitry Ishenko on bass, John Shannon on guitar and Jared Sims on tenor and baritone saxophones.

In R&B and soul music, the most important thing a drummer can do is to lock in with the bass player. Your bass drum and the notes of that bass line should almost sound like one instrument. This tune is built around the bass line and it's especially unique because you do *not* play the kick drum on beat 1. Andrea explains, "I always have the groove in mind when I start writing. I wanted a straight-16ths funky kind of thing. I had that bass line on beat 1 and it just didn't feel right. Putting it on the upbeat really drives it home. To help drummers, I always like to sing them a little bit of the hi-hat part and the bass line. That's something I feel all vocalists should know how to do. It really helps the drummer get the groove if they don't hear it."

Dmitry explains further, "normally my instinct would be to lay into the downbeats and connect with the drums in that way, but Andrea composed this bass line on the keyboard and it totally makes the tune."

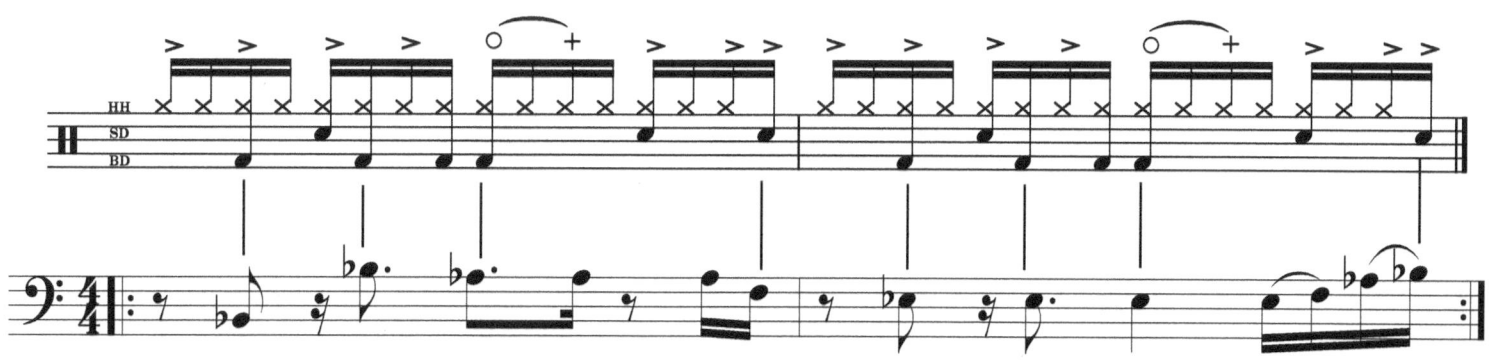

Notice how the notes of the bass part line up with the drum groove. No matter what you play in-between these accents, this hookup is the secret sauce that makes the tune feel good. Dmitry adds, "especially when things are so syncopated, you can lose where you are in the measure really easily. You still have to feel the grounded downbeats. Even if they're not being played, they're implied."

Now that we've gone over the groove, let's check out the form. This one starts with 4 bars of just the rhythm section, followed by some hits that the whole band plays in bar 4. Andrea says, "there's a lot of rhythm going on here. I love putting in hits and rhythmic stops. It really breaks up the tune and makes it more interesting."

STUFF YOU CAN USE

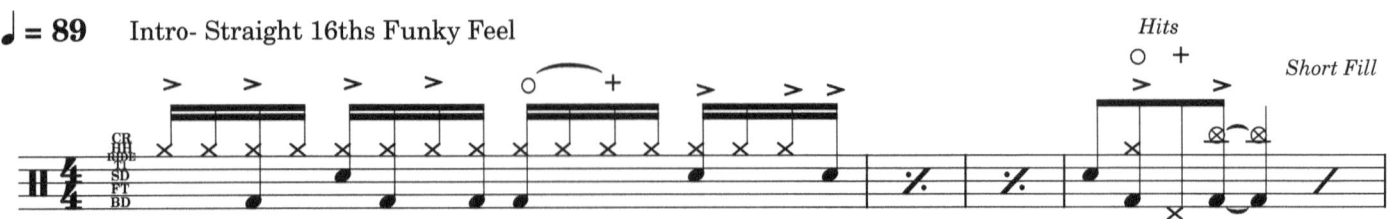

Keep grooving as the vocals enter for verse 1. When backing up a singer, the drummer's main job is to support the song and make it easy for everyone else to play their parts. This section is 8 bars long and then we come to the first chorus. At this point, the horns enter as the texture becomes thicker and the tune builds. Stick with the hi-hat instead of going to the ride and resist the urge to play too busy. Your job is to create a comfortable palette so all these textures can layer on top. Andrea says, "with a song like this, you just want that constant groove from the drums with that hi-hat. We want to keep the energy up without changing the groove."

Saxophonist Jared Sims adds, "the drums are providing the flavor of the tune. It's not just the dynamics, but also the approach and the meaning behind how I would attack it as a horn player. There's a million ways to play a shuffle or a backbeat or a swing. The drummer is defining the structure of what the beat is so I can lay my notes right in the pocket. It's not just chocolate or vanilla. There are a lot of other flavors in-between."

As the first chorus ends, there are some full band hits in measure 8. Repeat back to the top of the form for verse 2 and bring the volume down as the vocals enter. There's much less going on in the verses, and it's important to play with a sensitive touch and a keen ear. Guitarist John Shannon suggests that "in this style of music, it's always great for a drummer to be marking the form as we go and setting up the next part through fills or a change in their part. I always appreciate a drummer who dictates where the song is going because after all, the drums hold the most power potential in a small group setting."

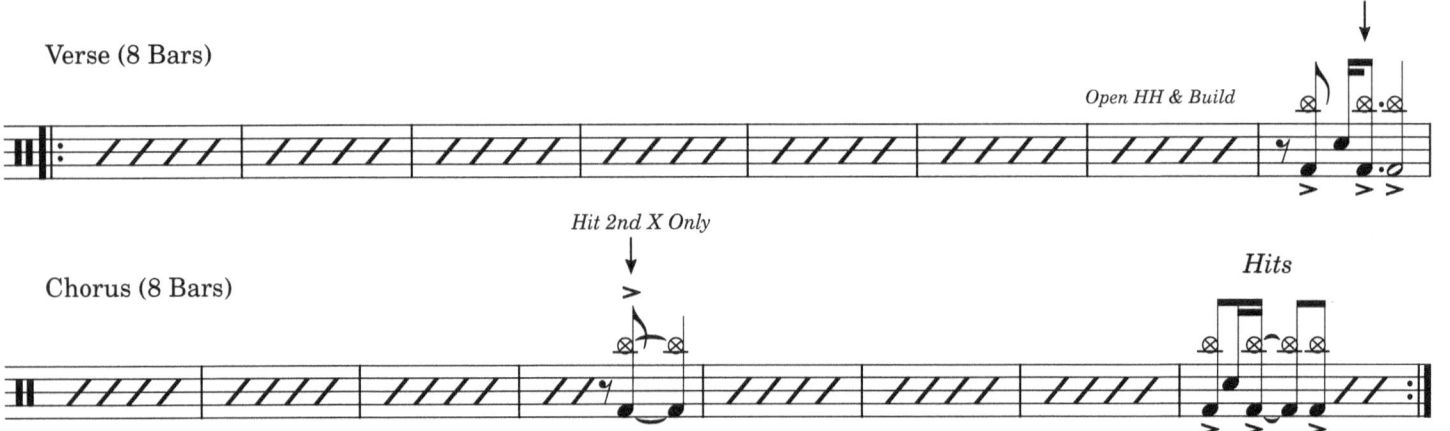

The second chorus signals another increase in the intensity, and we're also playing some hits with the rest of the rhythm section in measures 4 and 8. Make sure to count so you can nail those, and then play a little fill to signal that we're moving to a new part of the song.

The bridge is up next, and it's a big change in the vibe. The groove switches to a half-time feel on the ride cymbal and there is suddenly way more space. Andrea says, "this is the part where we just breathe. It's like a shimmery sound with the cymbals and the feel is way more laid back. We're just chilling and driving home those lyrics. I was kind of thinking of the breakdown in '24K Magic'

Charts, Lead Sheets & Road Maps

by Bruno Mars. That's our sexy breakdown section." Guitarist John adds that "as an improviser creating parts, when the textures of the kit change it lets me know where my parts can fit in and what they should be. If the drummer is playing the ride and not the hi-hat, that means the frequency from the hi-hat space is there for me to create on the guitar. The sonics from the drum kit are an important directive and compositional element of the song."

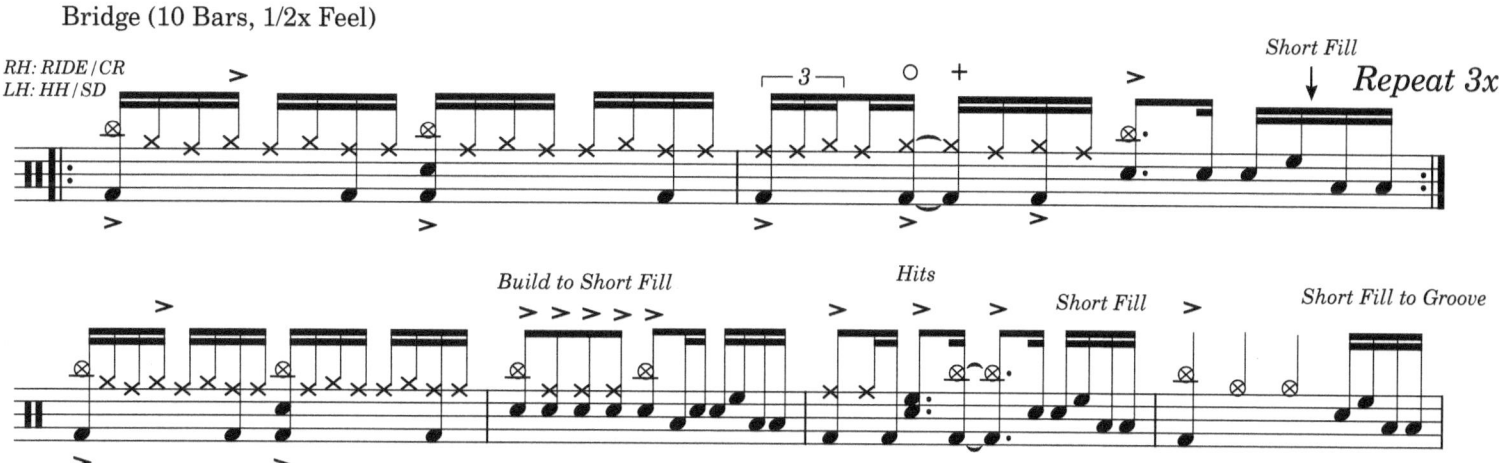

After the bridge, there are 2 bars of transition hits and small fills that serve as a slight reset before we head back into the original groove. Never stop counting and make sure to be clear and simple with your fills so you can help guide the band (or as my teacher used to say, "drive that bus!"). Jared adds, "as a horn player, I'm not thinking about the drums in terms of the specific parts of the kit. I hear it in a more intuitive way. In this style the drummer needs to give us the structural points. If I don't know a tune that well, those are like mileposts telling us where we need to go. It's gives horn players a little reassurance."

The last chorus is twice as long, and the first half is just bass and drums along with the vocals. Andrea says, "the groove is really important during that part. Just keep it constant and driving since it's just the bass and drums." After the first 8 measures, play a little fill to get us into the final part of the chorus and keep the intensity up as we build towards the end.

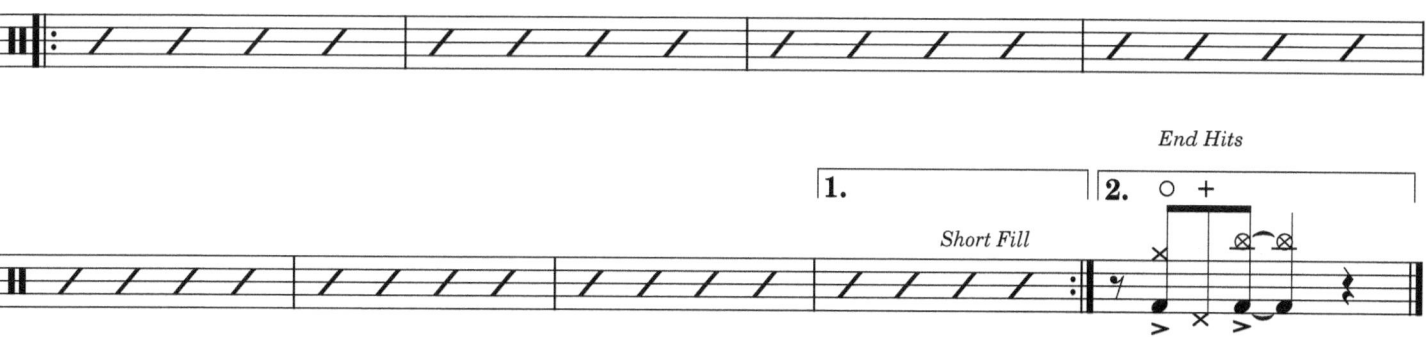

Andrea concludes, "this song is about being so head-over-heels for somebody that when you're away from them, you just want to be around them. It's like, 'I can't be away from you, I'm so addicted.' It's like how my dogs feel about me."

STUFF YOU CAN USE

"Always Leave Me Wanting More"

by Andrea Capozzoli

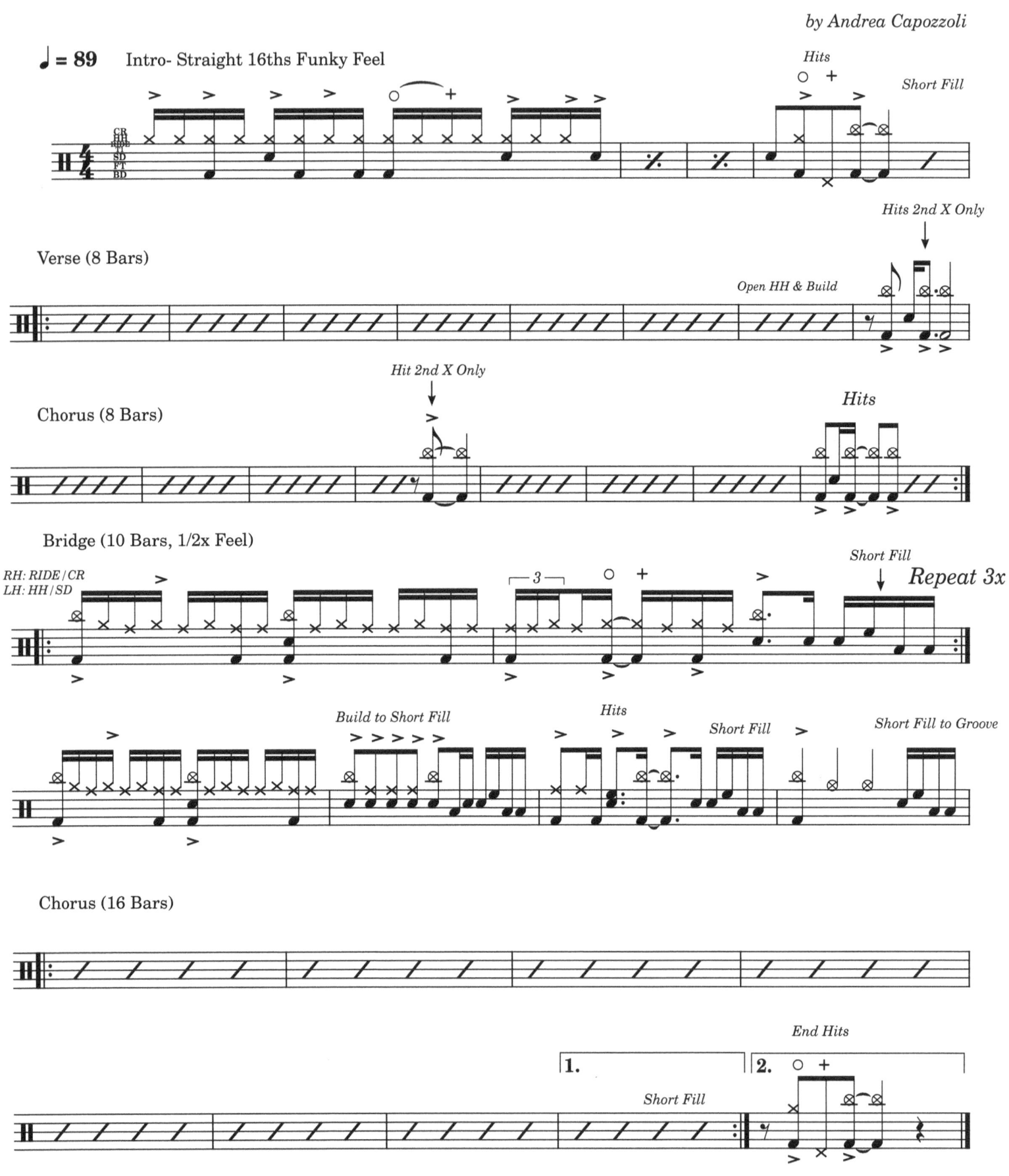

Charts, Lead Sheets & Road Maps

Maggie Scott, Andrea Capozzoli, Dmitry Ishenko & Rob
@ Ryles Jazz Club in Cambridge, MA
Photo by Ricky Hammerschmidt

Andrea recording @ C-Room Studio in Brooklyn, NY

Andrea, Rob, Dmitry & Jeff Ramsey @
Davis Square Theatre in Somerville, MA
Photo by Tina D'Ercole

STUFF YOU CAN USE

SONG WORKSHOP #12: "I'LL FORM THE HEAD"
BY MC FRONTALOT
FEATURING SCHAFFER THE DARKLORD & MISS EAVES

These next two tunes bring us into the world of hip-hop and feature MC Frontalot, the self-proclaimed "579th greatest rapper in the world." Frontalot is one of the progenitors of a sub-genre called "nerdcore," which is musically similar to other rap styles, but features quirky and fun lyrical content about science fiction, comics and other areas of interest to fans who identify as nerds and geeks.

Frontalot is actually known as the "Godfather of Nerdcore," and I've had the pleasure of playing in his band for the past few years. I have learned a lot about nerd things, and I've also learned that he is an excellent musician with a discerning ear who really knows what he wants from the drums in his music. Many hip-hop artists don't actually use live bands when they perform, so I asked Frontalot what attracted him to the idea.

"It's more fun to watch a band perform, and if you're down to just one member, it better be drums. When I started doing this in 2003, my first thought was, 'why would anyone want to see me up there rapping alone in the first place?' So I recruited my musician friends to back me up. It's nice to have a whole band doing versions of these songs every night because it makes the show an adaptable, living organism."

This first tune is called "I'll Form the Head" and features a couple other rap stars from this scene, Schaffer The Darklord and Miss Eaves. Everyone in nerdcore gets a stage nickname, and this track also includes keyboardist Gaby Alter (G Minor 7) and bassist Matthew Milligan (M-Audio). And me. I'm Beard Science.

This tune has a lot of verses done by a lot of rappers, and that means plenty of fun grooves and texture changes. The intro features this funky syncopated hi-hat groove for 8 measures.

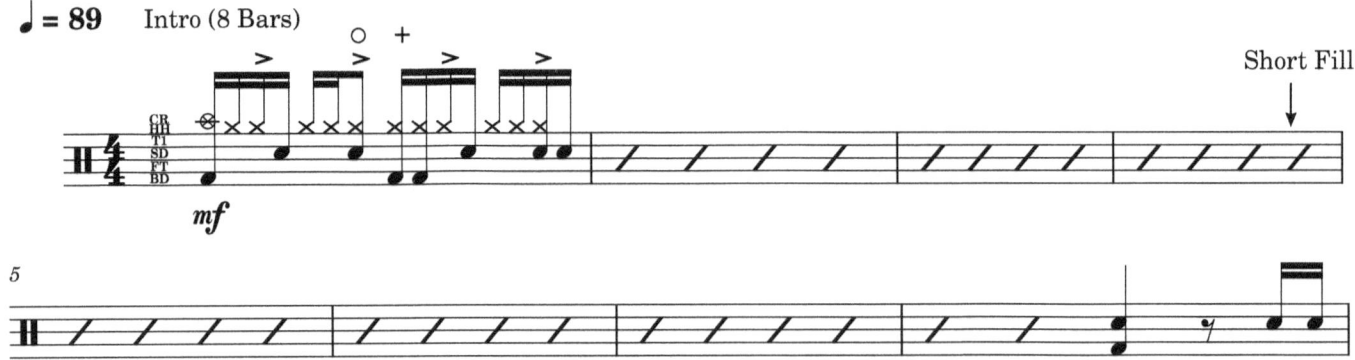

After a stop on bar 8 beat 3, the pattern changes to a more basic backbeat with some embellishments as Frontalot begins rapping. Keyboard player Gaby explains, "I think those little extra offbeat things make it funky. That's the pleasure. It's not always right on the beat." Make sure to lock in your bass drum with the bass player and repeat the 2-bar phrase without adding too much extra stuff. The figure on the last beat of the second measure lines right up with what the bassist is playing.

Charts, Lead Sheets & Road Maps

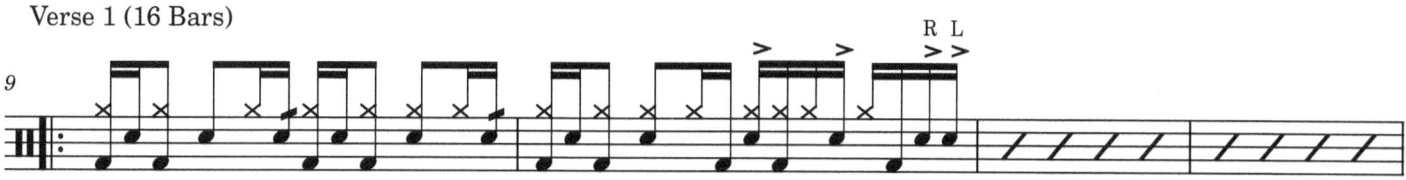

As we get to the first chorus, the energy and dynamics grow and the texture opens up as all the rappers join in. However, it's important not to get too loud right away. Frontalot explains, "when a drummer is playing too hard, I think it loses some sonic finesse and dynamic range with the ghost notes and other details."

After the first chorus, rapper Miss Eaves comes in to do verse 2. This groove is similar to verse 1, but has a little more bounce. Gaby explains, "the organ is playing with the snare on this verse. It's a call-and-response kind of thing and it's pretty sparse musically." Bassist Matthew adds, "it's our job to provide space for the lyrics to be delivered and lift it up without stepping on what's happening. Rapping is a very punctuated, specific thing and one misplaced fill could really derail the flow."

Play the hits in the last bar along with the lyrics and head into chorus 2.

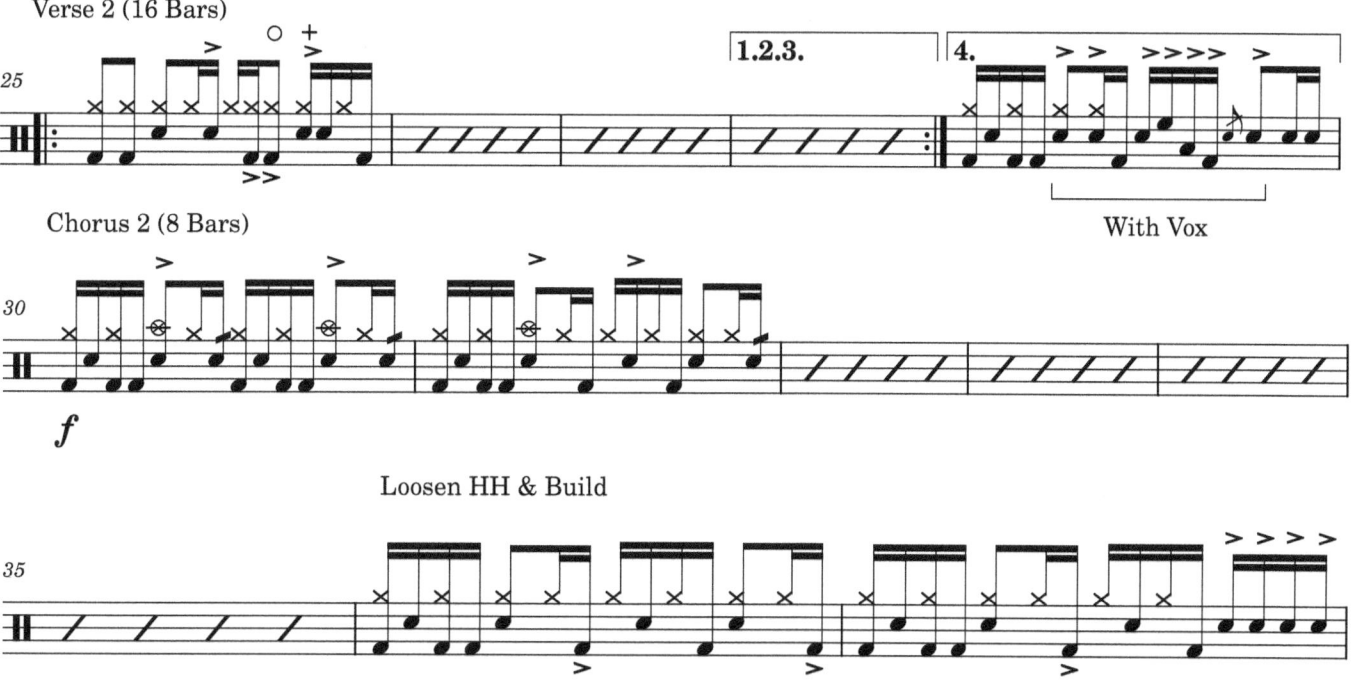

As we come out of this chorus, watch out for the rest during the first 2 beats of verse 3.

STUFF YOU CAN USE

In hip-hop this is called a "drop," and it's an incredibly important device in this style of drumming. As Matthew says, "you don't want to surprise a rapper with a hit or a drop. If you play a syncopated moment that they don't expect, you can really trainwreck a tune."

This verse features yet another groove change as Schaffer The Darklord begins rapping. There's a ton of space here as the bass and keyboards play sparingly. Besides being a talented rapper and comedian, Schaffer is also a drummer and sometimes accompanies himself during his own live shows (he also does hilarious impressions of famous drummers). "Playing drums for so long actually informs how I write my own songs. I think of lyrics as a percussion instrument. My songs are like drum solos with dirty words. Being able to combine these two disciplines onstage has totally changed my life."

The groove expands a bit in the second half of the verse as the keyboards become more busy and the intensity builds. Schaffer says, "it's a delicate balance. I want to hear a consistent beat from the drummer, but I don't want it to sound like a drum loop. That completely defeats the luxury of having a live drummer who can give it some flourish. The key is adding the right amount so it doesn't overwhelm the verses. I'm always so impressed with drummers who can do this artfully." Make sure to play the hits with Schaffer as you get into the third chorus.

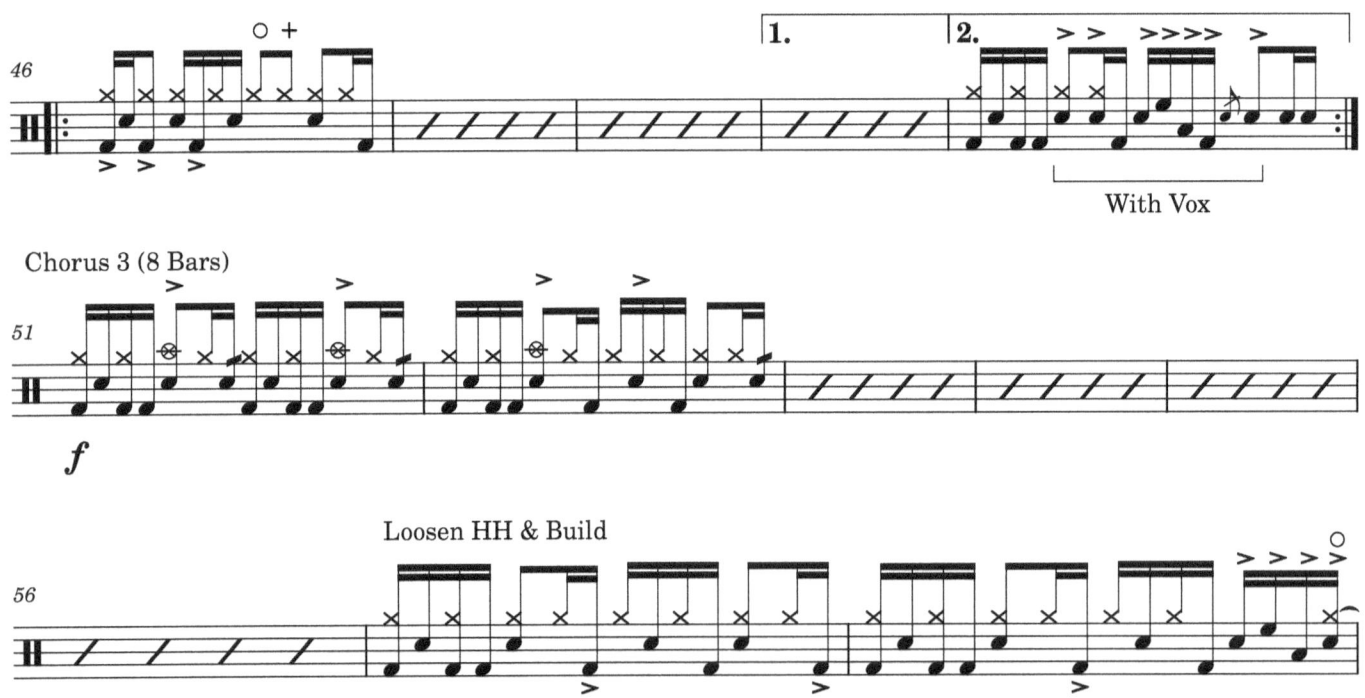

Then we hit the fourth and final verse as Frontalot returns with yet another groove.

Charts, Lead Sheets & Road Maps

Matthew explains, "on these four verses, it's a question of how to make them feel unique and musical interesting without stepping on the toes of the people who are rapping. Nothing we do can get in the way of the raps. But we also want to keep the song moving and give each verse its own flavor and feel."

Gaby adds, "the drums are playing a lot of cool little things and I think it sounds great that way. This is the moment where they take center stage."

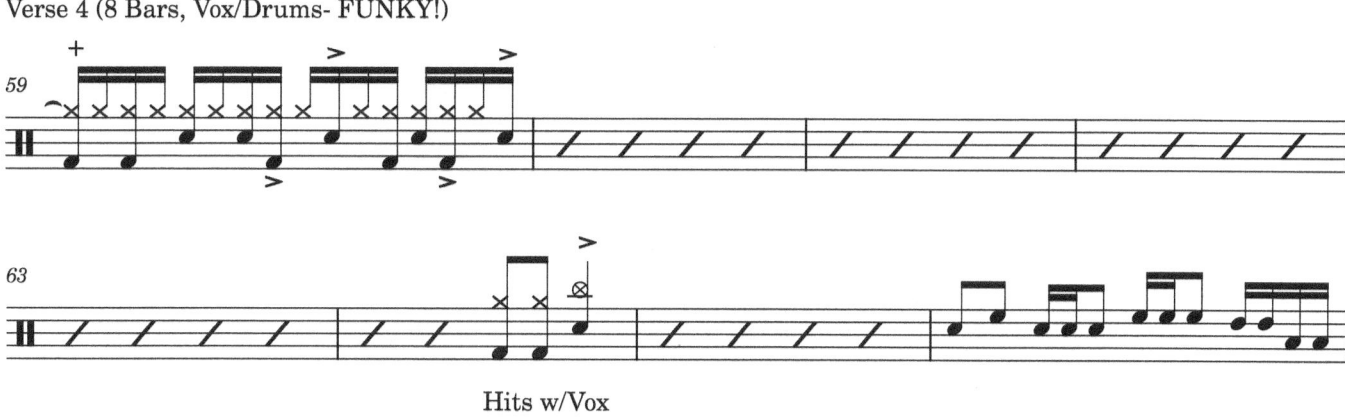

This groove is busier, more swinging and interacts a lot with the lyrics. Frontalot suggests, "it's all about the moments of rhythmic interplay between the drums and the vocal. An interesting rap vocal is slowing down and speeding up constantly. There are parts that go in and out of time where the drums should be more rigid, and parts that need the drums to feel those compressions and expansions with it. That's my favorite kind of drummer to work with."

After verse 4 (which is 8 bars instead of 16), we play the chorus again twice and we're out.

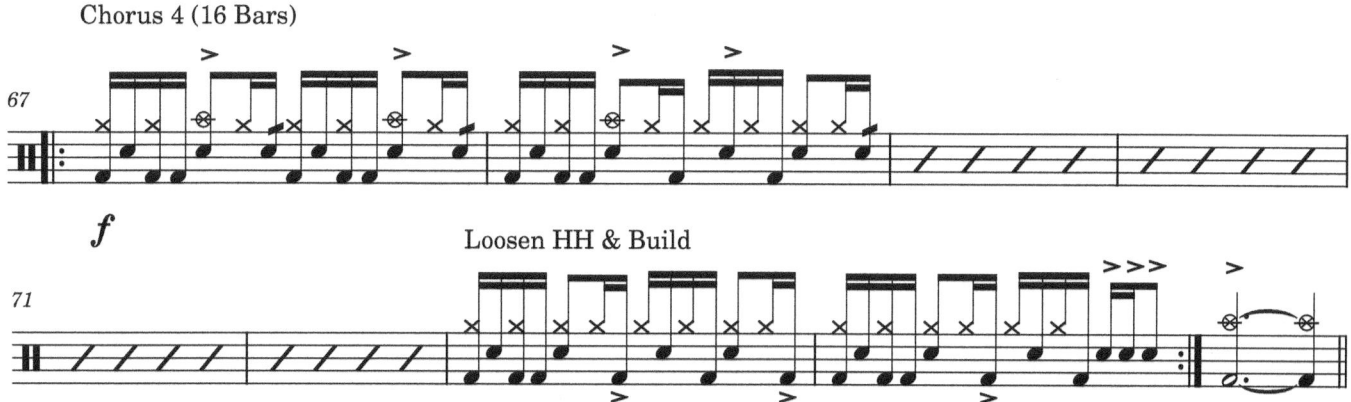

This is a long song with a lot of scene changes, but the key is to keep solid time, lock in with the bass player and really focus on supporting the lyrics.

Frontalot concludes, "you've got the whole circus in here. This song is about three pilots in the style of a Voltron-type team [a 1980s syndicated animé franchise] who lose a fight with a giant space alien because they can't agree on who is going to form the head of the giant mega-robot. The feel of the whole song musically is that we're having this animé bar fight that creates an absurdly funny, but scary tension. There's an opportunity for the whole song to creep up in urgency as it goes along, and the rest of the band has to do that. It should be subtle and it works nicely."

STUFF YOU CAN USE

Rob, Matthew Milligan & Gaby Alter @ The Paramount Theater in Seattle, WA

Schaffer The Darklord & Rob @ Snoqualmie Falls in Washington (Twin Peaks)

MC Frontalot & Rob in Boston, MA

Live @ Caesar's Palace, Las Vegas

Schaffer, sound man Nick Binary, Rob, Miss Eaves & MC Frontalot on tour

Charts, Lead Sheets & Road Maps

"I'll Form the Head"

Lyrics by Damian Hess, Shanthony Exum & Mark Schaffer
Music by Damian Hess, Gabriel Alter & David T. Cheong

♩ = 89
Swung 16ths Funky Feel

STUFF YOU CAN USE

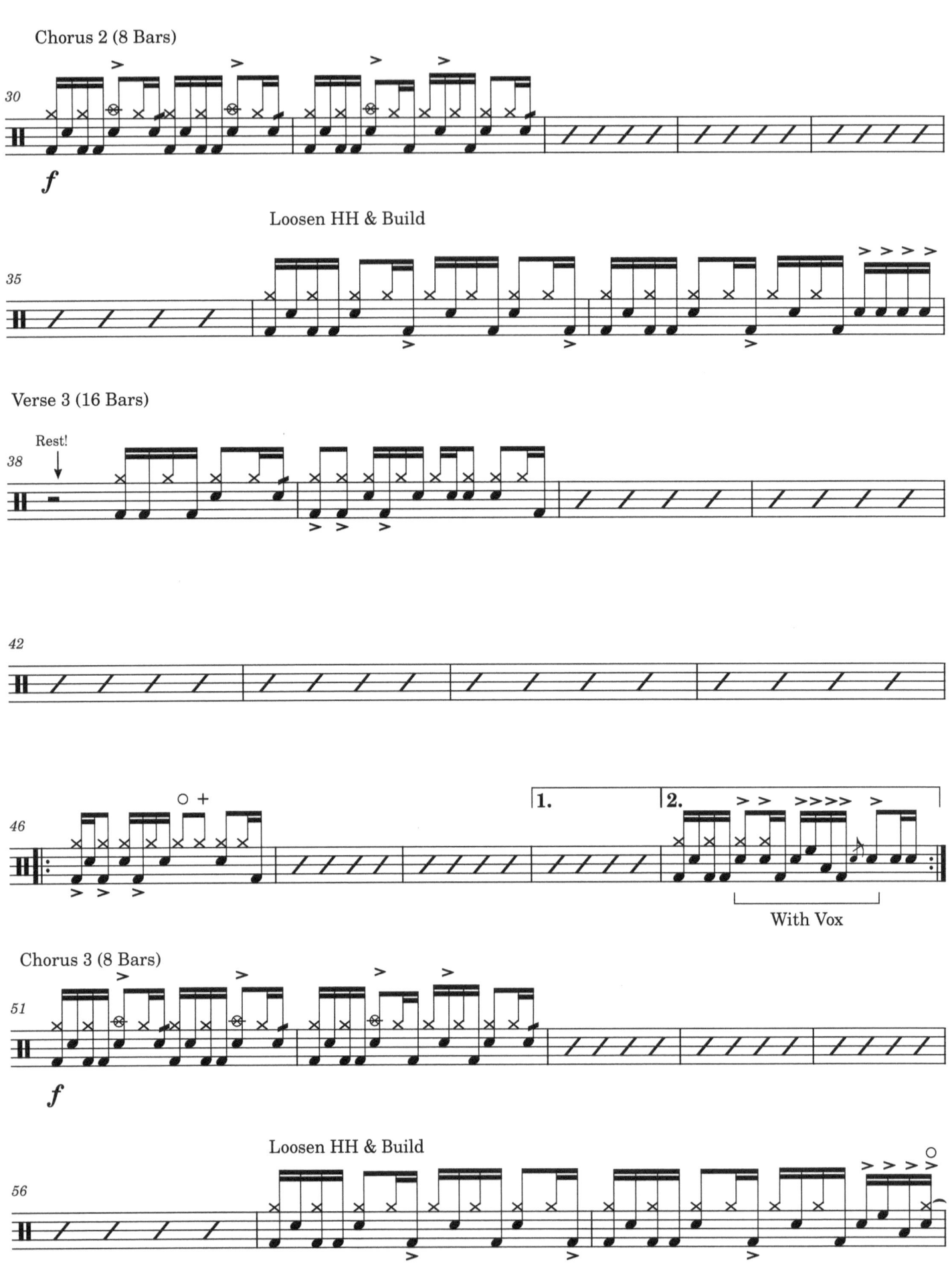

Charts, Lead Sheets & Road Maps

Verse 4 (8 Bars, Vox/Drums- FUNKY!)

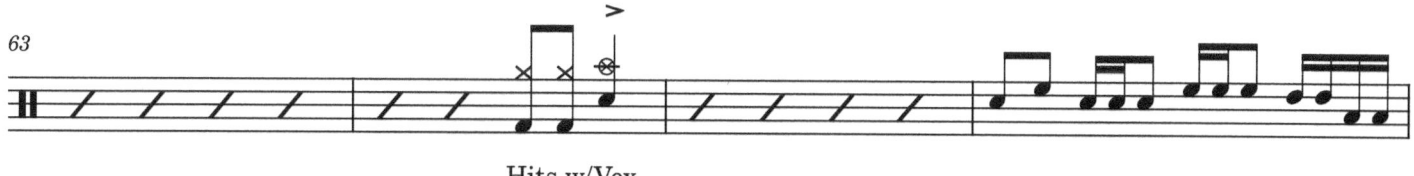

Hits w/Vox

Chorus 4 (16 Bars)

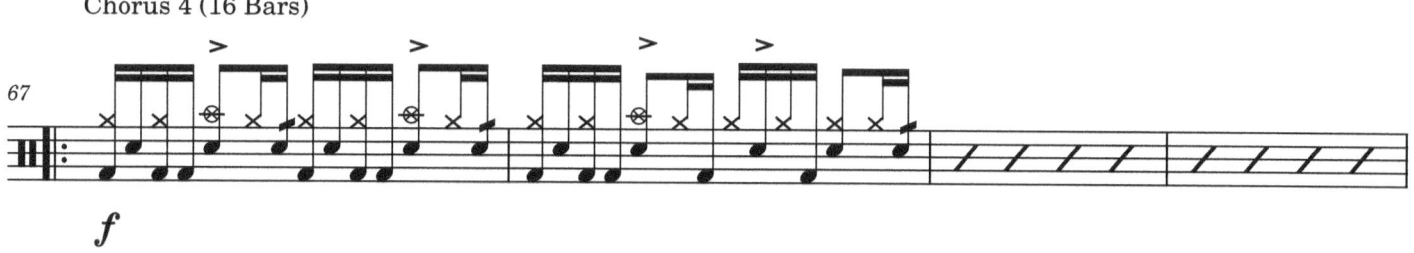

Loosen HH & Build

STUFF YOU CAN USE

SONG WORKSHOP #13: "CLICKBAIT"
BY MC FRONTALOT

This next track only has one rapper (Frontalot), but a lot of different grooves and feels. "Clickbait" begins with a New Orleans-style marching pattern on the snare, which as keyboardist Gaby Alter (G Minor 7) says, "takes up a lot of sonic space. It's not usually what you hear on a rap track, so my job is really to stay out of the way and create something that feels interesting and appropriate along with it."

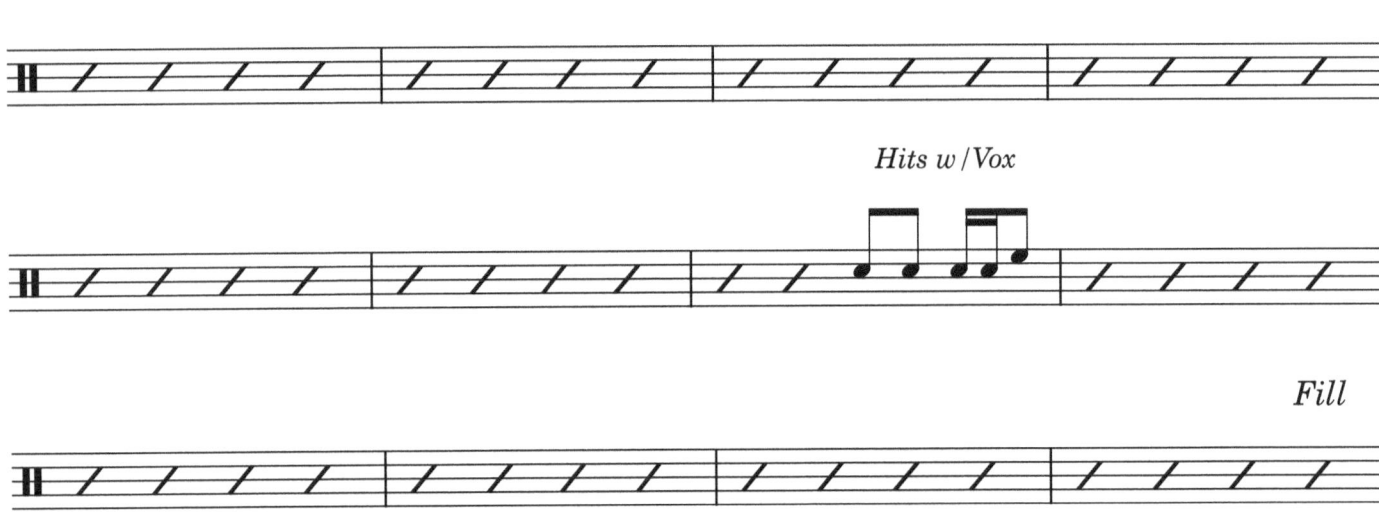

The vocals enter after 2 measures, while the drums carry the rhythm and the bass rests. Frontalot explains, "I was looking for some very pleasing disparate feels I could Frankenstein into a song shape. This tune is about the pettiest of gripes I could possibly have. I have a verified Twitter account, and about 6 months ago they suddenly started serving me a lot of ads after years of never seeing any. I got furious at myself for constantly clicking on them and furious at them for tricking me. As a song concept, it's like the different kinds of clickbait are searching for different attack vectors to get you into clickbait-land."

Make sure to catch those hits along with the vocals in measure 7 (the lyric is "your enlightenment"). Then we hit the chorus and the feel changes to a heavier backbeat groove with elements of funk and rock. Gaby suggests, "the drum part is much simpler as a way to have a respite and contrast with the verse." Make sure to lock in your bass drum notes along with bassist Matthew Milligan (M-Audio). He says, "this is a song where the chorus hook is clearly constructed and the bass line is really distinct."

Charts, Lead Sheets & Road Maps

Chorus 1 (8 Bars Backbeat Funk)

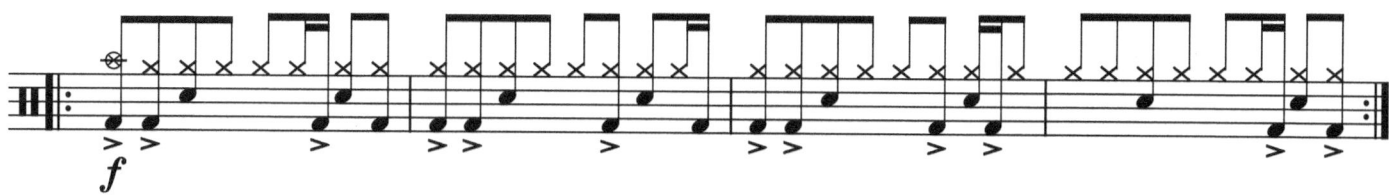

Frontalot further explains, "the chorus is uneasy and weird. It's like the feeling when you've surrendered to the clickbait and you're immersed and dirty and gross."

After 8 measures, we return to the New Orleans pattern for verse 2, but with a much edgier vibe and a few embellishments. The main textural change here involves the bass, which aggressively grabs center stage.

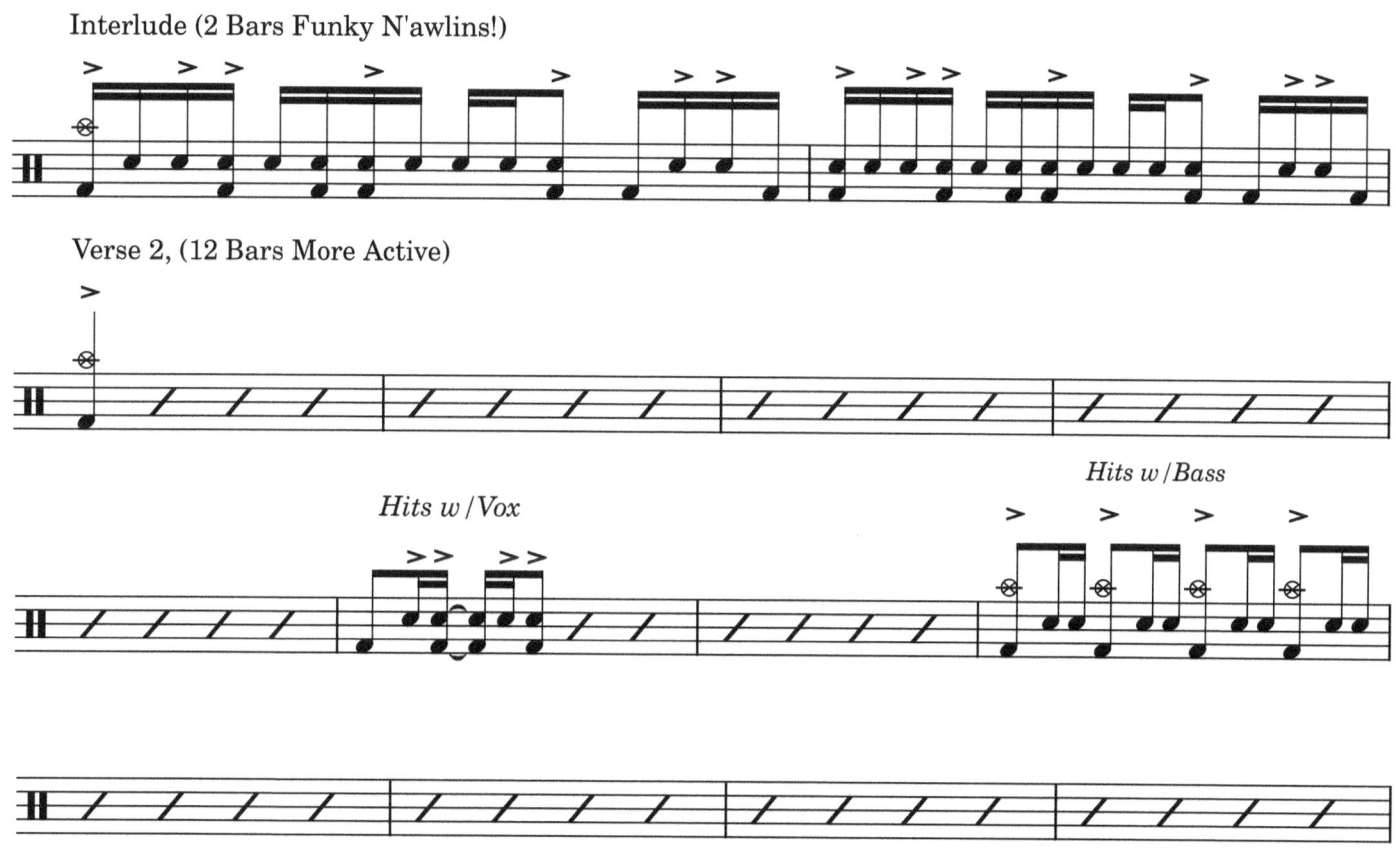

This verse has a much more assertive and almost angry vibe. Make sure to catch the hits in measure 6 with the vocals and measure 8 with the bass player. Frontalot says, "in verse 2, you become a grizzled veteran of these wars you've been roped into with the advertisers. A lot of the tonal stuff I'm doing is based off what I was hearing from the drums."

After another chorus, the third verse presents another feel change. This groove has a reggaeton vibe and shifts the texture from the snare over to the hi-hat. Gaby says, "this verse almost sounds sneaky to me. That hi-hat pattern is more subdued and creates a big shift in the mood. I'm using this synth-mallet sound which evokes a mysteriousness of the universe."

STUFF YOU CAN USE

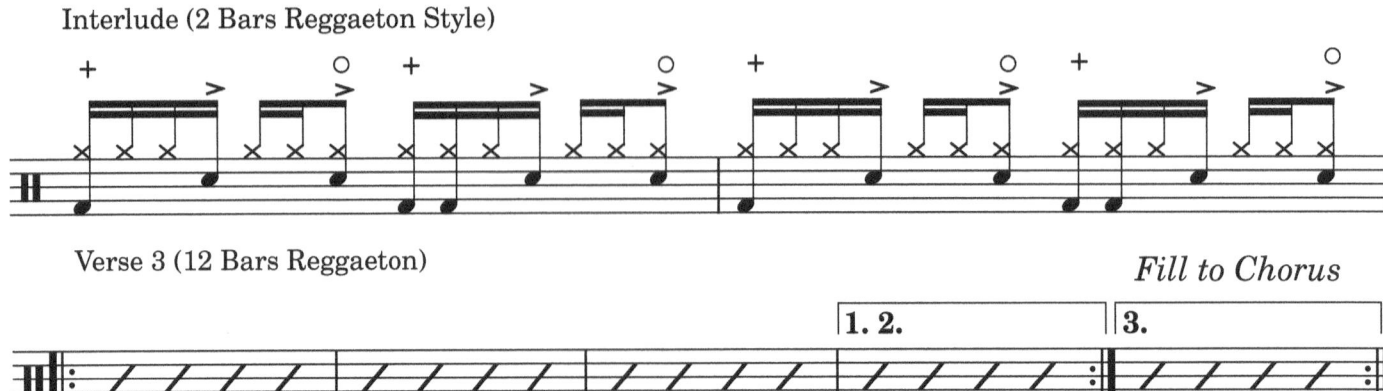

Matthew adds, "these verses are open to what we can do collectively to make them different and interesting. The idea is to give the song that forward momentum from start to finish." Frontalot says, "verse 3 is where you accept that it's futile to resist the clickbait."

After the reggaeton, we end with a double-length chorus which he describes "like an old-school Rick Rubin hit pulling the big sparse drums out and looping it so it morphs into hip-hop."

The key to this one is smoothly transitioning between these feel changes and supporting the lyrics. Frontalot concludes, "the rhythmic interaction between the drums and vocals is one of the main things that's pleasing about these grooves. The rhythm section leans on each other or the vocalist finds a moment to have interplay with what's going on with the band."

Rob & MC Frontalot @ SXSW in Austin, TX

Charts, Lead Sheets & Road Maps

Ken Flagg, Rob, MC Frontalot and Matthew Milligan @ MAGFest in Washington, D.C.

Excitement

STUFF YOU CAN USE

"Clickbait"

Lyrics by Damian Hess
Music by Damian Hess, Gabriel Alter,
Matthew Milligan & Rob Mitzner

♩ = 91

Intro (2 Bars Funky N'awlins)

Verse 1, (12 Bars Vox In)

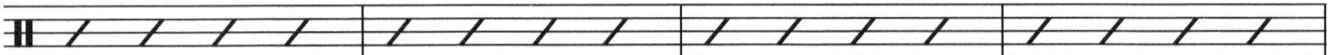

Hits w/Vox

Fill

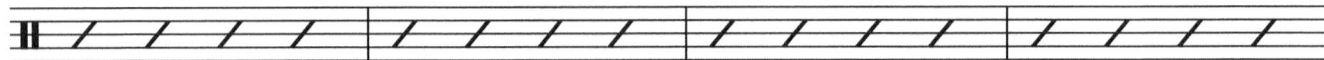

Chorus 1 (8 Bars Backbeat Funk)

Interlude (2 Bars Funky N'awlins!)

Verse 2, (12 Bars More Active)

Charts, Lead Sheets & Road Maps

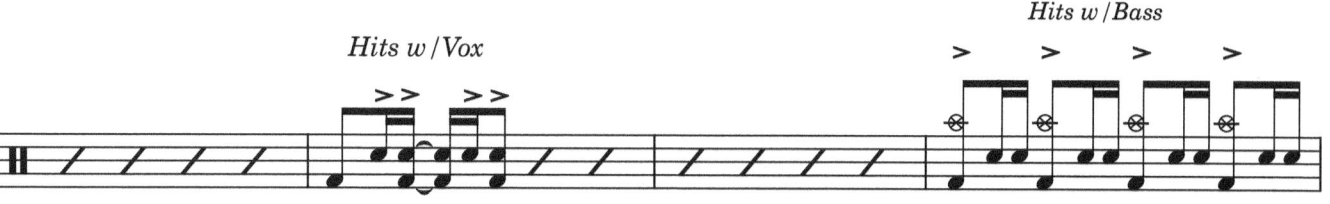

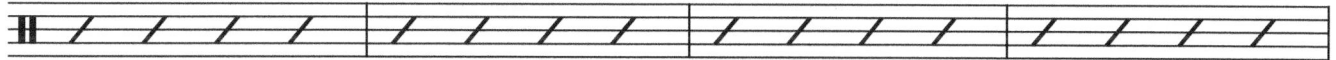

Chorus 2 (8 Bars Backbeat Funk)

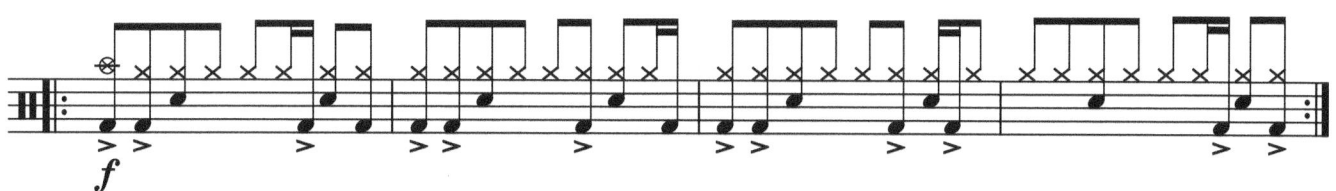

Interlude (2 Bars Reggaeton Style)

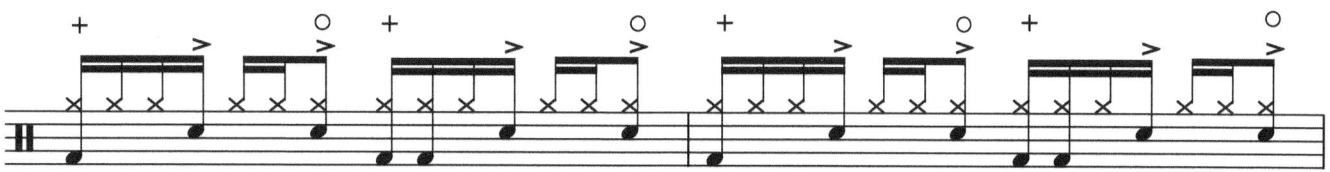

Verse 3 (12 Bars Reggaeton)

Chorus 3 (16 Bars Backbeat Funk)

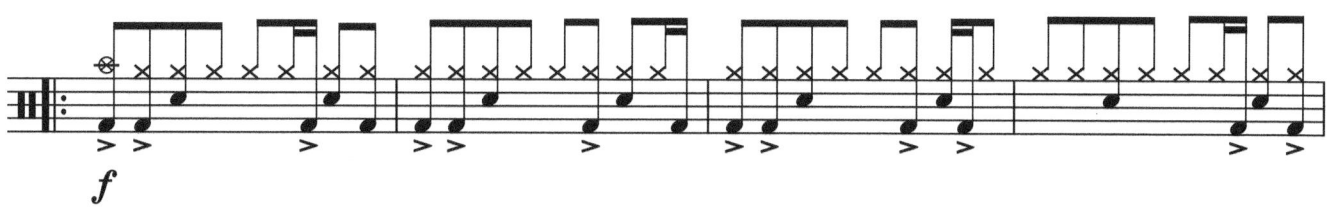

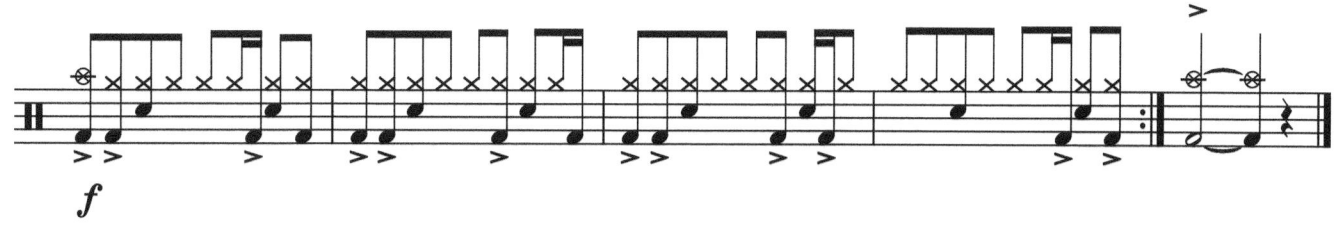

STUFF YOU CAN USE

SONG WORKSHOP #14: "GETTING CLOSER"
FROM THE MUSICAL *RADIOACTIVE*
BY WILL REYNOLDS & ERIC PRICE

These next two tunes by composer Will Reynolds and his writing partner lyricist Eric Price tackle a genre that many rock players may never have thought of exploring…musical theater! This style of drumming is really its own animal, but the skills it requires will also help you in absolutely every other style. Playing theater music takes good reading skills, a sensitive touch and the ability to switch between sections and feels quickly and smoothly. Will is an acclaimed composer and winner of many awards in this genre, but most importantly for us, he writes fantastic drum parts.

"In my music, I really rely on the drummer. Sometimes these songs change tempos four times and it can be a challenge to lay back and push forward in the right spots. When I'm developing a show, I actually like to give the drummer freedom to write the parts as they go along."

This first tune "Getting Closer," is from a musical called RADIOACTIVE about the life of Marie Curie, the Nobel Prize-winning scientist who discovered radium (and then ironically, died from radiation poisoning). Along with Will's music and Eric's lyrics, it features Broadway star Hannah Corneau on vocals and our friend Dmitry Ishenko on acoustic bass.

The tune begins in cut time, which means there are two beats per measure and each is worth a half note. Will explains, "it can be frustrating for a drummer with less theater experience to see cut time all over the place instead of 4/4. You need to know that the pulse stays the same, it's just what's emphasized that's changing. It's mostly written that way for the actors and the pianist who might have a harder time reading runs of 16th notes."

So let's read some cut time! It goes by fast, so get ready to count and stay on your toes.

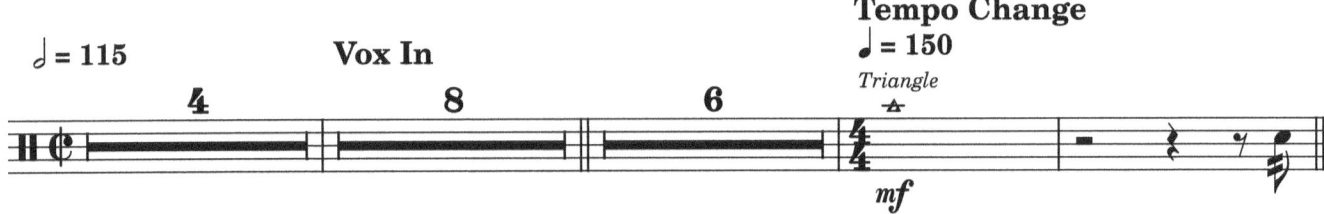

You'll also see a triangle part at the first tempo change. I have been gently teasing Will for years about what I call his "triangle fetish," but it's actually an important musical device. He explains, "I like to call the triangle, cymbal scrapes and rolls 'color percussion.' Much like jazz or any other style, this music has a tried-and-true vocabulary, and that triangle is like a shortcut to the audience's heart. It can be an emotional moment in the piece, a surprise or an idea. There's just a magical quality about it."

If you don't have a triangle on your kit, just use a cymbal bell and I'm sure he will forgive you. That triangle signals our first tempo change into 4/4, but the good news is that the pulse stays the same and there are 2 measures before the drums fully enter.

Charts, Lead Sheets & Road Maps

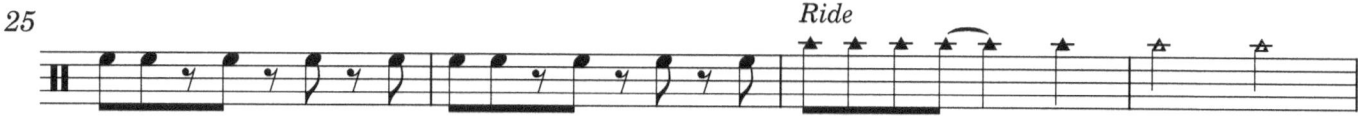

You will also notice that this is not a fully written-out drum part. Will says, "I imagine there will be kick drum and other things to flesh out this rhythm. I think a part that micro-manages the drummer can stifle creativity. I'd rather rely on the skill of the drummer to interpret based on what's going on around them."

Here's what I came up with:

After a few breaks in the groove for some "color percussion" on the ride cymbal, we transition into a marching-style pattern on the snare.

Then we hit letter B and transition back to *tempo primo* (the original tempo) in cut time for some gentle closed hi-hat. This goes by quite quickly, so stay alert! Also be mindful of the dynamic ups-and-downs over the course of each phrase.

STUFF YOU CAN USE

Then we have a cymbal scrape that signals a return to the rock groove in 4/4 time. Will states, "if the drummer hasn't memorized and internalized these two distinct feels, it's over. There's a sweet spot for these grooves and the trick is to not make them alike. The way they feel is driven by the lyrics. There are these emotional moments between Marie Curie and fellow scientist Pierre, whom she later marries. He's expressed feelings for her and she's saying 'I can't get closer to you while I'm getting closer to discovering radium.' These toms, snare and cymbals all represent different things that are happening in the lyrics and they really add to the emotion of the storytelling."

After another turn though the tom groove, we play the march on the snare again, followed by a brief hi-hat interlude that gets us to the end. Watch out, since that hi-hat groove looks visually similar to what we played at letter B in cut time. However this is in 4/4, so it's not as fast and has some different accents that follow the lyrics.

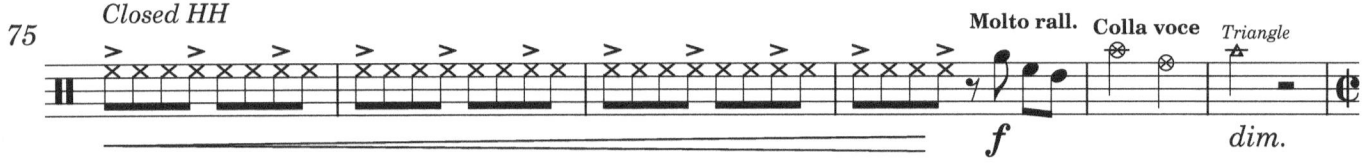

Then you'll see some more Italian terms. *Molto rallentando* literally means "slow down a lot" and *colla voce* is translated as "follow the voice," so listen carefully to the track and try to stay connected. We end with the hi-hat in cut time and Will concludes, "the drummer can be a big asset to a musical director or arranger if they can really capture the sound they're looking for."

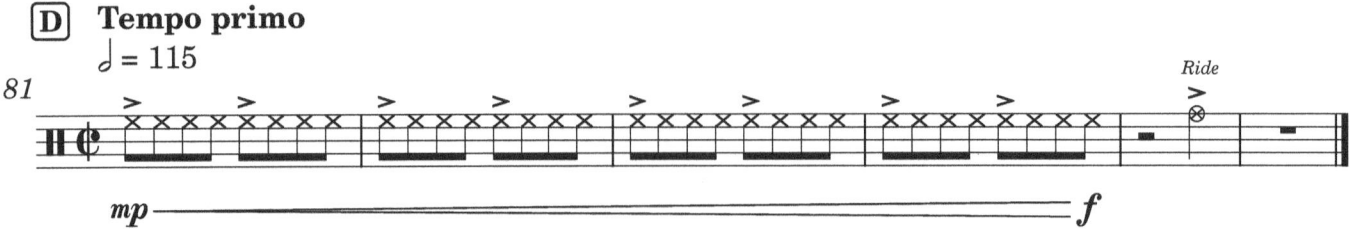

Charts, Lead Sheets & Road Maps

Rob @ The Seaside Lounge Studios in Brooklyn, NY
Photo by Thomas Mester

Will Reynolds, Deborah Abramson, Rob & Emilio Tostado after a performance of the musical STU FOR SILVERTON

STUFF YOU CAN USE

"Getting Closer"
from the musical
RADIOACTIVE

Music by Will Reynolds
Lyrics by Eric Price

Charts, Lead Sheets & Road Maps

STUFF YOU CAN USE

SONG WORKSHOP #15: "THE VIOLET HOUR"
FROM THE MUSICAL *THE VIOLET HOUR*
BY WILL REYNOLDS & ERIC PRICE

This next tune from musical theater writing team Will Reynolds and Eric Price is the title track from the show THE VIOLET HOUR, which chronicles the adventures of a young book publisher in early 20th-century New York. This one is sung and played by Will himself, with Dmitry Ishenko joining us on acoustic bass. The tune begins with…a very long rest!

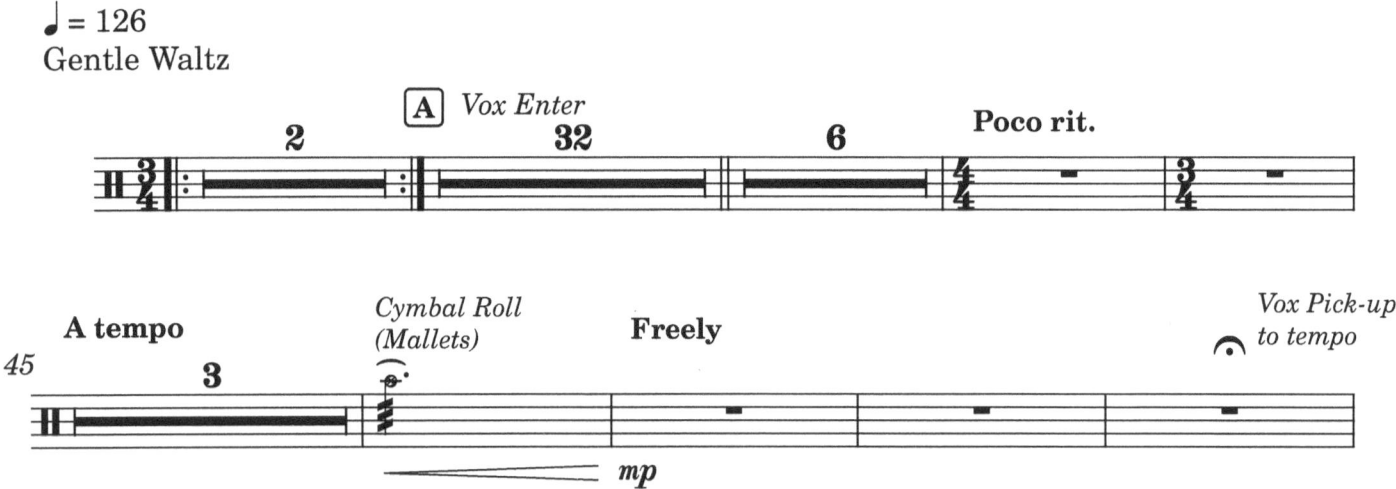

You might be wondering why we would choose a song that doesn't start with the drums actually playing. This book is all about *Stuff You Can Use*, and I feel that being able to count through rests and stay connected to the chart is one of the most important things a drummer can learn. I think this skill applies to any genre of music. Sometimes you don't play for the first verse of a rock tune and sometimes you lay out for an entire chorus of the bass solo in jazz. Either way, you need to count those rests and keep your place in the music.

Will explains, "in this genre, there could be a 9-minute sequence where you're laying out for a weirdly odd number of bars. Ultimately, it is absolutely on the drummer to count those bars and know the big shape of what's happening sonically. Sometimes using lyrical cues from the actors can be helpful in marking where you are."

This one is even trickier since the time is played "freely," meaning *there is no click track*. This enables the singer and accompanist to push and pull the time as they see fit, but it also means you need to use your ears and make sure to play that first cymbal roll in the right spot (it's an important "color percussion" moment).

Charts, Lead Sheets & Road Maps

After the *fermata* (which is a hold or pause), listen for the vocal pickup that gets us into a gentle brushes waltz groove.

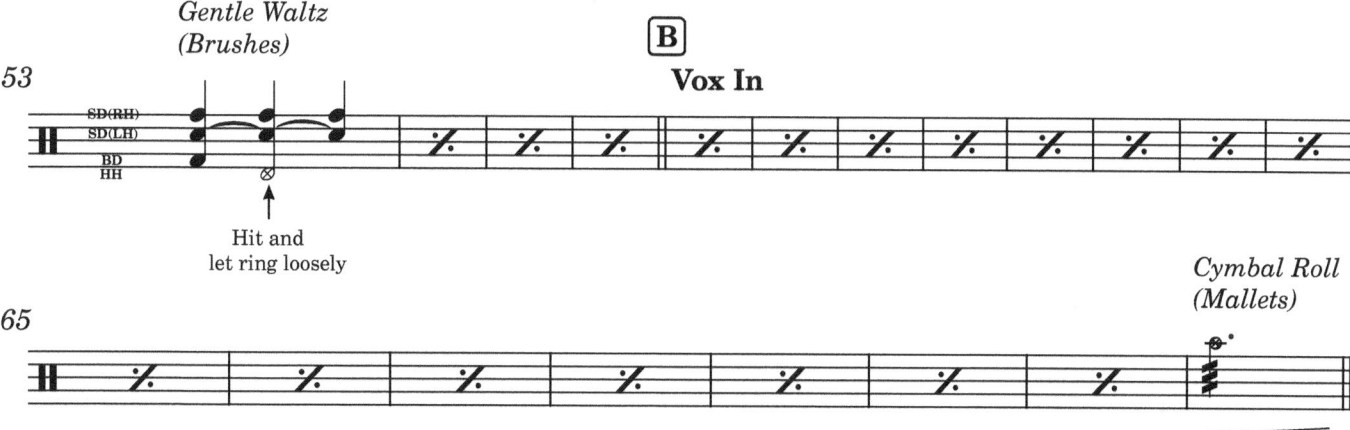

Stepping on the hi-hats and letting them ring on beat 2 of each measure matches the rhythm and tonal quality of what's happening in the piano. In the last bar of this 16-measure verse, the pattern ends and we have a cymbal roll. Since we don't have time to quickly switch to mallets, turn your brushes around and do the roll with the rubber part.

Will explains, "we want a perfect classical roll, but that's not always technically possible. So the drummer needs to find a way to deliver that dreamy rush that provides so much magic to the audience. A drummer needs to have 5-10 slightly different versions of these types of rolls to use in every situation even if you don't have a mallet in your hand."

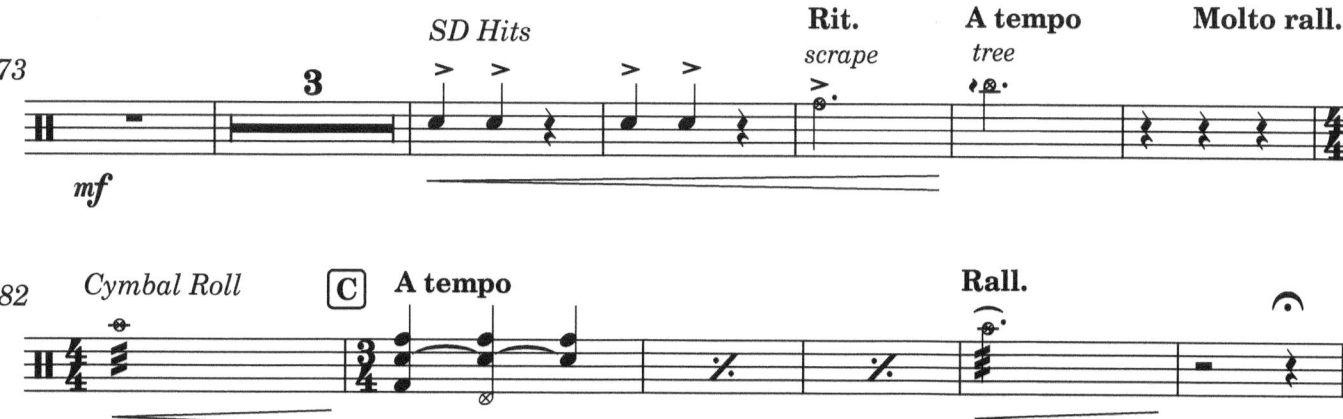

After the cymbal roll (or "swell" as it's sometimes called), there are 4 bars of rest, followed by some important snare hits that reinforce the lyrics and mark the climax of the tune. Lyricist Eric Price explains, "at this point in the show, the character has written his first novel. Its publication would mean a new start for him and a chance to finally secure his place in the world." Will adds, "any time we use the word 'moment,' we emphasize it in the music because that's what the show is about - moments that change a person's life."

Make sure to lock in those hits with that lyric, then flip one brush around to do the cymbal scrape. You'll also notice a "tree" (short for "mark tree") in the part, and if you don't have one of those, do another cymbal roll to help make that moment meaningful and big. You'll hear harps, bells and timpani, followed by another *molto rallentando*. There's a lot of stopping and starting here, but it's critical to stay engaged with the chart and use your ears as your guide since there is no click track.

STUFF YOU CAN USE

Then we're back to the waltz, but only for a few measures before another *fermata*. After this last dramatic pause, there are 8 more measures of groove before the "color percussion" takes over for a gentle finish.

This is a short tune, but there's a lot packed in. Having the skills to navigate though all these changes and switches will undoubtedly make you a better drummer in any style of music you play…and it will make the composer very happy!

Will Reynolds and Rob @ C-Room Studio in Brooklyn, NY

Charts, Lead Sheets & Road Maps

"The Violet Hour"
from the musical
THE VIOLET HOUR

Music by Will Reynolds
Lyrics by Eric Price

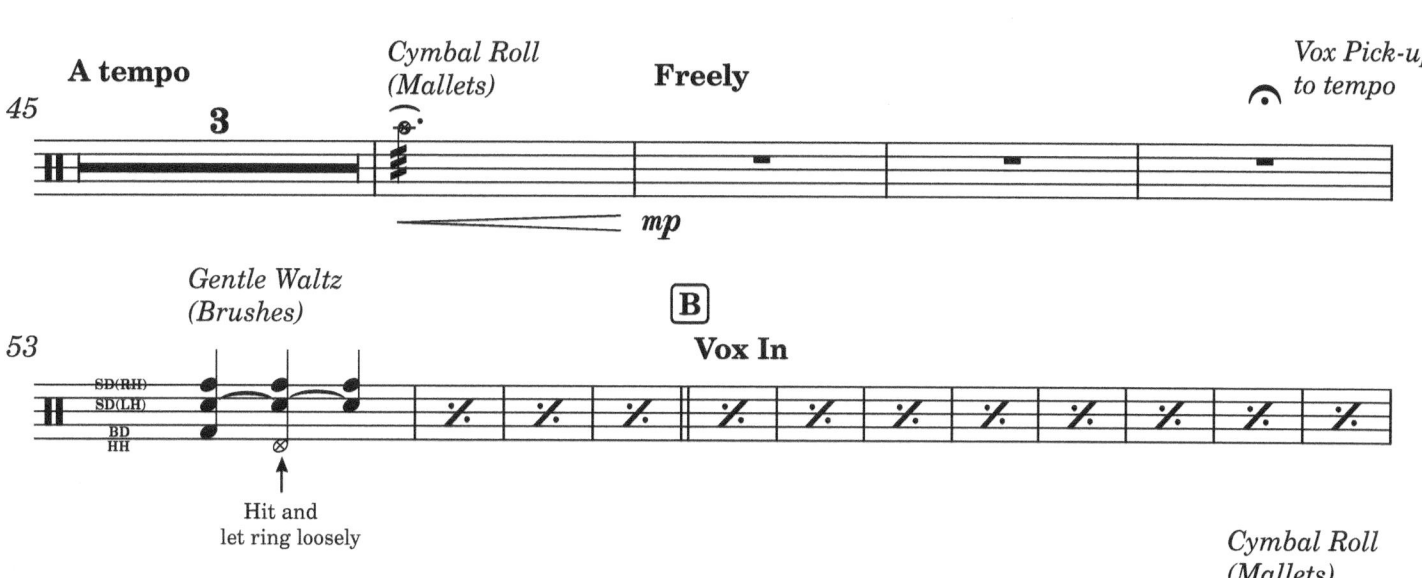
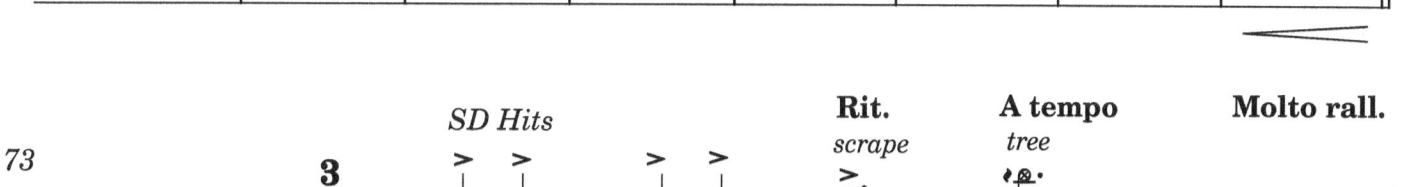

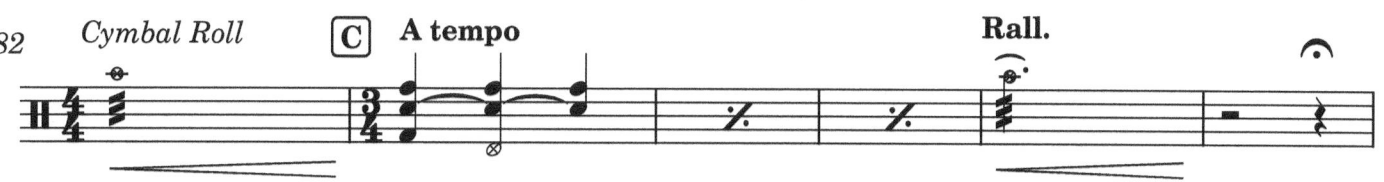
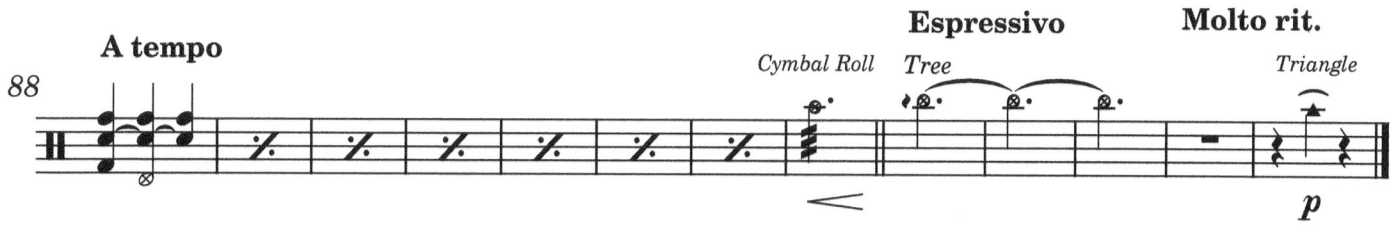

STUFF YOU CAN USE

SONG WORKSHOP #16: "INSURRECTION"
BY MICHAEL GALLANT

This next one is a rockin' instrumental by pianist and composer Michael Gallant. Michael and I actually played in a jazz quintet when we were in high school and reconnected in New York many years later. Now I play in his trio, where his biggest musical influences include The Bad Plus, Michel Camilo and Led Zeppelin…a very diverse selection! This group also features the omnipresent Dmitry Ishenko on electric bass.

The main groove is a funky backbeat with a few variations, but "Insurrection" is all about the dynamics, texture and intensity changes throughout the different sections. Michael explains, "I've found that in any music I like, you can't maintain a full-on fever pitch for the entire tune since it gets old very quickly. It's like dynamite. You have to use it tastefully."

The intro begins with some very quiet cymbal bell hits that line up with the piano.

After 8 measures, come in with a light ride cymbal/cross-stick pattern.

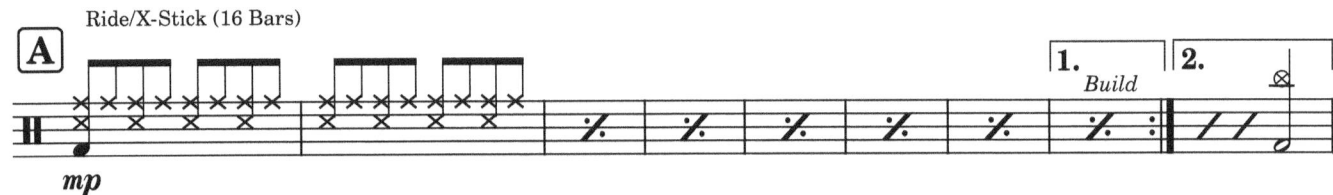

16 bars later, the texture changes again. After the hit on beat 3, count those rests and get ready to come in big with an open hi-hat groove. Michael explains, "I want some hard-rock Zeppelin action."

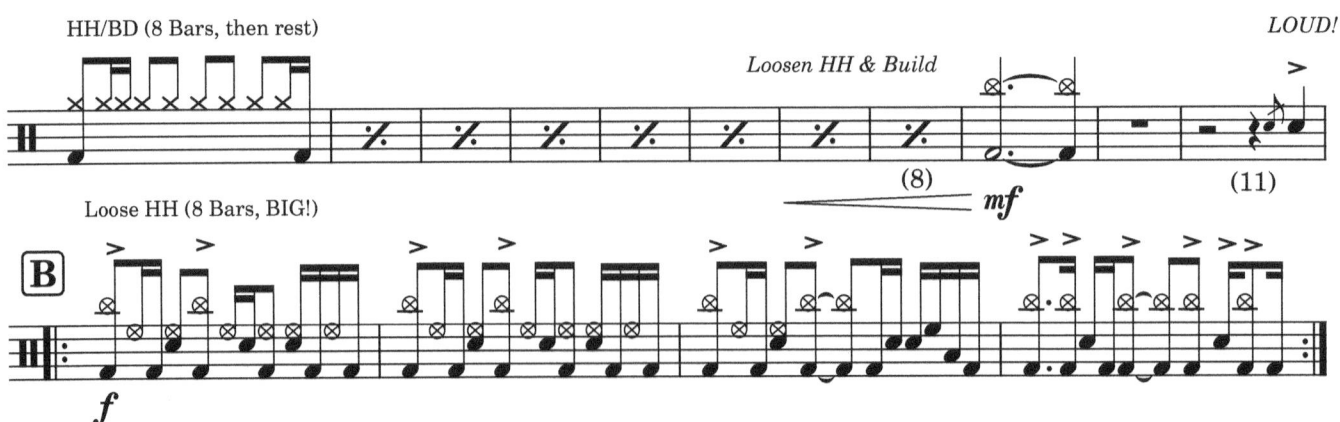

Charts, Lead Sheets & Road Maps

After 8 more bars the feel tightens a bit, although the bass and drums continue to lock in on a similar rhythmic pattern. Find Dmitry's bass notes with your bass drum.

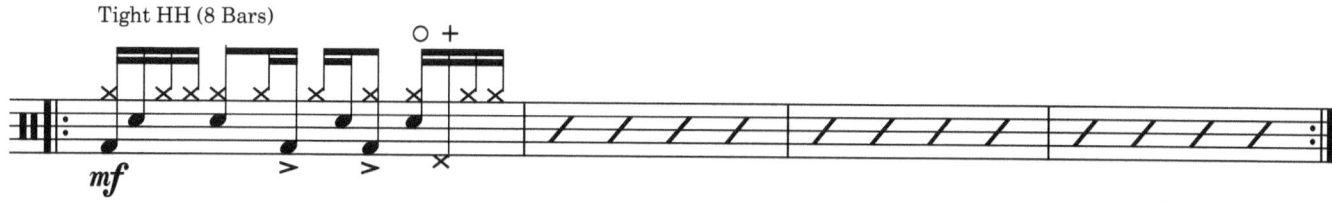

Then we play another 8 bars and the kick drum pattern changes slightly. This may seem like a small adjustment, but these variations keep the song moving so it doesn't get too static. Dmitry explains, "there are several build-ups and lots of peaks and valleys, so you don't want to get to your maximum dynamic level right away. You want to pace it and find the spot that is the actual climax and give it one hundred percent."

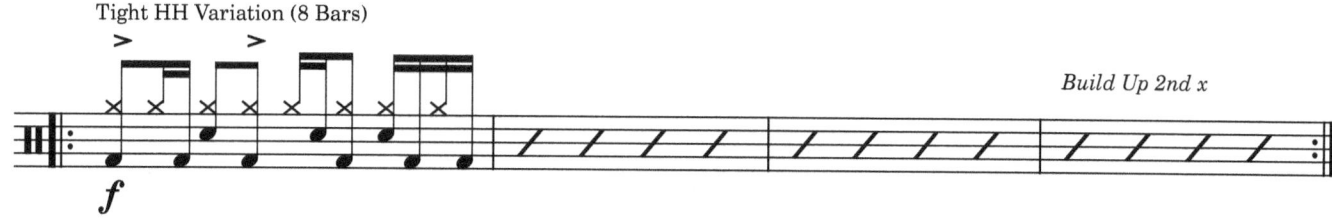

Then we do 8 more measures of the open hi-hat "Zeppelin" part from earlier, followed by a drastic change for the bridge section.

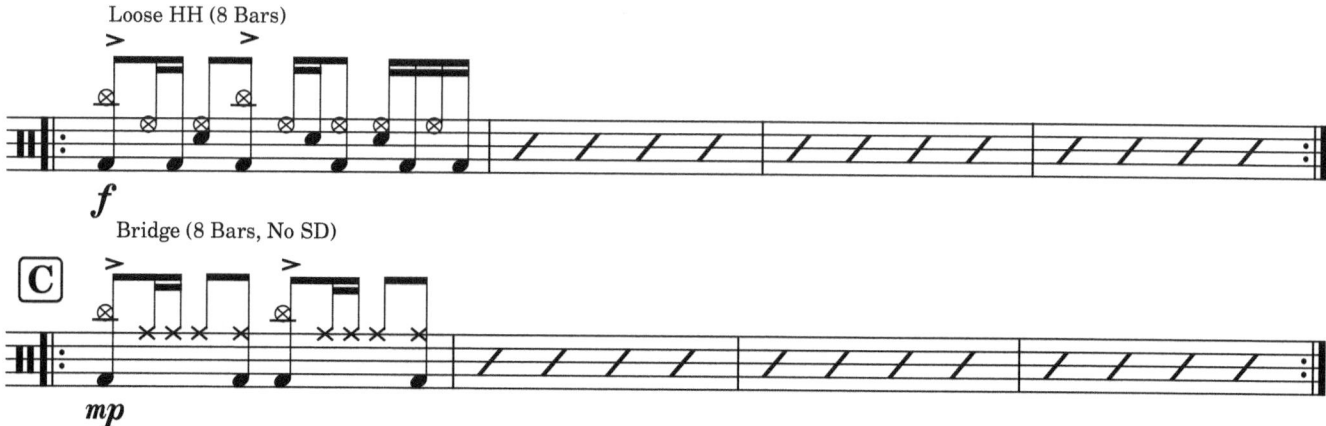

Michael explains that this section "gives the listener a little break before the final act, and the drummer really needs to read the energy of the band and react to it. There has to be a breath, otherwise the performance can feel dead. Even if it's intensely dead, it's still dead."

Then we play 4 more bars of groove before a big drum solo over some hits.

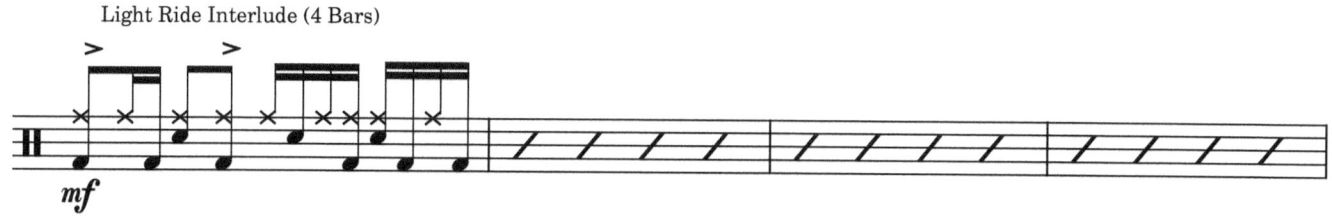

STUFF YOU CAN USE

Soloing over hits is one of the most important concepts a drummer can learn in any style of music. Michael says, "the piano and bass are more secondary here. We're supporting the drummer by giving some ideas to anchor the solo. Those hits provide a grounded base and the drummer can stick closely to them, or play around them and fly into the atmosphere. I want the drummer to approach this section as a composer and direct the flow." Try to develop some melodic ideas and build the energy of your solo as it goes along.

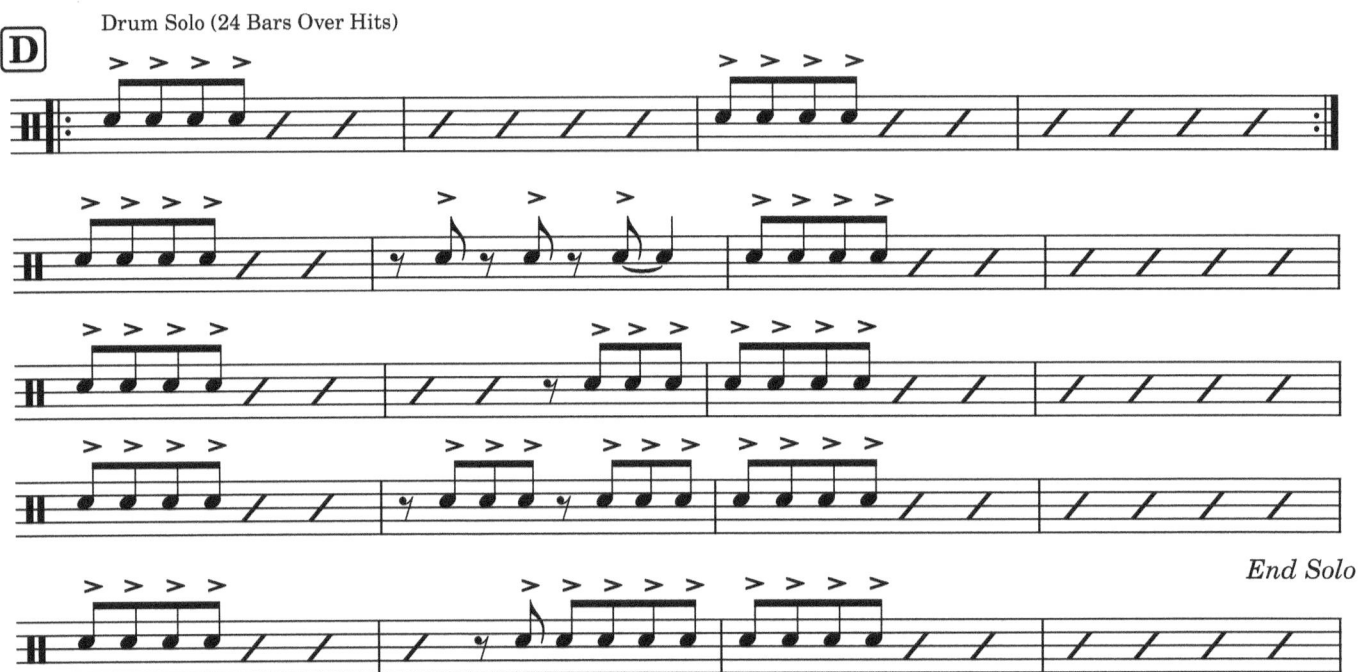

Dmitry adds, "in this case, I'm not interacting with the solo too much. Sometimes it's better just to mark the hits because the drums are playing off you or relying on you to show where it is. That way we can sync up in the most strategic moments." As the solo concludes, come back in with a vengeance and drive the band towards the end of the song.

Charts, Lead Sheets & Road Maps

As we reach the finish line, things start to…unravel. So I asked Michael why this tune is called "Insurrection."

"I really tried to capture the emotional footprint of what happened at the Capitol on January 6th. At the beginning, I wanted there to be storm clouds, something weird and intense going on. I didn't want this tune to be relaxed. It's supposed to be a little unsettled and the ideas come in waves. The drum solo is the point where the fury and rage become a destructive force and explode. And the end is a total disintegration of the main theme. It's an apocalyptic, chaotic, messy rock thing and I love it. Time-wise, I'm almost deliberately fighting with the drummer during this final part. I'm trying to push and pull and create tension like something is tearing. But you don't want it to fall apart too much or else it's just guys banging on instruments. Then we end on this suddenly happy little major chord. It just felt right."

Rob, Dmitry Ishenko & Michael Gallant @ The Smithsonian in Washington D.C.

Octomoose

Dmitry, Rob & Michael @ Tomi Jazz in NYC

STUFF YOU CAN USE

"Insurrection"

By Michael Gallant

Charts, Lead Sheets & Road Maps

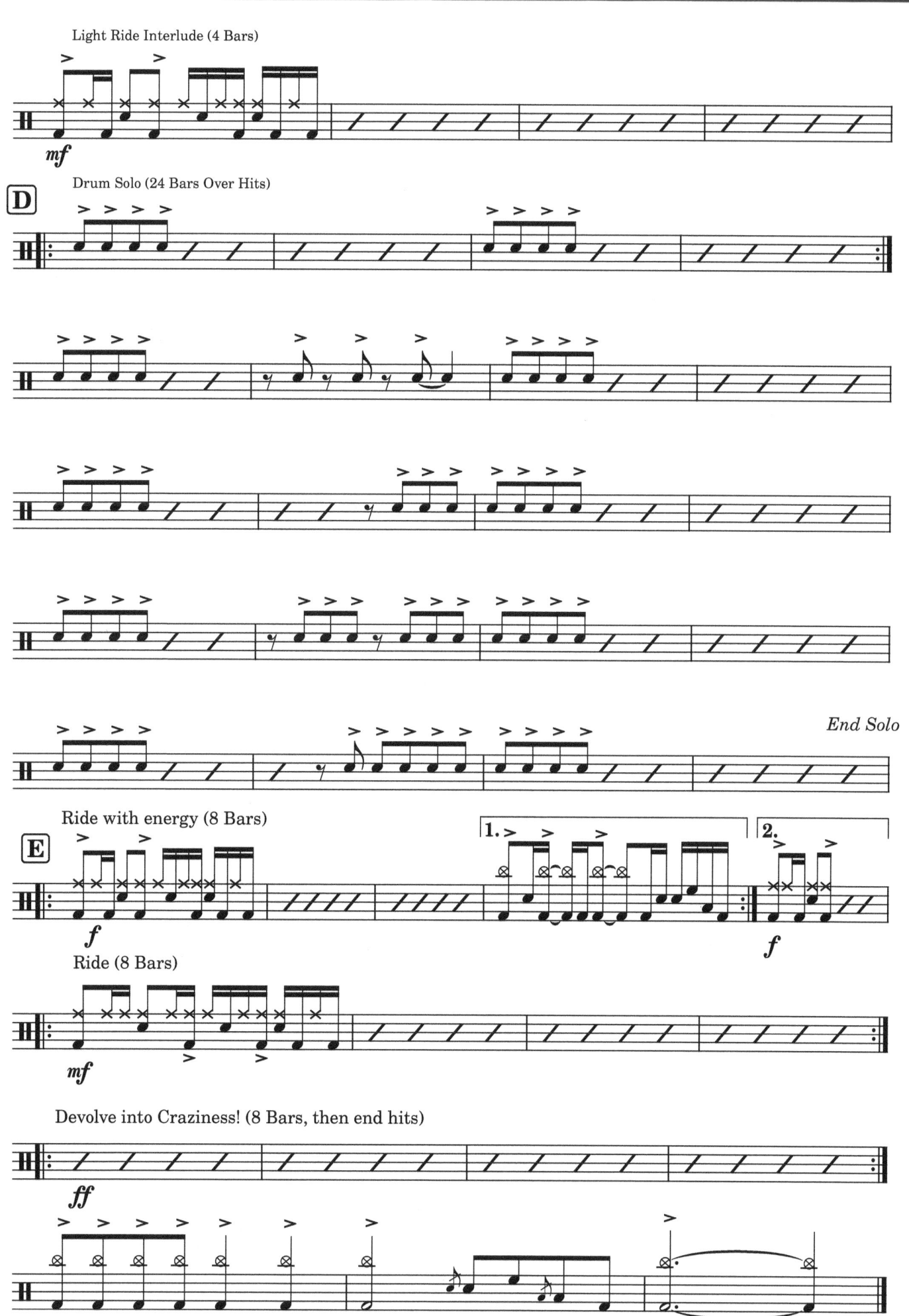

147

STUFF YOU CAN USE

SONG WORKSHOP #17: "MODERN JAZZ COMBO"
BY LARS POTTEIGER

This next tune is a piano trio piece written by Lars Potteiger and also features Dmitry Ishenko on acoustic bass. Lars is a longtime collaborator of mine who can play everything from jazz to classical, rock and R&B. As a composer, his biggest influences include Brad Mehldau, Ahmad Jamal and Bill Evans, and you can also hear many elements of classical chamber music in his tunes. The music he writes is challenging, a blast to play and often spotlights the drums.

This aptly titled song has a relaxed, straight 8th-note feel and dances through multiple time signatures and tempo changes. It finishes with a flourish, featuring a drum solo over a frenetic vamp. Buckle up!

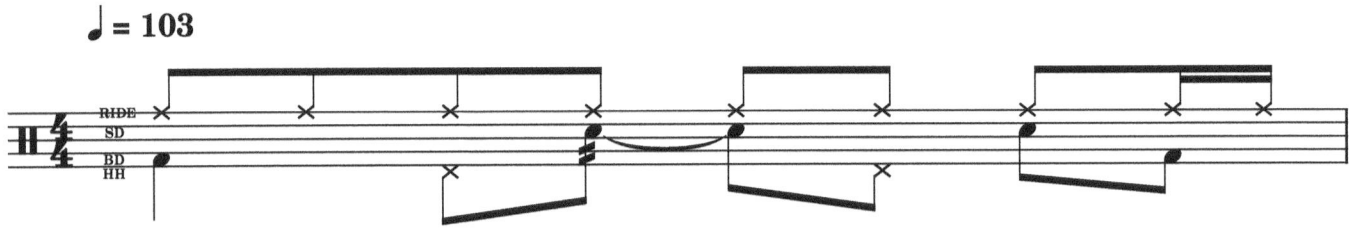

Lars says, "what I was going for in this piece is something that is 'through-composed' in nature. I didn't want it to be like a jazz standard with a shorter form, solos and variations. I'm thinking of it as more of a chamber music piece where we improvise over parts of the tune and tread that line between what is composed and what is made up by the players as we're playing it."

As you know by now, there are many different types of charts in this book and Lars wrote this one in the style of a lead sheet, but also as a score. This means that we can see both the melody, which is the top staff and the chords, which are on the bottom. As drummers, we have to be able to read all kinds of charts when artists throw them at us, and this one gives us a lot of information we'll use to play the form and hits along with the band. It also uses a concept called "rehearsal letters" to help us indicate the different sections. This is exactly the same as when we marked the verses and choruses in the rock tunes. The styles may be vastly different, but the same musical skills will help you in any situation. *Stuff You Can Use!*

The tune starts with a 4-measure intro with everyone playing this light groove which emphasizes beats 1 and the "and" of 2.

Charts, Lead Sheets & Road Maps

Then the melody enters and we play 19 more bars. Remember to keep counting and avoid guessing or assuming how many measures are in each section. Lars says, "I really want that straight-8th's feel to simmer."

When we get to letter B, stop on beat 1 of the 2/4 measure and play those 5 light hits in the 15/16 measure. This may seem tough at first, but try subdividing the 15 into groups of 3 and play it 5 times, making sure to land on the correct downbeat in the next bar. After a bar of 6/4, stop again on the 2/4 and play 5 hits, only this time in 4/4. This is essentially the same thing as 16/16, so we're just repeating the previous phrase with one extra 16th note added. Practice this slowly on your own at first until you get it.

STUFF YOU CAN USE

Lars suggests, "the hits create some nice ensemble moments and break up the monotony of that groove. I was really hearing the melody that way. It wasn't just me making it unnecessarily difficult for the rest of the band. That was just something I heard in my head and I just needed to figure out what container to put it in."

After the hits, we get back into the groove and play 9 measures until the bass solo.

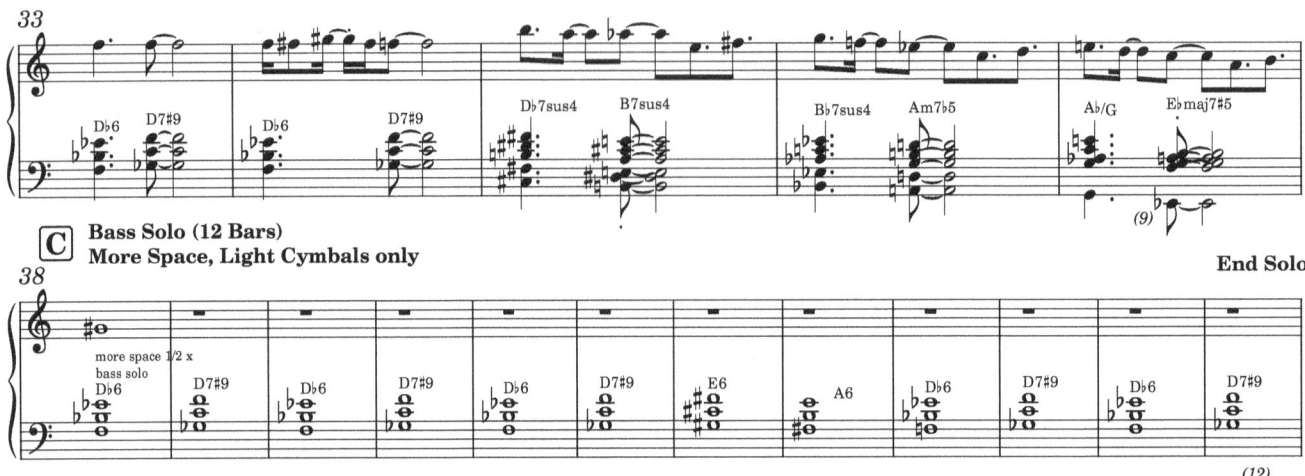

Dmitry explains, "there are three different approaches an accompanist can take when playing behind a bass solo. Number one is to clearly mark all the sections and almost be like a play-along track. Number two is doing that, plus being interactive if you hear an idea you want to grab onto. Number three is being completely contrapuntal and playing against what the soloist is doing. Personally, I prefer number two most of the time since it really outlines where the measure is. Give me a cushion to fall back on. It's normal to feel uneasy sometimes, and approach number three can cause you to second-guess yourself and ruin the flow of your improvisation."

Lars also suggests "gravitating more towards cymbal work gives your bass player some space. If you play a lot of bass drum, snare and toms it could interfere with the frequency of what he's playing."

Rob & Lars Potteiger enjoy pierogies @ The Ukranian-American Social Club in Reading, PA. Photo by Dmitry Ishenko

As the bass solo ends and we hit letter D, the band plays some hits together, followed by a short rest. It's ok for your cymbal to ring through this. Then we play some hits alternating between 3/4 and 5/4 time. This phrase could also be written as 2 measures of 4/4, so it's not quite as challenging as it looks.

As that section concludes, we have another rest and rejoin the original groove in 4/4. We play 4 bars, and then the piano solo begins. Lars says, "during the solo, I like the interaction with the drums a lot. We don't want to play a game of cat and mouse where we copy each other's ideas, it's more like a dialogue or a conversation. Some musical situations call for a more static approach, but in this case a little rhythmic interaction is cool. That's why it's important to have good ears so you don't make noise in the same space."

STUFF YOU CAN USE

Once the solo ends and we get to letter F, play those hits along with the band. Try to play very small "setups" between them to make the whole phrase more fluid and musical. Lars adds, "I don't want or need the drummer to play like a metronome since everyone is responsible for keeping the time. The hits are a framework, but we want it to be musical and connected as we move between them."

After the hits at letter F, we've arrived at the big moment…the drum solo!

But first, we've got a tempo change. Listen to the click track for one measure of this faster tempo before the solo vamp begins. It's a 7-measure phrase which repeats 4 times and the time signature changes *every single bar*. Sounds easy, no? Well don't worry, since I didn't nail this one the first time either! The key is to break it down piece-by-piece, practice slowly and try to internalize it so you're not counting frantically the whole time you're trying to solo.

Lars explains, "the tempo change creates a drastic left turn in the piece. What better way to get us out of that *ostinato* [repeating figure] we've been playing the whole time than to go to a new tempo and add hits to give it some energy for the drum solo. In this vamp, it's almost like things feel out of balance and connect at certain times. I just wanted the drums to settle into this thing that felt a little unsettled and just rage on it."

Charts, Lead Sheets & Road Maps

When you're soloing over any vamp, playing a few hits along with it is a good way to start your solo. However, as we talked about in the odd time section in the first half of the book, you don't want to get stuck in the vamp and not be able to develop any other ideas. My approach on this one was to join the bass player for a few of those low notes in the first couple of bars, and then sometimes play the hits in the 7/4 measure at the end of the phrase. But not all the time! The key is to dance in and out of playing in unison with the band versus playing against them. This is an advanced-level concept, but it's a great thing to think about even if you're just starting out with this style of music. Dmitry explains, "on the drum solo I'm just hanging on for dear life, tapping my foot and making sure I've got the hits all correct. I'm not interacting with the drums at all."

As the solo ends, we jump back in to the original tempo and end with a gentle cymbal roll on beat 3. Lars concludes, "it made sense to come back to that figure which was happening earlier in the piece. It makes the drum solo less arbitrary."

Dmitry Ishenko, Rob & Lars Potteiger

Soundcheck @ Yocum Institute in West Lawn, PA

STUFF YOU CAN USE

"Modern Jazz Combo"

By Lars Potteiger

Charts, Lead Sheets & Road Maps

155

STUFF YOU CAN USE

Charts, Lead Sheets & Road Maps

SONG WORKSHOP #18: "BLUES FOR BOB"

BY ROB MITZNER

We've reached the final tune in the book, and it's the most personal for me. I wrote this as a dedication to my late teacher Bob Gullotti. Bob was a legendary educator who influenced so many young players, as well as a monster jazz drummer with his group The Fringe. He has been my biggest influence on the instrument, and I'm eternally grateful for all the years he spent kicking my butt and pushing me to get better. Bob was all about *Stuff You Can Use* and I really hope he would have liked this book.

Bob always thought of the drums as a melodic instrument and you could hear it in the way he played. One of his core teachings was to have students play the entire Charlie Parker Omnibook melodically around the drumset, including the heads and transcribed sax solos. This was incredibly challenging since it would force you to reimagine the role of the drums and think like a horn player. So to record this tune, I got the best horn player I could find, the amazing Chris Cheek, to join Dmitry Ishenko and me. Chris spent years playing saxophone in Paul Motian's band and has also played with Brian Blade, Keith Carlock, Jeff Ballard and a long list of the world's finest drummers.

On this tune we're all playing the head in unison, just as Bob taught with the Charlie Parker book. This chart is in the style of a jazz lead sheet, so the melody and 12-bar blues form is written out once and then looped for the solos. It's important to keep track of where you are at all times and listen intently to the other players.

Chris says, "I like to interact with drums both rhythmically and dynamically. I remember playing with Paul Motian and being amazed at how many different ways he could make the cymbals sound. Good drummers do that with all the parts of the kit. They use their touch to achieve different types of sounds and add depth to the music so it's engaging. No matter how great the groove is, if it's the same dynamic level all the time, it can become monotonous. Whenever you have variations in the sound, it really helps the music breathe."

When you play the melody in unison with the sax and bass, stay on the snare for most of it and use the toms as "accent tones." For example, throw in a floor tom when there is a low-pitched note, a high tom for a higher note and play the hands together on the ending triplets to give it a thicker texture. Keep playing 2 and 4 on the hi-hat to help everyone stay together.

Dmitry says, "those triplets are the main event in this head. You can't fall into the trap of just taking them at face value the way they are written, or you might not be in sync with your bandmates. I approach it by really listening to the drums so we can agree on how much to lay them back or push them forward. I think pulling them back a bit makes the tune more grooving and really at ease."

After you play the head twice around the kit with the band, switch over to the ride and start swinging for the sax solo. I asked Chris what he's likes to hear from the drums during this solo:

STUFF YOU CAN USE

"Some people like drummers to be really active and do things to mess around with the time by approaching it in a more abstract or busier way. Personally, I like to play with drummers who have great time. It doesn't have to be complicated. It's like you're driving down the highway: whether you're at 55 or 70, if you're just cruising at that tempo there doesn't have to be anything tricky about the rhythm. On some level, rhythms that sound good also feel good physically. Drummers who are really musical are always asking, 'what does the music need in this moment?' Maybe it doesn't need much, and that's ok. I remember Motian was an extreme example and sometimes wouldn't interact at all. Nothing I could do would get any kind of response out of him. And then the next night on the same tune, he would be very interactive. In a way, it's like you're having a conversation. If the other person is always talking over you or finishing your sentences, it's hard to have a dialogue. I love to get ideas from the people I play with, and I think that's the joy of playing with good musicians. It takes you out of your own world and you become influenced by other people's ideas so you can experiment, explore and have fun."

Dmitry says, "you need to have the utmost awareness of what's going on at every moment. I'm almost splitting my brain into two halves. The first half is making sure the quarter-note feel is exactly right with the drummer, and that one of us isn't pushing or pulling. It's a very delicate balance and you have to make these decisions in a split-second to create that perfect cushion for the soloist. The second half of my brain is with the soloist. If you hear a phrase that you think is going to resolve on a certain beat, you can nail that with the soloist. You ultimately want to come up with a compromise to make them sound good. If everyone is together, it's beautiful music and that's what you want."

After the sax solo, Dmitry plays 2 choruses of bass solo. Switch over to the closed hi-hat or grab a pair of brushes to bring your volume way down and stay out of the tonal frequency of the bass. Chris suggests, "it's a really helpful thing for drummers to increase their sensibility about melody and harmony. That really translates to finding a balance on the drums and informs a good drummer's choices."

Dmitry says, "in this tune, there's no chordal instrument so all I've got is the drummer. The drummer doesn't have to play 2 and 4 the whole time on the hi-hat, and I don't want them to mark every single downbeat, but it's good to check in and make sure you're in the same place. If I realize we're not together, I'll make it into a thing and try to cover it up by repeating that rhythm so it seems intentional. Those are the secrets of jazz."

After two choruses of bass, it's the drummer's time to shine. One soloing trick I learned from jazz great Adam Nussbaum is to sing the melody of the song in your head as you solo. This will help you play interesting ideas that fit each part of the form while keeping you connected so you don't lose your place. Chris says, "this tune has a Thelonious Monk vibe with lots of space in the melody. Just listening to the tune kind of gives you a lot of ideas on how to play it. As an improviser, there's a lot to draw from to build a solo."

Charts, Lead Sheets & Road Maps

Dmitry adds, "if I feel that the drummer is going for a certain phrase in their solo, I might latch on to it to show I'm with them. But in some situations, the drummer just flies off and does their thing so I step aside and don't interfere."

Once you play those 24 measures, make sure to be as rhythmically clear as possible as you end your solo and go back into the unison melody.

Dmitry explains, "I would encourage drummers to be aware of the fact that everyone can't always follow everything you play. If you feel like people are getting lost or maybe it gets a little off and they shy away from you, go ahead and do your thing. But wherever you are in the form, be sure to mark the last 2 bars because you don't want the 'head out' to fall apart. Your audience is going to remember that and think 'these guys really screwed up this tune!'"

Then we play the head twice again in unison and end that last phrase with gusto. Chris concludes, "to me, what makes the difference between a good drummer and a great one is dynamics. That's what really helps you get inside the music. It's such an important thing to consider while you're playing."

This tune concludes our journey from the shed to the stage. I hope that these charts, videos, interviews and analyses have provided you with some valuable tools for your "oh sh*t" bag that you can take into any musical situation. Being able to adapt, listen, learn and evolve as a drummer is critical whether you're playing jazz, rock, musical theater or anything in-between. These skills truly are the *Stuff You Can Use!*

Bob Gullotti
Photo courtesy of his wife, Marion Campos

STUFF YOU CAN USE

"Blues for Bob"

By Rob Mitzner

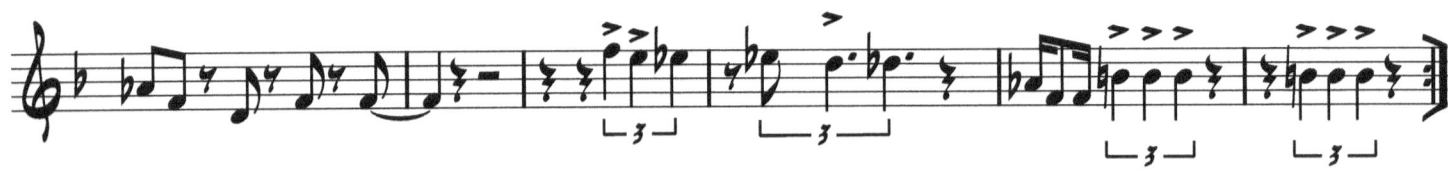

Head 2x In & Out, Played in Unison
4 Choruses Bari Sax Solo
2 Chorus Bass Solo
2 Choruses Drum Solo

Charts, Lead Sheets & Road Maps

Photos courtesy of Marion Campos

STUFF YOU CAN USE

GLOSSARY OF MUSICAL SLANG

Blowing: Solos.

Busy: A lot of notes.

Colla Voce: Italian term meaning "follow the voice."

Color Percussion: Triangle, cymbal scrapes, swells, mark tree and other auxiliary percussion designed to evoke an emotional audience response in theater music.

Contrapuntal: Two or more separate melodic lines played against each other at the same time.

Cut Time: Common in theater music, it has two beats per measure and each is worth a half note. It is technically 2/2 time.

Cymbal Swell: A roll with mallets that increases in volume to a climax point.

Dark vs Bright Tone: Cymbals tend to be brighter and take up a similar sonic space as horns, guitars and some vocals. The bass drum and toms are darker and inhabit the same space as the bass player.

Downbeat: Beat 1 of the measure. Also, the time the gig starts and a famous jazz magazine.

Driving: Pushing ahead or on top-of the beat. Also, how you get to the gig.

Drop: A short rest or musical break in hip-hop, which originated from producers deleting a beat or two from a recorded groove to give it rhythmic variation.

Fermata: A pause or hold in music of undetermined length.

4-on-the-Floor: Playing all 4 quarter notes on the bass drum.

Ghost Notes: Small notes played quietly within a pattern that enhance the feel. They are felt as much as heard.

Half-Time Feel: Half the notes, but in the same amount of time. An example is when the snare plays just once per measure on beat 3 instead of on 2 and 4. This creates the illusion of a slower tempo, but the metronome does not change. A "double-time feel" uses the same concept in that the time goes by at the same rate, but you're playing *twice* as many notes within each bar. An example of this is the snare playing 4 times per measure (on the "and" of each beat) instead of on 2 and 4.

Head In/Out: The head is the entire melody of a tune. The "head in" is played at the start of a song, while the "head out" is at the end.

GLOSSARY OF MUSICAL SLANG

Larry Graham: Legendary funk bass player with Sly and The Family Stone and one of the innovators of slapping (hitting the strings with your thumb percussively). Check out *Graham Central Station*.

Lead Sheet: A chart that gives you relevant information about the form, hits, groove and dynamics while leaving many details of exactly what to play up to each individual player. All band members will often read the same lead sheet and interpret it for their instrument.

Lift: A pause or rest in the groove in pop or rock music. It can be a small fraction of a beat or last a full measure or more.

Lock In: This is when the notes of your bass drum and the notes the bassist plays are perfectly aligned. It can also refer to a more general syncing of the groove between multiple band members.

Metric Modulation: A change in the time signature where the pulse in the original meter becomes a different subdivision in the new one. An example is the quarter note in 4/4 becoming a dotted quarter note in 6/8. The pulse itself remains the same, but the package we're putting it in changes.

Molto Rallentando: Italian for "slow down a lot."

"Oh Sh*t" Bag: Duffel in my Subaru with wrenches, cables, various fluids and everything I need to get out of a jam. Also the place you'll put all these grooves, tips and *Stuff You Can Use*.

On Top vs. Behind the Beat: The placement of the groove relative to the metronome tempo, which does not change.

Ostinato: A repeating musical phrase sometimes also called a vamp.

Pickup: A short rhythm before the downbeat of a song or section that brings you in.

Pocket: The feel of the groove.

Polyrhythm: Layering one rhythmic subdivision over another in the same amount of space. For example, 3 over 2 is three evenly spaced notes played with one limb, while two evenly spaced notes are played with the other over the course of one measure.

Proggy: Refers to progressive rock music where the time signature changes frequently.

Push: An anticipated note that occurs on the upbeat.

STUFF YOU CAN USE

Rehearsal Letters: Markers on the chart used to help refer quickly to different spots in the song.

Road Map: A shorthand guide you can write to help you learn the number of measures in each section, groove changes, dynamics and other important landmarks in a song. It serves as your driving directions for the tune.

Score: A chart that includes all the instruments on multiple staffs instead of just a single-instrument part.

Setup: A short fill which leads the band into hits or the next section of the song.

The Shed: Short for woodshed. To "get in the shed" is to engage in heavy and focused practicing.

Slap-Tap Technique: Using wrist action to accent every other stroke of an 8th or 16th-note hi-hat pattern. This will give it some shape and make it groove harder. It's not quite a bounce, but you do make one stroke for every two notes, hitting the second note as your hand is on the way back up.

Staccato/Legato: Italian terms for short and long notes. Staccato notes should generally be played on a drum, while legato notes suggest cymbals.

Staff: The set of five horizontal lines the notes are written on.

Stirring: Moving your hands in a circular motion around the snare while playing with brushes.

Texture: Refers to the overall sound quality, which combines the rhythm, melody and feel.

Through-Composed: A piece of music which does not have repeating sections. Every part is different than the previous one.

Timbre: The tone color or sound quality of a note. Each instrument and part of the kit has its own timbre.

Tip Jar: The place to grab some tools for your "oh sh*t" bag. Also the place you make the big bucks.

Top of the Form: The spot in a song where the melody begins.

Transcription: A chart written out note-for-note exactly as it is to be played.

2-Beat: A groove where the bass drum plays on beats 1 and 3, with the snare on 2 and 4.

GLOSSARY OF MUSICAL SLANG

2-Feel in Jazz: A bouncy swing feel emphasizing beats 1 and 3.

Vamp: A repeating musical figure.

Walking: When a bass player plays all four quarter notes of a swing feel in jazz or blues.

Word Painting: Writing lyrics that directly correspond to elements in the music. For example, saying the word "stop" as the tune abruptly stops, or using the word "high" on a high note.

FULL TRACK LISTING

All Tracks Produced by Rob Mitzner
All Drums Recorded @ C-Room Studio, Brooklyn, NY January, 2021
Dmitry Ishenko Bass Tracks 1-4, 7, 8, 11, 14-17 Recorded @ C-Room Studio

Groove #'s 1-53:
Dmitry Ishenko: bass
Rob Mitzner: drums
Mixed by Charles Burst

Song #'s 1-4: "Classic Breakdown," "The Conjuration," July 1," "Gowanus Mash"
Music & Lyrics by Vern Woodhead, © Woodhead Music 2020, All Rights Reserved
Vern Woodhead: vocals, guitars
Yana Davydova: guitars
Dmitry Ishenko: bass
Rob Mitzner: drums
Mixed by Charles Burst

Song #5: "Our Funeral"
Music & Lyrics by Simon Garrett
Simon Garrett: vocals, guitars
Matthew Milligan: electric bass
Rob Mitzner: drums
Mixed by Charles Burst

Song #6: "Escape"
Music & Lyrics by Simon Garrett
Simon Garrett: vocals, guitars, electric bass, synths
Rob Mitzner: drums
Mixed by Charles Burst

Song #7: "Sleep"
Music & Lyrics by Dave Ross
Dave Ross: vocals, guitars
Dmitry Ishenko: electric bass
Rob Mitzner: drums, hand percussion
Mixed by Mitch Rackin
Vocals & guitars recorded @ Behind The Curtains Media, Brooklyn, NY by Michael Abiuso

Song #8: "Worn Away"
Music & Lyrics by Dave Ross
Dave Ross: vocals, guitars
Dmitry Ishenko: electric bass
Rob Mitzner: drums, hand percussion
Mixed by Mitch Rackin
Vocals & guitars recorded @ Behind The Curtains Media, Brooklyn, NY by Michael Abiuso

Song #9: "Famous"
Music & Lyrics by Luke Buck
Luke Buck: vocals, guitars
Matthew Milligan: electric bass
Rob Mitzner: drums
Mixed by Charles Burst
Additional guitars & vocals recorded @ Behind The Curtains Media, Brooklyn, NY by Michael Abiuso

Song #10: "Without You"
Music & Lyrics by Luke Buck
Luke Buck: vocals, guitars, banjo, keyboards
Matthew Milligan: electric bass
Rob Mitzner: drums
Mixed by Charles Burst

Song #11: "Always Leave Me Wanting More"
Music & Lyrics by Andrea Capozzoli
Andrea Capozzoli: vocals, trumpet, keyboards
John Shannon: guitars
Jared Sims: tenor and baritone saxophones
Dmitry Ishenko: electric bass
Rob Mitzner: drums
Mixed by Charles Burst

Song #12: "I'll Form The Head" (Unplugged '21)
Lyrics by Damian Hess, Shanthony Exum and Mark Schaffer
Music by Damian Hess, Gabriel Alter and David T. Cheong
Published by Nerdcore Fervor Conglomerated (ASCAP)
MC Frontalot: raps
Gabriel Alter (G Minor 7): keyboards
Matthew Milligan (M-Audio): electric bass
Rob Mitzner (Beard Science): drums
w/special guest rappers Schaffer The Darklord & Miss Eaves
Mixed by Charles Burst

Song #13: "Clickbait"
Lyrics by Damian Hess
Music by Damian Hess, Gabriel Alter, Matthew Milligan and Rob Mitzner
MC Frontalot: raps
Gabriel Alter (G Minor 7): keyboards
Matthew Milligan (M-Audio): electric bass
Rob Mitzner (Beard Science): drums
Mixed by Charles Burst

Song #14: "Getting Closer," from the musical RADIOACTIVE
Music by Will Reynolds, Book & Lyrics by Eric Price
Hannah Corneau: vocals
Will Reynolds: piano, programming
Dmitry Ishenko: acoustic bass
Rob Mitzner: drums
Mixed by Charles Burst

Song #15: "The Violet Hour," from the musical THE VIOLET HOUR
Music by Will Reynolds, Book & Lyrics by Eric Price
Based on the play by Richard Greenberg
Will Reynolds: vocals, piano, programming
Dmitry Ishenko: bass
Rob Mitzner: drums
Mixed by Charles Burst

Song #16: "Insurrection"
Music by Michael Gallant, © 2021 Gallant Music LLC, All Rights Reserved
Michael Gallant: keyboards
Dmitry Ishenko: electric bass
Rob Mitzner: drums
Mixed by Charles Burst

Song #17: "Modern Jazz Combo"
Music by Lars Potteiger
Lars Potteiger: piano
Dmitry Ishenko: acoustic bass
Rob Mitzner: drums

Song #18: "Blues for Bob"
Music by Rob Mitzner
Chris Cheek: baritone sax
Dmitry Ishenko: acoustic bass
Rob Mitzner: drums
Mixed by Charles Burst

ACKNOWLEDGEMENTS

We've reached the point where I get to thank everyone who helped me get this massive and somewhat crazy project over the finish line. This list includes family, friends, colleagues, collaborators, teachers and a wide variety of folks in the music industry I've met over the years.

But let's start with my Mom. I started playing guitar at age 5 and took piano lessons all through my childhood years in the Washington D.C area. While I liked learning tunes from my Dad on guitar, these piano lessons were (to put it kindly), rather creatively uninspiring. When I turned 12, I had to choose an arts class for middle school with the choices being home economics, woodshop and concert band. Little did I know that this would be the most important choice of my entire life. I wanted to do the band, but guitar and piano were not options. One night at dinner, my Mom blurted out, "why don't you try the drums?" I still wonder if she knew she was signing up for years of ear-splitting noise, scruffy friends tracking mud into the basement, driving me to and from gigs and later, nervous late nights waiting for me to get home. I think she knew and she signed up anyway. The rest is history, so thanks Mom. You were right, and I still can't sew or use a power saw.

Next are my teachers. I wouldn't be a drummer without them either. My first band teacher Frankie Ball was a giant man with a booming voice who tolerated no riff-raff. But beneath his gruff exterior was a warm and funny person who got me going on learning rudiments, traveling to band festivals and working as part of a group. **Stuff You Can Use.** Years later before he passed away, the school had a concert in his honor. At the end, he pulled me aside to give me his most important and lasting wisdom on being a professional musician. With a mischievous twinkle in his eye he whispered, "make sure you get paid." Thanks Mr. Ball.

My first drum teacher was Steve "Freelance" Larrance. Steve was the original inspiration for this book and spent his early days playing with everyone from Tina Turner to Little Feat and Miroslav Vitous. He could nail every single style, and he did it with serious flavor and groove. He instilled that in me from day one, and many of the patterns in this book are derived from his teachings. Later in high school, I would sub for him on gigs around town, with one particularly memorable occasion where he accidently booked himself to play two weddings at the same time. We met in the morning and switched drumsets, with me setting up his kit at the second gig and then going to relieve him mid-song at the first. Talk about getting thrown into the deep end! **Stuff You Can Use.** Steve, as you used to say to me all time quoting the Duke, "I love you madly." This book is for you.

It's also for the late Bob Gullotti, my teacher throughout college and beyond, as well as my biggest influence on the instrument. Even though Bob was an avant-garde jazz heavyweight, he drilled me on everything from David Garibaldi's "Future Sounds" to the Garwood Whaley snare drum books and his unique polyrhythmic exercise, "The Table of Time." As you read about in the "Blues for Bob" section, he taught me touch, technique, melodic soloing and most importantly, how to interact with the rest of band. **Stuff You Can Use.** Bob, this is for you too.

In college at Brown University, I played in the big band led by Matthew McGarrell, and in a combo coached by Dave Zinno. Matt taught me how to really drive a band and he also taught me how to be a pro. I can still see him up there waving his arms cajoling me to give those 15 horn players a good ass-kicking. That was probably the most fun I've ever had playing drums. He also got me in with some local Rhode Island big bands where he (in his late 40s) and I (not yet old enough for a legal beer), were easily the youngest members. We played "In the Mood," "Pennsylvania 6-5000" and "Sing, Sing, Sing," and the bandleader (who was pushing 90) would stand up there with his baton before the first tune and ask, "did everyone take their pills?" The band would explode in laughter, but we weren't sure if he was kidding. I loved those old guys. *Stuff You Can Use!*

Dave Zinno is a world-class bassist and my first rhythm section guru. He'd have the pianist, guitarist, bassist and me visualize different scenes and play free-jazz. ("You're in the woods and a bear is chasing you," or "you're underwater floating above a coral reef.") What a fun mental exercise to unlock true creativity and improvisation as part of a group. More *Stuff You Can Use!*

In addition to these seminal figures in my life, I want to express gratitude to my drum companies who have helped me enhance my sound and take it to the next level. Paiste Cymbals and Tim Shahady hooked me up with with a gorgeous spread of Swiss metal to film these tracks for the book. These guys have a perfect cymbal for every musical situation. *Stuff I Can Use*. Hendrix Drums has had my back for years, and they make the best snare drums around. Thanks to Rhett Hendrix for believing in me when I was a kid wandering the halls of NAMM, and to Joe Fazzio and the team for always supporting me. Roger Johnson is my artist rep from Remo, which is fortunate because he knows more about drumheads than anyone I've ever met. Remo is the gold standard, and I've been playing them since age 12. Also, thanks to the folks at Drumdots who make these little polymer dampening gels I can't live without in the studio or onstage.

I'd also like thank my sister Jen, my nieces Mia and Emma, and most of all, my partner Rebecca. This book would never have happened without her support and encouragement. Also, Dmitry Ishenko, my rhythm section compadre for life. This wouldn't have happened without him either. I'd also like to express gratitude to my friend Dan Shinder for helping me formulate the early stages of this project, along with designer Ricky Hammerschmidt, engineering wizard Charles Burst and camera guru Albert Bickley. Also, thanks to each and every one of these amazing musicians! They made this project come to life.

Finally, I'd like to thank Rob Wallis, Joe Bergamini and Hudson Music for believing in me and helping make this dream a reality. One of the best parts about choosing a career as an artist is that you never stop learning, growing and acquiring new skills. Though it may sound cliché, I discovered through this project that great things are possible if you surround yourself with the best people and allow them to elevate you far beyond what you could achieve on your own. These collaborations are what make being an artist the best job in the world. We are always stronger together. This is truly the **STUFF YOU CAN USE!**

ABOUT THE AUTHOR

New York-based session drummer Rob Mitzner has recorded for Billboard Top-10 charting albums, films, Broadway shows, and performed at Lincoln Center, The Smithsonian, Caesar's Palace, The Blue Note, Boston Symphony Hall and for President Obama in his hometown of Washington D.C. He has been featured in national publications such as *Downbeat* magazine and *Modern Drummer*, and his credits include over 50 commercially available albums across many genres. When he's not playing or touring with the wonderful artists in this book, Rob spends his days at C-Room Studio in Brooklyn cutting drum tracks, shedding funky electric bass and writing articles for various publications. As a tribute to his late teacher Bob Gullotti, he live-streamed a 3-hour performance of the entire Charlie Parker Omnibook, playing the melodies and transcribed sax solos around the drumkit. He was recently featured on the national TV show "Trending Today" on Vice, and regularly appears on Drum Talk TV. Rob holds a B.A. in Music and Political Science from Brown University, and is a proud endorser of Paiste Cymbals, Remo Drumheads, Hendrix Drums and Drumdots.

www.robmitzner.com

The last day of filming @ C-Room Studio, Brooklyn, NY January 2021